Histories of Crime

HISTORIES OF CRIME

BRITAIN 1600–2000

Edited by

Anne-Marie Kilday

and

David Nash

First published 2010 by
PALGRAVE MACMILLAN

Palgrave Macmillan in the UK is an imprint of Macmillan Publishers Limited, registered in England, company number 785998, of Houndmills, Basingstoke, Hampshire RG21 6XS.

Palgrave Macmillan in the US is a division of St Martin's Press LLC, 175 Fifth Avenue, New York, NY 10010.

Palgrave Macmillan is the global academic imprint of the above companies and has companies and representatives throughout the world.

Palgrave® and Macmillan® are registered trademarks in the United States, the United Kingdom, Europe and other countries.

ISBN 978–0–230–22469–8   hardback
ISBN 978–0–230–22470–4   paperback

This book is printed on paper suitable for recycling and made from fully managed and sustained forest sources. Logging, pulping and manufacturing processes are expected to conform to the environmental regulations of the country of origin.

A catalogue record for this book is available from the British Library.

A catalog record for this book is available from the Library of Congress.

10 9 8 7 6 5 4 3 2 1
19 18 17 16 15 14 13 12 11 10

Printed in China

This volume is dedicated to the memory of our much loved colleague,
Professor Detlef Mühlberger

Contents

Acknowledgements

The editors would like to thank the numerous people who have helped in the writing of this book. First, we would like to express our thanks to staff at the National Archives, the National Archives of Scotland, the National Library of Scotland and the Bodleian Library, Oxford for their patience and helpful advice. We would also like to thank each of the contributors to this volume for their hard work and in particular, their patience and grace when dealing with our many queries. We would like to thank Julie Richards for help with the index.

We would also like to thank those involved at Palgrave Macmillan in the production of this book, from embryonic idea to published work. Thanks go to our commissioning editors Beverley Tarquini and Kate Haines and to our editorial contacts Ruth Ireland and Jenni Burnell. We would also like to thank our anonymous reviewers for their helpful and important contributions.

Notes on Contributors

Joanne Bailey is Senior Lecturer in Early Modern History at Oxford Brookes University. Her publications include *Unquiet Lives: Marriage and Marriage Breakdown in England, 1660–1800* (2003) and journal articles on marriage and the law. She is currently preparing a book on parenting in England, *c*.1760–1800.

Shani D'Cruze is currently Honorary Reader in the Research Institute for Law, Politics and Justice at Keele University. Recent publications include (with S. Walklate and S. Pegg) *Murder: Social and Historical Approaches to Understanding Murder and Murderers* (2006) and, with L. Jackson, *Women, Crime and Justice since 1660* (Palgrave, 2009).

Anne-Marie Kilday is an Assistant Dean (Teaching and Learning) and a Principal Lecturer in History at Oxford Brookes University. She is currently working on a monograph entitled *The Unforgivable Crime? A History of Infanticide in Britain* for Palgrave. Recent publications include *Women and Violent Crime in Enlightenment Scotland* (2007) and, with K.D. Watson, a special issue of the journal *Family and Community History* (2008).

David Nash is Professor of History at Oxford Brookes University and has worked and published extensively in the area of the history of blasphemy, blasphemous libel and religious crime/law for over fifteen years. His previous books include *Blasphemy in Britain: 1789–Present* (1999) and *Blasphemy in the Christian World* (2007). He is a Director of SOLON: Promoting Interdisciplinary Studies in Bad Behaviour and Crime and has given advice to MPs and evidence to the House of Lord Select Committee on Religious Offences (2003). He is about to publish a monograph on the history of shame (with Anne-Marie Kilday).

Judith Rowbotham is a Director and co-founder of SOLON: Promoting Interdisciplinary Studies in Bad Behaviour and Crime, an Associate Research Fellow of the Institute of Advanced Legal Studies and a Reader at Nottingham Trent University. An interdisciplinary scholar, she specialises in criminal and legal studies and crime history. Recent work includes: 'Turning Away from Criminal Intent: Reflecting on Victorian and Edwardian

Strategies for Promoting Desistance Among Petty Offenders', *Theoretical Criminology*, 13(1) (2009), 'Miscarriage of Justice? Post-colonial Reflections on the "Trial" of the Maharajah of Baroda, 1875', *Liverpool Law Review* 28 (2007), *Criminal Conversations: Victorian Crimes, Social Panic and Moral Outrage* (edited with K. Stevenson, 2005) and 'Innocent Recidivists? Contested Presentations of Women and Girls *c.*1850–1900', in M. Porrot (ed.), *Recidivism: A European Perspective* (2005).

Heather Shore is a Senior Lecturer in Social and Cultural History in the School of Cultural Studies at Leeds Metropolitan University. She is the author of *Artful Dodgers: Youth and Crime in the Early Nineteenth Century* (1999). She has also co-edited two collections: *Becoming Delinquent: British and European Youth, 1650–1950* (with P. Cox, 2002) and *The Streets of London: From the Great Fire to the Great Stink* (with T. Hitchcock, 2003). She has also contributed to a number of journals and books. She is currently writing a history of the metropolitan underworld.

Kim Stevenson is Senior Lecturer in Law at the University of Plymouth and Co-Director of SOLON: Interdisciplinary Studies in Crime and Bad Behaviour. Her main research interests are sexual offences, particularly from a historico-legal perspective, and she has published a number of articles in this area. She is also the lead editor of Blackstone's Guide to the Sexual Offences Act 2003 (2004).

Chris Williams is a Lecturer in the History Department at the Open University. He has published work on the history of policing in the UK, covering topics such as police reform and nineteenth-century urban history, historical criminal statistics, the decline in autonomy of urban police forces in the twentieth century, the early history of CCTV and the links between colonial and 'home' police and private payment for policing services. He is also actively engaged in promoting the preservation of records and artefacts relating to criminal justice history, and their presentation to the wider public.

Sarah Wilson is a Lecturer in the School of Law at the University of York. Her key research interests are equity and trusts, and especially financial crime, past and present, and her approach to both have strong law and history dimensions. Much of her work seeks to look at experiences from past societies in terms of identifying patterns of continuity and change in identifying 'issues of today' and finding possible solutions for them.

Introduction

David Nash and Anne-Marie Kilday

Popular and academic interest in crime and law has never been greater. Students study the subject of crime and its context in increasing numbers on history, criminology, media, film, social policy, and legal studies courses. Crime and legal issues are also avidly read and followed by the wider public through a wide range of media. Studies of crime and the law are also areas which inform the investigation of social and cultural history in ways that a previous generation of historians could scarcely imagine. This book offers a detailed and informed synthesis of the important research undertaken in crime and the contexts associated with it during the last few years.

Exploring crime and the law through recognisable themes highlights the value of looking at current issues through an historical microscope. Criminological debates about the nature of policing, the murder of children and the history of offences against property and against the body are perennial, but urgently deserve a greater understanding in terms of their wider historical context. It needs to be remembered that this context can be shaped by the different legal systems in England/Wales, Scotland and Northern Ireland, respectively. There are, however, also areas which are exciting growing interest, informed by contemporary debates such as the relationship between law, ethnicity, religion and morality, as well as more detailed gender-specific analyses of deviance and criminal behaviours. Alongside this, whole categories of crime remain poorly understood, or the academic work in the area is not widely known. These are similarly in urgent need of informed investigation for the benefit of students and general readers alike.

This book shows the evolution of attitudes towards criminality through time as well as changes in society's responses to it. Legislative strategies, policing approaches, criminal justice and public reactions to community safety have all changed through history, and an appreciation of this is important for modern British culture. Moreover, considering laws and crimes as specific themes is particularly useful for escaping the temptation to view the law and, indeed, 'crime' as a monolithic entity which is studied with agendas which reflect this. The identity of criminals and the means/ motives behind criminal practices also similarly have a history which needs to be traced on a more 'human' scale than has previously been the case. This is done through analysing violent and non-violent criminality across gender and time and through comparative analyses. The use of the more 'human' scale of specific offences and areas also enables the book to investigate, for the first time, the consequences of crime and criminal activity from the victims' perspective. From here it is possible to analyse society's wider attitudes and fears associated with criminal behaviour as well as aspects of attitude to the law and legal systems over time.

The purpose behind this book is not to replicate texts which produce an overall history of crime and the law since 1700, of which there are many good examples.[1] Instead it hopes to fulfil something of a different purpose. Whilst it is readily possible to discover straightforward and chronological histories of crime which cover this period, it is not always possible to gain an easy way into the debates that go with this. The work of all the authors within this book brings together expertise in both the history of crime and the history of the law, and in all chapters these are discussed alongside one another. Each chapter uses the research findings of the authors concerned, giving students access to the very latest research in this area. However the discussion of this, undertaken by each author, occurs alongside an accessible analysis of the historiography within which this research has an important place. This discussion is contextualised alongside scholarship both past and present and, occasionally, with some guesses about the future direction that academic and policy debates may follow. Where appropriate, each chapter has also addressed wider debates beyond crime and criminality, whilst important texts which relate to and explain these have been considered and discussed. Thus this book, and the chapters within it, offers a multifaceted and flexible way into the further study of crimes in context.

The book does contain a number of chapters that (even through their title) clearly suggest subject matter that is not explicitly or entirely about 'crimes' as such. These include chapters covering subjects such as the underworld, moral crimes, the death penalty and policing. This is because the wider history of crime, and how society has dealt with it, demands coverage of these issues as the essential context. Crime and contemporary perceptions of its practitioners has led commentators to create the conception of a criminal underworld and, in many cases, theorise about its practices.[2] Similarly the issue of morality, and the construction of so-called moral crimes is the context within which a society thinks about the wickedness or otherwise of its own population. It also allows a society, at any moment in time, to theorise what the consequences might be of allowing immorality to foster bad behaviour and criminal activity. Likewise, for society to maximise the quality of life for its citizens, it needs to prevent crime and, where possible, catch criminals. Thus any consideration of the history of crime must encounter and analyse the strategies, tactics and philosophies implemented by forms of law enforcement and policing.

Theft is a crime that has been, and will always be, with us. Nonetheless our consideration of crimes in context means that it has proved impossible to contain a single analysis of this offence within the confines of one chapter. Doing so would have compromised the exploration of issues discussed in a number of other chapters, particularly the ones by Wilson on fraud and Shore on the underworld. We have also been conscious during the construction of this book, of the comparative (and remarkably surprising) absence of work on the long-term history of theft in its traditionally understood form. This, for us, was in stark contrast to the developing work on the underworld which saw theft as merely one small part of a much larger environment for crime and criminality. Similarly, the recent arrival of historical analyses of Victorian fraud have also emphasised that new areas of research related to other aspects of property crime were receiving important scholarly attention at the expense of conventionally understood practices such as theft.[3]

We consider that for the reader to make the best use of the contents of this book, it would help to hold a number of enduring and important themes in their mind whilst reading. Noting both the perennial importance of some themes, and the episodic appearance of others, is a significant factor in making the link between a history of crime and its contemporary reality.

Readers of the chapters on homicide, moral crimes and the death penalty in particular will readily note how the use of the death penalty was severely limited because so many offences demanded it. As the reader will discover, late eighteenth- and early nineteenth-century society had prescribed the ultimate penalty for many crimes, yet in most areas the reader will come across a well-documented reluctance to convict where a capital sentence was likely.[4] This was clearly the starting point for a long-term debate on the nature and purpose of punishment, a debate which clearly spilled into other areas of the law. Arguments related to penal policy were characterised as debates about whether punishment was a form of retribution which society could justify, or whether punishment should be aimed at some form of reformation of the individual concerned. One lesson from looking at this debate is that it would be a mistake to simply suggest that the issue of retribution belonged to an uncivilised past and that the reformation concept should be squarely identified with 'modern approaches'. It is noteworthy, for instance, that some modern legal theoreticians are prepared to suggest that society exacting retribution alongside restorative justice is a wholly legitimate function of the law in contemporary society.[5]

Just as the detection and apprehension of criminals is clearly an essential part of policing the community, all societies have to deal with the issue of what to do with the miscreants they catch. A long-term perspective upon this would suggest that British society has clearly been unable to make up its mind about the function and effectiveness of its punishment regimes. Shame punishments may have functioned in close-knit communities, but were deemed increasingly ineffective from the early nineteenth century onwards.[6]

As will become apparent, the rationale of the 'Bloody Code' lost its logic by the first third of the nineteenth century. That is, indeed, if it was ever anything more than the spontaneous expansion of a reactive system based on precedent. Another solution to widespread criminality, transportation to the colonies, rose and fell during the period under discussion and was phased out by the end of the 1850s, implying, at the very least, a mixed judgement upon its value and effectiveness.[7] The use of gaol, prison and other forms of confinement at home was the solution chosen to replace this, and this arguably brings our view of punishment up to the present day. However, it is emphatically clear that the issue of punishment is scarcely resolved. Contemporary society is home to vastly overcrowded prisons, whilst the media host a series of changing and emotionally-charged debates around the fitness of sentencing and punishment. Some even concede that the era of incarceration has failed to provide the solutions that its theoreticians, from Bentham onwards, propounded.[8] There is even a hunt for alternatives, with the discussion of 'cheaper' shame punishments and restorative justice.[9]

Another fundamentally important theme that runs through the whole book – and makes appearances in every chapter – is the issue of the media and media representations. From its appearance at the start of our period in the chapbooks and other forms of popular literature which were circulated to the populace around the time of executions, the role of print culture in crime and the perception of it has grown dramatically in both volume and sophistication.[10] Popular ballads were also themselves methods of transmitting and storing perceptions and value judgements about crime, criminals and the reaction of authority to them. The period covered by the book also witnessed a considerable growth in the reporting of crime in both local and national newspapers. These media outlets, throughout our time period, were capable of describing criminal incidents, the actions and mechanisms of various policing measures, and of course the actions of the judiciary system in processing and deciding the fate of defendants.[11] But clearly newspapers also went further and were involved in the business of opinion formation. Newspaper editorials could spread knowledge of individual crimes and their apparent ferocity. These could also construct images and perceptions of the individual criminal and sometimes of an entire criminal class. Editorials could also monitor and pass comment upon the actions and effectiveness of attempts to police crime and may even have had considerable influence in shaping how these were undertaken. It is also important to remember that newspapers contained a vast number of reports from throughout the country. Showcase trials and editorial copy were syndicated throughout the country by the mid-nineteenth century, so that the consequences of crime in London could be read about in provincial drawing rooms. However the reverse was equally true; notable cases that occurred on the Celtic fringe and the provinces could equally find their way into the London newspapers.[12] Court reporting itself also grew in sophistication and it has been satisfactorily established that much of this work was undertaken by junior members of the legal profession seeking to supplement their own meagre incomes.[13]

We should also not forget that many of the stories conjured up and inspired by the reporting of court cases became the inspiration for popular fiction which would appear in newspapers, periodicals and the earliest magazines. The rise of the novel very quickly gave birth to a number of different genres which drew heavily on crime for their inspiration and subject matter.[14] The twentieth century saw this trend develop exponentially as the unit costs of publishing fell, precisely as literacy rates and levels of discretionary spending grew.[15] The impact of the crime novel and 'whodunit' is almost impossible to gauge satisfactorily, but there are certainly some issues that are worth pondering. For many people, for most of their lives, their only encounter with crime and the law would have been from thinking about the subject matter they encountered in the newspapers and novels. Indeed the encounter with popular depictions of crime may have been the place where a vast number of people learned about crime, and developed opinions upon it. Thus it is scarcely too far-fetched to suggest that the popular media in a very real sense shaped what the public thought about everything, from punishment for theft to the moral arguments for the use of the death penalty.

The twentieth century saw the reach of the printed word (with its growing taste for 'true-life' depictions of crime) augmented by the power of cinema and television. Once again the depiction of crime and criminality was further expanded, this time with a growing sensationalist and graphic quality. All areas of crime and most areas of the context behind it found their way into films depicting everything from the motivations of individuals, to the structures which regulate the law and, indeed, criminal activity itself.[16] Television very quickly latched on to the power and popularity of crime as a central story in the dramas it broadcast. A particular impact of television was its portrayal of policing activity, and in Britain each decade arguably had its own constructions of the archetypal policemen and police role, supplemented, we should remember, with alternative versions which arrived from the USA. The 1960s saw *Z Cars* depict everyday police work for the viewing public whilst the BBC's *Dixon of Dock Green* (resurrecting a character from the celebrated and iconic 1950s film *The Blue Lamp*) concluded each episode with a homily on the nature of police work and morality. The 1970s introduced a new dynamic of associating the police simultaneously with glamour and seediness, personified by ITV's *The Sweeney*. The 1980s saw growing diversity and the continuation of some older themes, perhaps best represented by the contrast between the action and grisliness of *Taggart* and the refined pondering of wider morality in *Inspector Morse*. The years since then have seen depictions of police work blur even further, with new generations of crime drama supplemented by a growing trend to produce 'true-life' television.

The historical period covered by this book also witnessed significant technological changes over the whole era. These have inevitably had a considerable impact upon the nature of crime and control of crime within society. We have already heard about the power of print culture in influencing popular reactions to crime, but there was also a technical innovation in the use of information that informed and created the attitude of authority towards the phenomenon. Although crime statistics were not invented during this period, their systematic collection, analysis and presentation represented a significant technological innovation.

Police work itself obviously benefited from the ability to use technology to combat crime. New methods of acquiring and preparing evidence and the growing acceptance of new types of evidence, made possible through the application of technology, inevitably made fighting crime a more effective proposition. New inventions, such as fingerprinting (in the nineteenth century) and genetic profiling (in the twentieth century), had to be accepted by the legal process, but once this had been achieved, some elements of police work could be transformed and made significantly more effective.[17] The ability of the police to respond to incidents in progress became more satisfactory with the harnessing of telephone and radio technology and other elements of procedure. Crime prevention was arguably made possible through the use of motor transport, which made routine patrols more extensive and more effective.[18] We might also argue that crime prevention is one particular area that has seen the most significant investment in recent years, with the widespread and growing application of other electronic surveillance technology.[19]

However the growth of technology also has a darker side, which we should also consider. New technology has changed the shape of crime itself. Certainly it has been suggested, for example, that the new wave of theft and larceny which occurred from the end of the eighteenth century onwards appeared because there were simply more high-value portable items available to steal![20] Thus, we should factor into our account of theft in the last 300 years that changes in the ownership and desirability of movable goods were clearly a factor in the incidence of larceny of all kinds. We might also say that technological innovations meant that some types of crime could benefit from what economists call the economies of scale, which may have been a factor in crime becoming more organised.[21] Technological innovations were also arguably responsible for changes in the nature of larceny itself. The growing sophistication of the financial and banking sector presented new opportunities for white-collar larceny in the form of fraud.[22] We need only look around our own age (with the spread of the Internet) to learn the lesson that the arrival of new technology allows crime and criminality to modernise, as much as it allows the forces of law and order to move forward in the fight against them.[23]

Another enduring issue that appears in all areas of the book is how crimes and their context have a distinctly gendered dimension. We will obviously notice that some crimes are almost exclusively the preserve of one gender or another (the obvious example covered by this book being infanticide).[24] But gender also has an important role to play in how we regard those of both sexes considered guilty of crime and criminal activity. Our whole perception of the reality of sex crimes and how they come to be perpetrated is deeply rooted in how a given society and members of it consider the nature of male and female sexuality at any given moment.[25] This is even more pertinent to society's changing attitude to same-sex relationships.[26] Morality and behavioural standards alter over time, as does society's expectations of what is seemly and unseemly behaviour between the sexes. Society invariably carries its images of how men and women should behave in the sexual arena and brings these to the judgement of any guilty party it finds. These images are reinforced and reiterated in the media, which reports upon court cases and creates opinion around these. There is no better example of this than the different treatment accorded to male and female individuals found guilty of murder – yet even this has changed over time.[27] Although not universally accepted, it has been common for historians to suggest that women receive different treatment from the courts and judicial system than men do.[28] Certainly it can be argued that society and the media have frequently tried to make male and female murder defendants fit into a number of gender-specific stereotypes.

However, it should also be mentioned that the perceptions of gender identity have further influenced the participation of the respective sexes in both policing work and, indeed, criminality itself. The involvement of women in the police-force has lagged significantly behind the use of male officers, and full participation in the whole range of policing activities only altered with the coming of gender equality.[29] From an earlier period, when they were confined to dealing with the issues associated with women and children, women police workers should now expect the same range of career opportunities open to their male colleagues. Career opportunities for women thieves in the pre-modern period were often predicated upon the sexual desire of the victim and their expectation associated with certain forms of provocative female behaviour.[30]

One last overarching theme that should help the reader to make sense of the material which follows is to consider how much the history of crime and its context turns around questions of the supposed civilised nature of society. On the one hand, it would be quite easy to equate increased levels of crime with increased lawlessness, and thereby the supposed threat to the long-term health of 'civilisation'.[31] However, as the last section suggested, changes in society allowed crime to evolve as much as policing methods.

Likewise we might consider that a liberalising of punishment regimes should be considered a noted mark of a civilised society. But as Michel Foucault has warned us, we should think of this merely as forms of punishment changing from regimes in which deterrence is deemed effective, to those in which surveillance has taken over.[32] Importantly, Foucault's suggestion waved aside the idea that this was a more civilised solution, suggesting that the institutionalisation of an individual was an altered form of brutal punishment rather than a more obviously humane and civilised one.[33] As society itself changes, at any given time, that society invariably hosts a dialogue about what punishment is actually for. One specific reference point within this debate is usually an assessment of how civilised a society is, or has become. A specific marker of this is society's discussion of the death penalty. This debate considers what the effective and just punishment is for those who take the life of another or commit some commensurably serious crime. In this issues of deterrence, retribution and justice are held up to a supposed standard of what is civilised and what is not. Intriguingly, it is worth remembering that the answers to this question are scarcely easy, intelligible and straightforward. An important indicator of this is given by looking at the current state of affairs in the USA. Rather than a single answer to what is just and civilised in the use of the death penalty, individual American states (during the historical period covered by this book) adopted individual responses to this question. In this, they generally argued for local standards of morality that they felt they could justifiably defend against the occasionally contrary opinion of the Federal government and other states within the Union.[34]

Thus from these themes we now proceed to introduce the contents of the book and outline what will be discussed in each chapter. We have formatted each chapter to make its contents as user-friendly as possible to the potential reader. Each chapter contains an introduction to the crime/offence or subject covered in which contemporary and historic understanding is introduced. This is followed by a section which outlines the fundamentally important chronology of each subject. This is not simply a timeline or list of what happened when – it is an exploration of the legal context that has shaped the history of each subject. Inevitably, this section of each chapter has entailed each author determining the relative and sometimes absolute importance of events, policies, reactions and innovations. The historical analysis of each subject is then followed by a section entitled 'historiography'. This section brings together the work of historians who have studied the area in question. In this, the analytical themes they have highlighted are showcased and investigated. Where there has been disagreement between historians over facts, analysis or interpretation, this has also been emphasised. The fourth section of each chapter illuminates and provides valuable examples of the themes and analysis present in both the chronology and historiography sections. The last section in each chapter is a summative conclusion.

David Nash's chapter, which commences the book, outlines how society has dealt with the issues associated with what he has termed 'moral crimes'. This section has been chosen to start the book because it outlines a particularly early conception of where crime and criminality originated and, as such, provides the perfect context for the discussions of other crimes which follow. This society believed that lesser moral failings, if allowed to escalate, would invariably lead to greater and more dangerous moral infractions.

The chapter highlights two particular offences that, whilst both having a modern dimension, also display important elements of a changing historical and legislative context. The first of these is the history of blasphemy which demonstrates how a crime, the control of which was explicitly linked to the maintenance of order, mutated into one in which defending the rights of the individual in league with the establishment came to be the accepted norm. The second of these is what might loosely be termed 'homosexual crimes' within a society coming to terms both with the freedom of the individual and its role in legislating to protect the vulnerable. Both of these are considered in relation to the changing moral climate that informs both the long-term attitude to morality and the associated episodic 'moral panics' that later swept Regency, Victorian and Edwardian England.

The sections on blasphemy indicate the extent to which this 'offence' was regarded as a serious threat to the moral and social stability of society and the safety of the realm. Nash outlines the changing legal and political perspectives on blasphemy and points out that prosecutions for the offence were born out of a concern that blasphemous behaviour had the potential to corrupt the minds of the populace. Thus, the seemingly modern concept of press and media censorship stemmed from the debates over religious freedom which began way back in the seventeenth century and evolved over time. Arguments over how to define blasphemy have acted as a focal point for historical studies of this offence. The history of blasphemy, and its more recent recasting as a species of hate crime, emphasise its longevity and the extent to which its status acts as a barometer of public opinion.

In a similar way, the sections on homosexuality reflect the almost symbiotic relationship between legal attitudes to this species of activity and public opinion more widely. Whilst once considered a most heinous crime, over time, homosexuality has come to be largely regarded as an acceptable lifestyle choice. The chapter emphasises the complex nature of attitudes towards homosexuality through an exploration of the issues of 'consent'. Although prosecutions were regularly difficult to convene, due to strict rules of evidence, it is clear, nonetheless, that just as with blasphemy, homosexuality was viewed as a moral concern which could corrupt the sensibilities of the impressionable. The degree of toleration for homosexual activity altered over time, as historians have shown; even beyond 1967, when the 'offence' was finally decriminalised.

Joanne Bailey's chapter on cruelty and adultery illuminates some harrowing and provocative instances of marital disharmony. Initially, the chapter traces the changing definition of spousal cruelty both with regard to the legal context and in relation to societal notions of 'appropriate' behaviour. Bailey then goes on to examine how spousal cruelty was reported, 'managed' and explained over time and challenges the simplistic notion that marital abuse became 'privatised' after the dawn of the nineteenth century. The influence of evolving media portrayals of domestic violence is also investigated in order to demonstrate how certain publications were used as political tools, whilst others promoted the notoriety of certain episodes or suggested the existence of stereotypical victim and aggressor types.

The remainder of the piece outlines how attitudes to extramarital encounters were shaped by the sexual double standard which existed for most of recent history, and suggests, that in times of crisis, adulterous behaviour and its repercussions came to be seen as a visible and viable threat to the moral and social order. As was the case with instances of marital cruelty, media attention directed towards illicit extramarital relations sensationalised this kind of behaviour (especially episodes involving public figures) and exposed these scandals to wider society. For these reasons adulterous practices had to be regulated at worst, and eradicated at best, although the methods used to attempt this varied across time and across cultures, until consideration of these matters came to reside in the conscience of individuals.

Anne-Marie Kilday's chapter on infanticide begins by emphasising the longevity of the crime and notes the fact that attitudes towards the offence have changed considerably over time. Kilday points out that in early history infanticidal behaviour was regularly condoned in some cultures and wholly rejected in others. However, by the dawn of the seventeenth century, most European countries had put statutory provisions in place in an attempt to curb the practice of newborn child murder, particularly by young, unmarried women. Since that time, Kilday explains, attitudes towards infanticide have become more nuanced and measured, and increasingly, efforts have been made to understand why this crime has been committed and why it still exists today.

The chapter then goes on to provide an overview of the historiography related to infanticide and discusses the four key themes of scholarly interest. These are an analysis of the individual, regional and national experiences of newborn child murder; an investigation of attitudes towards infanticide and infanticidal women; an appreciation of the literary and cultural context for infanticide; and finally, an understanding of the motives behind this form of criminality. Many of these themes are then illuminated in Kilday's discussion of six case studies from around the UK. The chapter finishes by outlining some avenues for future research and indicates how incomplete our understanding is of this emotive and complex crime, and the individuals who committed it.

Kim Stevenson's chapter deals with the emotive crime of rape, which, for a range of reasons, is one of the most complex offences that the judicial authorities have to contend with. As Stevenson makes plain from the outset, instances of rape were and are notoriously difficult to investigate and any evidence gleaned is generally considered problematic and open to question. Historically, the legal context for rape has been determined and shaped by men. Thus, the overwhelmingly gendered nature of this crime has resulted in the prolonged subordination of women, especially in the arena of the courtroom. For the historian, difficulties in tracking down appropriate source material relating to rape have been compounded by the obvious methodological problems associated with the analysis of data relating to sexual assault. The so-called 'dark figure' of unreported or unrecorded crime looms large in relation to rape and sexually motivated violence more generally. In this chapter, Stevenson traces the legal response to rape throughout history, highlighting definitional problems, the contested issue of consent and the influence of the notion of respectability on judicial opinion. The case studies employed in the chapter illuminate all of these themes, and in addition, they reflect that although the legal definition of rape has been clarified more effectively in recent times, problems still remain, and a low conviction rate prevails.

Shani D'Cruze's chapter on murder and fatality begins by providing a brief overview of trends in homicide since the early modern period. The initial sections focus on recurring themes such as honour, gender and race, as well as murder within the domestic setting and more exceptional forms of homicide, such as serial killing. The chapter then moves on to explore the criminal justice system's response to murder and homicide, through an examination of changing attitudes towards violent behaviour throughout history and across cultural and legal contexts. Historians of fatal violence have been largely preoccupied with providing an explanation for the commonly accepted decline in homicide rates over time. The most common theory discussed by historians in relation to this question is the notion of the 'civilising process'. D'Cruze analyses the appropriateness of Elias's work as an explanatory framework, and indeed challenges the statistical evidence which points to an historical decline in unlawful fatality. The infamous case studies which conclude the chapter emphasise the commonly complex nature of homicidal episodes, the nuances of judicial responses to fatal violence and the perpetual fascination that this kind of criminal activity holds for the public at large.

Heather Shore's chapter on the criminal underworld and organised crime exposes the evolving nature of criminal networks throughout history, and explores the complexities of the relationships that existed between the criminals, the authorities, the media and the public. The chapter explains why London acts as a nucleus for the criminal underworld, and identifies certain features such as kinship, territory and violent behaviour which transcend most chronological and spatial boundaries to become the inherent characteristics of criminal networks and the so-called 'criminal class'. Yet, Shore makes clear that an unambiguous and comprehensive definition of organised crime has proved fairly elusive and contentious, and as a result, historians have fashioned their understanding of this form of criminal activity through a range of interdisciplinary frameworks.

The case studies in this chapter reveal much of the mythology associated with organised criminals, from thieving rogues and highwaymen to gang lords and robber barons. This notoriety and celebrity, perhaps most strongly evidenced by the modern media's obsession with gangster culture, stands in stark contrast to the implacable attitude of the authorities when faced with violent recidivists. As Shore indicates, the character from the criminal underworld, if detected and prosecuted, could expect harsh treatment from the courts.

Sarah Wilson's chapter on fraud begins by examining whether or not the perpetration of this kind of activity can be usefully analysed alongside other, more readily identifiable forms of criminality. Although cost-intensive, it seems that fraud fails to achieve the same recognition as other types of property theft, which are generally regarded as more overtly threatening and thus more serious. Although this kind of attitude is beginning to change over the course of the more modern era, the transition is slow and inconsistent. Wilson then goes on to describe how historians of white-collar crime have largely been preoccupied with two interrelated issues – respectability and class. Notions of both of these factors have seemingly altered over time within the contexts of changing economic fortunes, evolving business practices and emerging technologies. The case studies included in this chapter illuminate these key historiographical concerns to great effect. In addition, definitional debates and discussions of potential common characteristics amongst the perpetrators of fraudulent criminality across history are also examined. This is pertinent alongside the influence of white-collar crime on policy making and legislative change in more recent times. As this chapter makes clear, white-collar offences, and fraud in particular, are crimes of our past, our present and our future, and as such, they should merit more of our attention.

Chris Williams's exploration of the history of policing provides a welcome counterpoint to the chapters which focus on criminality and criminal behaviour. The piece begins by tracing the evolutionary nature of policing provision, from the old 'reactive' system of constables and nightwatchmen, through to a new 'proactive' and more centralised system, heralded initially by the establishment of the Metropolitan Police in 1829 and then further enhanced and modified by subsequent legislative changes over the course of the next 150 years. However, this transition, as Williams is quick to point out, did not happen overnight, nor was it a smooth or uniform process. The transformation in attitudes towards the role and function of policing over time is then explored alongside the extensive influences of cultural change and technological advancement on policing methods. This exemplifies just how different policing activity is today, compared with the early modern period. The chapter then moves on to examine the various nuanced approaches that historians have adopted in their analysis of policing and detection since the 1970s, with a particular focus on issues of legitimacy and causation. Several other key themes emerge from this review, which are then illuminated by the detailed case studies. These include the notional fear of serious crime (especially theft) and police responses to it; the development of appropriate methods for dealing with insurrection;

the concept of the police as 'domestic missionaries', and debates over the spread of expertise and the preferred hierarchical structures operating within and across the multifarious layers of the police force as a whole.

The volume concludes with Judith Rowbotham's chapter on the history of capital punishment after 1750. This piece charts the various shifts in attitudes towards execution over the last 250 years and highlights the particular social, legislative and political contexts where reconsideration of this punishment strategy was conducted. The chapter begins by exploring the early history of execution and examines the rationale behind the inclusion of certain capital offences in the statute book. A discussion of the 'effectiveness' of the 'Bloody Code' then follows, which culminates in an exploration of the debates around the comparative 'usefulness' of capital punishment in the first half of the nineteenth century. The chapter then builds on this material, in order to investigate the increasingly, but varied, organised opposition to the death penalty which gained momentum throughout the modern period until the final debates on the issue in 1964. The media involvement in this campaign is given particular attention in order to emphasise how complex, controversial and indeed divisive the issue of capital punishment has been throughout history, and this theme is also picked up in the chapter's exploration of the historiography on the subject. The specific issues of performativity and professionalization are examined in some detail throughout, and are especially explicated by the selected case studies which testify to the longevity of the debates surrounding the death penalty which continue still to this day, despite the fact that the last criminal execution in Britain occurred well over forty years ago.

Notes

1. See for instance B. Godfrey and P. Lawrence (2005) *Crime and Justice 1750–1950* (Cullompton: Willan); B.S. Godfrey, P. Lawrence and C.A. Williams (2008) *History and Crime* (London: Sage); S. Carroll (2007) *Cultures of Violence: Interpersonal Violence in Historical Perspective* (Basingstoke: Palgrave Macmillan); B. Godfrey, C. Emsley and G. Dunstall (eds.) (2003) *Comparative Histories of Crime* (Cullompton: Willan); R. McMahon (ed.) (2008) *Crime, Law and Popular Culture in Europe, 1500–1900* (Cullompton: Willan); C. Emsley (2005) *Crime and Society in England 1750–1900* (2nd edn, Harlow: Longman); V.A.C. Gatrell, B. Lenman and G. Parker (eds.) (1980) *Crime and the Law: A Social History of Crime in Western Europe since 1500* (London: Europa) and J.S. Cockburn (ed.) (1977) *Crime in England 1550–1800* (London: Methuen).
2. See for instance R. Sindall (1990) *Street Violence in the Nineteenth Century: Media Panic or Real Danger?* (Leicester: Leicester University Press); J.J. Tobias (1967) *Crime and Industrial Society in the Nineteenth Century* (London: Batsford) and J.J. Tobias (1979) *Crime and Police in England 1700–1900* (Dublin: Gill & Macmillan).

3. There are, of course, some exceptions that should be considered, but these are primarily case studies which are limited in scope and/or chronology. For example, T.C. Whitlock (2005) *Crime, Gender and Consumer Culture in Nineteenth Century England* (Aldershot: Ashgate); D. Palk (2006) *Gender, Crime and Judicial Discretion 1780–1830* (Woodbridge: Boydell); C. Herrup (1984) '"New Shoes and Mutton Pies": Investigative Responses to Theft in Seventeenth Century East Sussex', *Historical Journal*, 27:4, 811-30; J.M. Beattie (1986) *Crime and the Courts in England 1600–1800* (Oxford: Clarendon Press) and H. Shore (1999) *Artful Dodgers: Youth and Crime in Early Nineteenth Century London* (Woodbridge: Boydell).

4. See for instance various chapters in this volume, as well as Beattie, *Crime and the Courts*, especially Chapters 8, 9 and 10; P.J. King (2000) *Crime, Justice and Discretion in England 1740–1820* (Oxford: Oxford University Press), especially Part III, and V.A.C. Gatrell (1994) *The Hanging Tree: Execution and the English People 1770–1868* (Oxford: Oxford University Press).

5. For further discussion see L. Moran and B. Skeggs (eds.) (2004) *Sexuality and the Politics of Violence and Safety* (London: Routledge).

6. For further discussion see D.S. Nash and A.M. Kilday (forthcoming 2010) *Cultures of Shame: Punishing Moral Lapses in the West 1500–1900* (Basingstoke: Palgrave Macmillan).

7. For further discussion see Beattie, *Crime and the Courts*, Chapters 9 and 10.

8. For further discussion see N. Morris and D.J. Rothman (eds.) (1996) *The Oxford History of the Prison: The Practice of Punishment in Western Society* (Oxford: Oxford University Press), especially Chapters 3, 5 and 8.

9. For further discussion see the introductory chapter in Nash and Kilday, *Cultures of Shame*.

10. For further discussion see L.B. Faller (1987) *Turned to Account: The Forms and Functions on Criminal Biography in Late Seventeenth- and Early Eighteenth-Century England* (Cambridge: Cambridge University Press); A. Fox (2000) *Oral and Literate Culture in England 1500–1700* (Oxford: Clarendon Press); A. Halasz (1997) *The Marketplace of Print: Pamphlets and the Public Sphere in Early Modern England* (Cambridge: Cambridge University Press) and S. Clark (2003) *Women and Crime in the Street Literature of Early Modern England* (Basingstoke: Palgrave Macmillan).

11. For further discussion see J.R. Walkowitz (1992) *City of Dreadful Delight: Narratives of Sexual Danger in late-Victorian London* (London: Virago); L. Brake, A. Jones and L. Madden (eds.), (1990) *Investigating Victorian Journalism* (London: Macmillan); L. Brown (1985) *Victorian News and Newspapers* (Oxford: Clarendon Press); L. Perry Curtis (2001) *Jack the Ripper and the London Press* (New Haven and London: Yale University Press) and A. Smith (1979) *The Newspaper: An International History* (London: Thames & Hudson).

12. For further discussion see Nash and Kilday, *Cultures of Shame*, Chapter 7.

13. See the discussion in J. Rowbotham (2005) 'Criminal Savages? Or "Civilizing" the Legal Process', in J. Rowbotham and K. Stevenson (eds.), *Criminal Conversations: Victorian Crimes, Social Panic, and Moral Outrage* (Columbus: Ohio State University Press), 91–105.

14. For further discussion see M. Priestman (1998) *Crime Fiction from Poe to the Present* (Plymouth: Northcote House) and M. Priestman (1990) *Detective Fiction and Literature: The Figure on the Carpet* (Basingstoke: Macmillan).

15. Although this focuses on working-class tastes for classical literature, see J. Rose (2001) *The Intellectual Life of the British Working-Classes* (Newhaven, CT and London: Yale University Press), 365–92 for a discussion of the availability of cheap and popular books.

16. See for example S. Chibnall and R. Murphy (eds.) (1999) *British Crime Cinema* (London: Routledge) and J. Curran and V. Porter (eds.) (1983) *British Cinema History* (London: Weidenfeld & Nicolson).

17. For further discussion see for instance C. Emsley (1996) *The English Police: A Political and Social History* (Harlow: Longman); P. Rawlings (2002) *Policing: A Short History* (Cullompton: Willan); G. Blaney (ed.) (2007) *Policing Interwar Europe: Continuity, Change and Crisis, 1918–40* (Basingstoke: Palgrave Macmillan); J. Bunker (1988) *From Rattle to Radio: History of Metropolitan Police Communications* (Studley: Brewin Books) and Chapter 8 in this volume.

18. For further discussion see B. Weinberger (1995) *The Best Police in the World: An Oral History of British Policing* (Aldershot: Scolar Press).

19. For further discussion see E. Zureik and M.B. Salter (eds.) (2005) *Global Surveillance and Policing* (Cullompton: Willan); R. Coleman (2004) *Reclaiming the Streets: Surveillance, Social Control and the City* (Cullompton: Willan) and T. Newburn and S. Hayman (2001) *Policing, Surveillance and Social Control* (Cullompton: Willan).

20. For further discussion see Beattie, *Crime and the Courts*, Chapter 4.

21. For further discussion see Beattie, *Crime and the Courts*, Chapter 4; Emsley, *Crime and Society*, Chapter 7; Shore, *Artful Dodgers* and J. Duckworth (2002) *Fagin's Children: Criminal Children in Victorian England* (London: Hambledon Continuum).

22. For further discussion see Chapter 7 in this volume and M. Levi (1987) *Regulating Fraud: White Collar Crime and the Criminal Process* (London: Tavistock); A. Bequai (1978) *White Collar Crime: A 20th Century Crisis* (Lexington, MA: Lexington Press); S. Wilson (2003) 'Law, Morality, and Regulation: Victorian Experiences of Financial Crime', *British Journal of Criminology*, 46, 1073–90 and G. Robb (1992) *White Collar Crime in Modern England: Financial Fraud and Business Morality, 1845–1929* (Cambridge: Cambridge University Press).

23. For further discussion see Y. Jewkes (2003) *Dot.Cons: Crime, Deviancy and Identity on the Internet* (Cullompton: Willan) and Y. Jewkes and M. Yar (eds.) (2009) *Handbook of Internet Crime* (Cullompton: Willan).

24. For further discussion see Chapter 3 in this volume as well as J. Kermode and G. Walker (1994) 'Introduction', in J. Kermode and G. Walker (eds.), *Women, Crime and the Courts in Early Modern England* (Chapel Hill and London: University of North Carolina Press), 1–25; M.L. Arnot and C. Usborne (1999) 'Why Gender and Crime? Aspects of an International Debate', in M.L. Arnot and C. Usborne (eds.), *Gender and Crime in Modern Europe* (London: UCL Press), 1–43 and A.M. Kilday (2007) *Women and*

Violent Crime in Enlightenment Scotland (Woodbridge: Boydell), especially the introduction and Chapter 1.

25. See J. Weeks (1989) *Sex, Politics and Society: The Regulation of Sexuality since 1800* (2nd edn., London: Longman), 114 and passim.

26. For further discussion see A. Grey (1992) *Quest for Justice: Towards Homosexual Emancipation* (London: Sinclair-Stevenson).

27. For further discussion see J. Knelman (1998) *Twisting in the Wind: The Murderess and the English Press* (Toronto and London: Toronto University Press) and S. D'Cruze *et al.* (2006) *Murder: Social and Historical Approaches to Understanding Murder and Murderers* (Cullompton: Willan).

28. See for instance P.J. King (2006) *Crime and the Law in England 1750–1840: Remaking Justice from the Margins* (Cambridge: Cambridge University Press), Chapters 5 and 6.

29. For further discussion see L.A. Jackson (2006) *Women Police: Gender, Welfare and Surveillance in the Twentieth Century* (Manchester: Manchester University Press).

30. See for instance J.M. Beattie (1975) 'The Criminality of Women in Eighteenth Century England', *Journal of Social History*, 8, 90.

31. For further discussion see J. Carter Wood (2004) *Violence and Crime in Nineteenth Century England: The Shadow of our Refinement* (London: Routledge).

32. For further discussion see M. Ignatieff (1978) *A Just Measure of Pain: The Penitentiary in the Industrial Revolution 1750–1850* (London: Macmillan).

33. See M. Foucault (1979) *Discipline and Punish: The Birth of the Prison*, trans. A. Sheridan (Harmondsworth: Penguin).

34. For further discussion see S. Banner (2002) *The Death Penalty: An American History* (Cambridge, MA and London: Harvard University Press); L.P. Masur (1989) *Rites of Execution: Capital Punishment and the Transformation of American Culture 1776–1865* (New York and Oxford: Oxford University Press) and E. Steelwater (2003) *The Hangman's Knot: Lynching, Legal Execution and America's Struggle with the Death Penalty* (Boulder, CO: Westview Press).

1 Moral Crimes and the Law in Britain since 1700

David Nash

1. Introduction

This chapter considers the history of how crime has been related, throughout the historical past, with the idea of collapsing moral standards. At a fundamental level, how a society considers the morality of its citizens is frequently a clear indicator of how it conceives its governing role. How far should a government's laws and policies aim to protect its citizens from harm (either that perpetrated by others or themselves)? How much is this intention compromised by the phenomenon of individual rights and liberties which effectively evolved during this period? The history of these also shows us how the moral paternalism of the State has partially (but interestingly not wholly) been defined as constituting 'the public interest'. More intriguingly, this demonstrates the inherent balancing act that any liberal democracy, such as the UK, must face up to. Essentially, government laws have to balance the protection of the vulnerable against permitting freedoms that enhance the lives of individuals. Since the arrival of urban societies, governments and policing authorities have expressed concerns about the growth of so called 'moral crimes'. These are 'crimes' that are considered to have wider impacts outside the context of the individual crime. Drunkenness, for example, may not be a significant problem on its own, but in the domestic sphere, it may lead to accidents or interfamilial violence. In the public sphere, it may lead to interpersonal violence, public order offences, theft or other crimes.

These particular issues are demonstrated through looking at two 'crimes' that contemporary society does not consider to be crimes at all, homosexuality and blasphemy. The UK's Judeo-Christian heritage has also regulated what it perceived to be sexual 'crimes', such as prostitution and homosexuality, in the belief that it was protecting society and individuals. A more dangerous crime was blasphemy, which brought the judgement of God down upon societies which did not punish it. Blasphemy also challenged divine authority and thus undermined the earthly authority represented by the law. Such conceptions, which appear perhaps anachronistic now, were extremely relevant to seventeenth-century society. A unified approach to these problems was to consider the issue to be one of moral reformation. This emphasised society's duty to legislate around drink, public manifestations of sexual behaviour, issues around public speech and the protection of religious belief. However, one of the striking things that emerges from this is how episodic and uncoordinated attempts to 'control' moral and social ills actually were over the 400 years in question.

2. Chronology

Many of the publicly expressed concerns about morality really appear in their modern form at the end of the seventeenth century. The restoration monarchies of Charles II and William and Mary took an especial interest in fostering conformity and legislating against social ills.[1] Within this legislation, we get a clear picture of what these societies found objectionable or challenging, and how legislation against these behaviours so frequently emanated from clerical authorities who were charged with policing and regulating moral conduct within this society.

From the early seventeenth century, there was a real offensive which believed that preventing small transgressions would in turn prevent bigger ones. Between 1601 and 1628 parliament passed no fewer than ten bills intended to combat the evil of drunkenness. The moral, and increasingly expensive, 'crime' of bastardy was targeted with five bills between 1606 and 1627. Profaning the Sabbath and blasphemy were tackled through nine parliamentary bills between 1601 and 1628, whilst seven different bills addressed the menace of profanity and swearing between 1601 and 1624.[2] This crusade against the populace's moral condition was aided by a variety of private organisations that took it upon themselves to observe, report and combat moral evils. Organisations like the Society for the Promotion of Christian Knowledge and the Society for the Reformation of Manners systematically investigated the petty moral misdemeanours of the populace.

In the London of the first two decades of the eighteenth century, for example, the Society for the Reformation of Manners pursued drunks, Sabbath breakers, profane swearers, gamblers, proprietors of bawdy houses and 'lewd and disorderly' individuals. Whilst low-level campaigns against gambling and drunkenness were a constant feature of the Society's activities, its high-profile campaigns against the other offences frequently ebbed and flowed.[3] During the French Revolutionary Wars, moral concerns were explicitly linked to political radicalism. The revolution was associated with immorality and the overturning of the natural order. Conservative commentators, such as the prolific pamphleteer Hannah More, spoke out against the levelling principles of Thomas Paine and the atheist Jacobin ideas filtering through to the English populace after 1790.

a) Blasphemy

Blasphemy in particular was seen as a profound threat to the social order of the late seventeenth century and beyond. It was a crime which threatened the psychological underpinnings of the law and thus threatened the whole social and moral order. Crucial to this was the enduring belief in providence. It was believed authority and order still relied upon God's favour – to displease God upset the moral and social order, bringing the country to ruin. Crimes in this period – much more so than after 1820 – were regarded as challenges to the existing social and political order. The modern offence of blasphemy stems from the end of the seventeenth century, when its challenge to morality became associated with wider challenges to the safety of the realm. These were part of a general campaign mounted against misbehaviour throughout Europe which resulted in analogous action.[4]

The main blasphemy statute which was active during the modern period was enacted in 1698 and became known as the 9 & 10 William c. 32. Although this was intended to provide a method of censuring and controlling speech crimes associated with sedition, it also suggested a fear of providential judgement upon the nation-State. Its preamble saw 'impious opinions' as simultaneously 'tending to the dishonour of Almighty God' as well as being 'destructive to the peace and welfare of this kingdom'. This statute made it an offence to deny the Christian religion or the divine authority of the scriptures or to preach polytheism. The punishments prescribed by this statute were to be graduated, starting with removal from office for a first offence, leading to legal disabilities and eventually to three years' imprisonment.

The Statute linked the instruments of State with the Church established by law, and this was exemplified in the previous judgement of Sir Mathew Hale in the case against John Taylor in 1675. Hale argued that religion and the law were so inextricably linked that religion was itself 'part and parcel' of the laws of England. Thus an attack upon the Church established by Law was an assault upon the laws of England and the peace of the community. Although the statute was never used successfully, it strongly coloured the debate about the status of blasphemy as an offence in English Law.[5] As we can see, the law was also explicitly intended to protect the Established Church and subsequent attempts to extend it to cover other branches of Christianity and other faiths were unsuccessful.[6]

An example of how this was applied in practice demonstrates the policing imperative that governed thinking at this time. Peter Annet's indictment in 1763 for publishing the *Free Inquirer* is revealing in its language of how corruption of morals occurred as a process. Annet was punished for his opinions, which rather sum up eighteenth-century authority's attitude to the evil that blasphemy spawned:

> tending to blaspheme Almighty God, and to ridicule, traduce, and discredit his holy scriptures ... thereby to diffuse and propagate irreligious and diabolical opinions in the minds of His Majesty's subjects, and to shake the foundations of the Christian Religion, and of the civil and ecclesiastical government established in this kingdom.[7]

By the 1790s the hard-hitting ideas of Paine's *Age of Reason* led to Thomas Williams being prosecuted in 1797. As has been suggested, the godless ideas of the French Revolution produced almost total panic in England's governing classes. This is perhaps summed up in the name of the new organisation which policed morality. No longer did it have the mild title 'Society for the Reformation of Manners' but it had the actively combative title 'Society for the Suppression of Vice'. Such groups in the first quarter of the nineteenth century were both authoritarian in defence of the social order and filled with individuals who genuinely believed they were acting in the best interests of the nation.[8] The writings of Hannah More and the Conservatives noted that Jacobin wickedness removed the hope of salvation in the next world – thus at a stroke removing the poor's incentive for morally upright behaviour. In moving against profanation of the Sabbath, the Constable's advice manual (which went through several editions) in 1818 declared this was necessary because a sacred Sunday 'humanizes, by the help of society and conversation, the manners of the lower classes; which would otherwise degenerate into a sordid ferocity and savage selfishness of spirit'.[9] These thoughts owed much to an association between behaviour which displeased God and manifestations of his divine displeasure. The Constable's advice on profanation and swearing argued that it gained 'force from the peculiarly awful circumstances of the times in which we live'.[10]

Where blasphemy was linked to a seditious contemporary political climate or encouraged conservative fears of unorthodox religious views, then prosecutions would be more likely. Thus it is no surprise to see prosecutions during the French Revolutionary and Napoleonic Wars (Thomas Williams in 1797, Daniel Isaac Eaton in 1812).[11] In the years of trade depression and political anxiety after the War's conclusion, there was a similar flurry of cases around the offences committed by the political radical Richard Carlile and his circle.[12] These cases tested the boundaries of what was acceptable criticism of religion. Defendants usually argued from the dock that their rights of free speech were being challenged in the name of a discredited attempt to maintain orthodoxy and order. These prosecutions were generally instigated by the Society for the Suppression of Vice with the connivance of the government.

Nonetheless, the high tide of draconian prosecutions had ebbed by the end of the 1830s. In 1841 the Royal Commission's Report into the Criminal Law emphasised that the law of blasphemous libel had, at times, been somewhat liberal in its operation. In particular, it emphasised that the law, if strictly applied, was capable of encompassing all criticism of the Christian religion within its orbit, but that the legal system had graciously declined to do so. Thus it argued that the law punished only those who were 'vulgar and unthinking' – this particular judgement on the blasphemer was to reappear in subsequent decades, with mixed consequences.

The 1841 Commission was also anxious to demonstrate that it did not stifle free-speech debate as its opponents claimed, declaring:

> There is no instance, we believe, of the prosecution of a writer or speaker who has applied himself seriously to examine into the truth of the most important of all subjects, and who, arriving at his own convictions of scepticism or unbelief, has gravely and decorously submitted his opinions to others, without any wanton and malevolent design to do mischief. Such conduct, indeed, could not properly be considered as blasphemy or profaneness; and at the present day a prosecution in such a case would probably not meet with general approbation.[13]

Richard Carlile and his shopmen would have been somewhat aghast at this declaration. Although the Commission had been selective in its judgements, there was a recognition that the law had to be coherent and defensible to retain public support and that it was only used in extreme circumstances. This was, in reality, a brake upon the application of the law in practice, rather than a specific removal of the theoretical reach of the law. Although blasphemy has generally lacked a conclusive *mens rea* (as a crime of strict liability), this assertion of the quality of objection to religion and the manner in which it was made has often acted as the closest measure that the law has for deciding culpability for the crime of blasphemy.

The real discredit of the Common Law of blasphemous libel was caused by the case in 1857 against the mentally unstable Thomas Pooley, who had taken to daubing his locale (Liskeard in Cornwall) with blasphemous graffiti. Despite his incoherent performance in court, Pooley was convicted and sentenced to 21 months' imprisonment. During this sentence Pooley's mental condition worsened, prompting John Stuart Mill to mention the issue as a species of barbarism in his treatise 'On Liberty'.[14]

The eventual realignment of the law to acknowledge the transition in public taste occurred some twenty-six years later in the famous Foote, Ramsey and Kemp case of 1883 (see below). The judgement that the offence was an issue of manner persisted, and this was evident in the numerous attempts to get the Statute and Common law offence repealed. When Charles Bradlaugh attempted to do so in 1889, the bill was roundly rejected by 143 votes to 48. Interestingly, some members of parliament still believed that removing the offence of blasphemy would imperil the moral safety of the community. One speaker remarked: 'While we punish those who killed the body, the Bill would allow men to murder men's souls with impunity.'[15]

Similarly, the law's retention was still regarded by some as fulfilling useful and valuable purposes. When, for example, repeal of the laws was contemplated in 1913 and a deputation told the Home Secretary that the law was 'an anachronism', an official at the Home Office profoundly disagreed with this view, declaring:

> First it is said that the law under which defendants are tried is old and obsolete. This is untrue: the law of blasphemy is on the contrary a striking instance of the common law adapting itself to the times and changing in accordance with a general change of view in regard to religious matters.[16]

In the Edwardian period in England the laws of blasphemy protected the public from inflammatory speeches as much as blasphemous publications. When Harry Boulter appeared before Justice Fillimore, this new emphasis on issues of public order was confirmed. The prosecution established that opinions hostile to religion could now legitimately be discussed in private. However the dangers individuals like Boulter posed were significant, since they attracted considerable crowds, if his views were unchallenged in public. The issue was encapsulated in Boulter's threat that 'if I knew a man who believed in Christianity, I would kill him'. When Boulter was found guilty, the judge proposed leniency explicitly upon a promise of future acceptable public conduct.[17]

Public order issues meant that local police constables were more prepared to consult the Home Office about potential trouble. It was this that accounted for the prosecutions of Thomas William Stewart, John William Gott, Ernest Pack and Thomas Jackson. All four, as members of a militant quasi-anarchist organisation, were scarcely innocents caught by an insensitive and aggressive law. Ernest Pack in particular also spoke to crowds about Malthusian birth-control issues, sometimes blending the two sub-jects together. For the police and Home Office, this connected blasphemy with obscenity and a potentially double-headed challenge to decency. The trial of Thomas William Stewart noted that 'a man was free to speak as he pleased on religious matters, but not as to morals'.[18] In 1912, when Thomas Jackson and Frederick Chasty were both prosecuted, the 1847 Town Police Clauses Act was used since it forbade 'profane or obscene language'.

An important landmark case which centred around the rights of athe-ists and unbelievers to criticise religion was not actually about a specific religious incident at all. When a devoted secularist, Charles Bowman, left a significant financial legacy to the National Secular Society (NSS), the Bowman family argued in court that the Society's work involved the deliberate act of blasphemy as understood by the Common Law. The Law Lords eventually rejected the family's case on the grounds that the law would trust an institution to behave responsibly. The judgement meant that the secularist aims of the NSS were no longer contrary to law and, more importantly, opinion on such matters could be expected to alter over time in the light of changing moral climates.

Nonetheless, the issue of private thoughts and morality were a central part of the *Gay News* case of 1977. The periodical *Gay News* was pros-ecuted by Mary Whitehouse, who inherited the mantle of the Vice Society and the Society for the Reformation of Manners. The paper had published a poem by James Kirkup which depicted Christ as a promiscuous homo-sexual amid an arguably obscene illustration. Despite defences from John Mortimer, Bernard Levin and others that *Gay News* should be considered a 'serious' publication, the paper's editor (Dennis Lemon) was convicted, after appeal to the House of Lords, and received a 12-month suspended sentence.[19] What was pertinent to the law was that the prevailing view about manner of discussion was overturned. The *Gay News* case remade the law so that a prosecution case merely had to prove the fact of publica-tion and no longer foregrounded the manner of that publication.

The law was not significantly tested in the distance between 1977 and its repeal in 2008. The Salman Rushdie case demonstrated that blasphemy would be preserved only as a residue of Christianity. Thereafter, much action was invested in preventing the act of offence rather than prosecuting it once it had occurred. This was particularly obvious in the case against the film-maker Nigel Wingrove, who produced an experimental piece on the erotic visions of St Teresa of Avila. In this film, Wingrove's Teresa interacted in a sexual manner with the body of the crucified Christ. Using what Wingrove would later term 'prior restraint', the British Board of Film Classification refused the film a certificate on the grounds that it might be blasphemous, ignoring the Home Office dictum that private prosecutions against material functioned as the barometer of public opinion.[20] Perhaps the death knell for the Common Law of blasphemous libel came in the case brought against the television broadcast of *Jerry Springer the Opera* in January 2007. In this, the magistrate ruled that the BBC should be regarded as a responsible organisation that understood what it was undertaking. This, for the first time, took the view prevalent in continental Europe which protected the producers of books, films and images provided sufficient warning was given as to the content's likelihood of causing offence. This was the final recognition that the law had no absolute duty to protect religion as a moral system and that it would instead protect the providers of culture and ask consumers to be more responsible about their viewing choices.

b) Homosexuality

Homosexuality began the period studied by this book as theoretically one of the worst of crimes, but by the end of the period had been decriminalised and subsequently recognised as merely a lifestyle choice. Most historians accept that the 'crimes' associated with homosexuality stem from the Tudor period. The 1533 Buggery Act made sex with a man (or an animal) a capital offence, and this was confirmed by subsequent statutes in 1540 and 1562. The last of these represents the final codification of these early attempts to legislate against homosexual activity. A judgement in 1718 confirmed that the offence of buggery also applied to the act with females.[21] Again connected with various societies for moral reformation, the early eighteenth century witnessed a panic about homosexual behaviour and such societies often entrapped unfortunate individuals.[22] Like other areas of the 'Bloody Code', the capital sentence was seldom used or even contemplated. In this instance, stringent laws of evidence were required to secure a conviction and the persistent failure to supply medical evidence generally meant the material fact of the accusation of buggery was left unproven. In most cases, these strict rules of evidence discouraged prosecutions and the use of the capital sentence.[23] There was, certainly, an unwillingness to use the full sanction of the law against private homosexual activity which did not possess a tendency to corrupt the morals of the impressionable. Netta Goldsmith noted that by 1830, homosexuals were far less likely to be executed than property criminals finding themselves prosecuted under the lesser offence of assault with intent to commit.[24] Nonetheless laws were still created with the intention of proceeding against the activity as a moral canker.

From the early seventeenth century, sexual approaches to an individual of the same sex could be interpreted as an attempt to break the law, emphasising that the vast majority of prosecutions were brought by private citizens in this period. In 1749 a law made sodomy illegal in the navy, which again showed evidence that homosexuality was viewed as a moral concern with an innate corrupting influence.[25] In 1781, a judicial ruling required the emission of sperm to complete the offence. This was further complicated by the fact that many prosecutions foundered on the inability to provide reliable witnesses. Much of the ability to prosecute in this area hinged upon the denial of consent by one of the parties involved or a demonstrable failure to obtain consent. After 1807, a sexual partner of a defendant needed their evidence corroborated in court and, if both parties were consenting to the act, additional corroboration was required. Thus consensual sexual acts that occurred behind closed doors would generally escape prosecution. The problems of proceeding with prosecution of the major offence meant that so many potential cases were redirected into the work of the lesser summary jurisdiction. These also were, significantly, offences that were of an obviously more public nature. Unproved charges were frequently reduced to ones of indecent assault, whilst subsidiary charges included soliciting the offence, conspiracy to, and incitement to commit the act. Summary jurisdiction also heard cases that were brought under offences such as vagrancy, indecent exposure, suspicion and lesser sexual acts that stopped short of penetrative sex.[26]

The 'short-circuiting' of the capital offence came to an end in 1828 when the rules of evidence no longer required evidence of the admission of sperm. A.D. Harvey saw this as arguably the culmination of a changed attitude which marked the first third of the nineteenth century.[27] The theoretical use of the death penalty was removed in 1861 as a result of the Offences against the Person Act. In 1885 the situation changed again with the Criminal Law Amendment Act, which specifically defined homosexual crimes and the sentences these would receive. Central to this was the famous Labouchere Amendment. This was the 11th clause of the Act, which provided that:

> Any male person who, in public or private, commits, or is a party to the commission of, or procures or attempts to procure the commission by any male person of, any act of gross indecency with another male person, shall be guilty of a misdemeanour, and being convicted thereof shall be liable at the discretion of the court to be imprisoned for any term not exceeding two years, with or without hard labour.

This is generally seen as the moment all homosexual activity became the target of the law as well as introducing the offence of 'gross indecency'. The Amendment also rendered illegal acts in private which might be said to have escaped the reach of earlier laws. Nonetheless, the public nuisance of homosexual approaches and importuning were further targeted under the 1898 Vagrancy Act, which made them summary offences.[28]

The Labouchere Amendment was made notable because it was followed by two separate incidents which highlighted the issue of the authority's attitude to homosexual activity. The first of these was the Cleveland Street scandal of 1889–90. This involved newspapers reporting upon police actions against a homosexual brothel housed at 19 Cleveland Street in London's West End. The story confirmed many prejudices that existed about immoral practices within the English aristocracy and even as far as the monarchy itself – since it was rumoured that the Duke of Clarence had been involved.[29] The second influential incident was the trial, conviction and imprisonment of Oscar Wilde in 1895, which brought the issue of homosexuality and the law considerable notoriety. Wilde was found guilty of a violation of Clause 11 of the Criminal Law Amendment Act of 1885. This also coincided with an obviously less tolerant attitude towards homosexual practices which historians have noted for the late nineteenth and early twentieth centuries.[30]

Further significant change occurred only in the middle of the twentieth century when something akin to a homophobic moral panic gripped the nation in the aftermath of the Second World War, with a spectacular increase in police activity against homosexual men. Matt Houlbrook noted that cases brought in the Metropolitan Magistrates Court in 1947 saw a threefold increase from 211 (in 1942) to 637 (in 1947). The gap between this situation and the pre-war world is graphically emphasised by figures for 1938, which showed 134 prosecutions for sodomy compared with 1,043 in 1954.[31] Other hints that the moral climate had changed are given credence by noting that conservatively-minded individuals were entering office. These included the committed Roman Catholic Sir Theobald Mathew at the office of the Director of Public Prosecution and Sir John Nott-Bowes as Metropolitan Police Commissioner. The Sexual Offences Act of 1956 reaffirmed that buggery was an offence that could be committed by any person with another, whether privately or publicly.

Into this strained atmosphere came the Wolfenden Committee of 1957, which eventually recommended the decriminalisation of most aspects of homosexual intercourse. The Committee's report redrew a distinction between public and private acts, which effectively had existed before the Labouchere Amendment. Whilst stressing how public acts had a tendency to damage order and decency, the Committee removed private homosexual acts from the purview of the policeman and the psychiatrist, with its declaration that there was no link between homosexuality and mental instability.

Homosexuality was finally decriminalised in 1967 when private acts between two consenting men over 21 years of age were no longer deemed illegal. Since that time a number of high-profile campaigns have sought to lower the age of consent or bring the differing situation in the Celtic fringe into line with the British mainland. In 1994 the age of consent for homosexuals was lowered to 18, and to 16 in 2001. In Northern Ireland a related measure brought the age down to 17.[32] These last legislative measures were mindful of the equality agendas that had become an essential part of equating British law with European Union law, and harmonised how the law would deal equally with male and female sexuality.

3. Historiography

a) Blasphemy

The historiography of blasphemy has been somewhat episodic, whilst legal commentaries were generally prompted by the sudden need for an investigation of the case law. Defining blasphemy has proved a methodological problem in itself and this has attracted different approaches from historical and literary studies and other disciplines. Legal histories similarly cannot produce a coherent definition of the offence.[33] It is frequently noted that many of the precedents established are sometimes vague or ambiguous so that some of the historiography must be sought within the legal pronouncement of judges themselves. Nonetheless, most commentators agree that the offence consisted of a systematic attack upon the sacred Christian beliefs of another sufficient to cause a form of insult and injury. Since the law in England only protected the Anglican Church established by law, this was considerably Anglo-centric before the arrival of considerations around European law forced a rethink.

The first systematic historian of the subject was Hypatia Bradlaugh-Bonner, daughter of the secularist leader Charles Bradlaugh. Bradlaugh-Bonner's work stemmed from free-speech arguments for the law's repeal to show the law's persistence as clearly anachronistic and anti-modern.[34] G.D. Nokes's legal commentary of 1928 thought it was aiding lawyers by noting that attacks upon the Trinity, the existence of God, the attribution of human passions to God, denial of Christ's birth, good works, teachings and resurrection had all been the subject of prosecutions.[35] However, producing such a supposedly authoritative list of possible offence criteria has had its shortcomings, since subsequent generations have uncovered new ways to offend. Another approach to the legal history of blasphemy has been the portrayal of those ensnared by the common law of blasphemous libel as martyrs for progress. This is the impetus behind Arthur Calder-Marshall's 1972 work *Lewd, Blasphemous and Obscene*, which rather celebrated its own libertarianism and optimism in the wake of the *Oz* obscenity trial which, like the earlier *Lady Chatterley's Lover* trial, were iconic moments for the counter-culture's victories for liberty of expression against a stuffy establishment. Thus Calder-Marshall saw the resolution of issues around blasphemy as both inevitable and a clear consequence of unconditional abolition.[36]

Historiographical approaches since the 1990s have been manifestly less optimistic. The Salman Rushdie affair questioned assumptions about blasphemy that had been commonplace within the previous 20 years. First, it was shown to be relevant to non-Christian communities and that the existing law's provision of religious protection was thus inadequate. Secondly, the assumptions about Christian society inexorably secularising were also shown to be misleading. Richard Webster's work placed blasphemy in a longer tradition of Western cultural clashes with the East and noted that Western conceptions of justice and free speech were scarcely value free. Wholly supportive of the Muslim case, Webster noted how the parochialism of English law was itself a dangerous anachronism.[37]

The two historians who have attempted long chronological studies of blasphemy are Leonard Levy and David Nash. Levy noted how often blasphemy persisted as an accusation used by rulers to consolidate power or to justify action against politically or socially dangerous groups.[38] In various works David Nash has noted how the history of blasphemy runs counter to attitudes associated with secularisation, as well as noting how its endurance was aided and abetted by the persistence of providential readings of the world. These sometimes led strong blasphemy laws defending supposedly moral and Christian Britain from the cosmopolitan standards of behaviour tolerated in what anxious moral commentators saw as a decadent Europe. Blasphemy's recasting as a hate crime provided a clear mandate for government concern and communities who would potentially use prosecution as an affirmation of identity. The communal response to blasphemy which characterised the early modern period was replaced by a legal approach which emphasised individual rights. With the transformation of blasphemy laws into hate-crime laws, the State's reinvolvement in prosecuting blasphemy has arguably brought the older communal-based approaches back into vogue.[39]

b) Homosexuality

Much of the literature associated with homosexuality and the law has also been related to historical investigations of the arrival of homosexual identity. Jeffery Weeks, for example, noted that the original Henrician Buggery Statute of 1533 and subsequent attempts to police related offences scarcely acknowledges the existence of a separate homosexual identity. As Weeks suggests, it was the commission of specific sexual acts that was targeted rather than types of person.[40] This demonstrates both a fear of the activity as a moral contagion and a suggestion that temptation was a more relevant consideration for eighteenth- and nineteenth-century society than the sexual orientation of the individual. Weeks, like Foucault, examined the interplay of social forces and the rationale of institutions to classify and process individual reactions to behaviour as a means of defining the homosexual. Alongside the discourses of sexologists and psychiatrists, Weeks thus sees the Oscar Wilde trial as 'clear evidence in the later decades of the nineteenth century of a development of a new sense of identity amongst many homosexual individuals, and a crucial element in this would undoubtedly have been the new public salience of homosexuality, dramatised by the legal situation'.[41]

Other historians, such as Harry Cocks, have strongly emphasised that legal procedure against homosexuals problematised the issue of privacy.[42] The role of blackmail, even when used by the sensationalist press, introduced other problems of its own for Victorian society.[43] A focus upon the legal history, such as that adopted by Harry Cocks, emphasises how specific legal cases brought discussion of homosexuality into the limelight and, occasionally, how readings of these incidents potentially produce a distorted analysis. For example Cocks suggests that the impact of the Labouchere amendment is coloured by interpretations that focus upon its declaration that private homosexual acts had come under the law's coverage. He argues that this assumes that all private acts before this date would escape legal intrusion. This has shifted focus upon the period before the legal 'watersheds' of the late nineteenth century. Thus consideration of the legal history of homosexuality, so Harry Cocks suggests, uncovers a much broader and more 'everyday' version of its legal history which describes the application of the law as 'familiar' and rather more removed from the 'sensationalist' and individual 'scandal' approach.[44]

This has focused upon how readers and historians should regard the repressive mechanisms and deployment of law and other institutions. In many respects, one of these arguments is also important in relation to all modes of behaviour deemed immoral at particular times in the historical past. Most consider that official silence about homosexual activity and practices produced sophisticated subcultures that thrived upon their fundamentally illicit nature.[45]

Other historiography has focused upon interpreting forms of legislation and placing them in a wider context. In this, attention has been drawn to the Wolfenden Report and some scholars have shown that it examined the policing of sexuality in its entirety. Thus concerns about homosexuality were placed alongside concerns about other threats to the moral sanctity of family life, such as divorce and adultery. Whilst the Wolfenden report may have received the accolade of being the liberal forerunner of decriminalisation, its credentials for being a humanitarian way forward may be questioned. David Selfe and Vincent Burke have suggested that Wolfenden followed a utilitarian perspective with the intention of minimising harm. In the end, its conclusions merely questioned whether legal proceedings were the most efficient and appropriate way to deal with the 'problem' of homosexuality.[46] In many respects, this might echo the conclusions that most modern societies come to in allowing a moral problem to move away from the central focus of the law and of unofficial policing agencies. However, in recent work, Leslie Moran has revisited the issue of how systems of control and regulation have defined the identity and status of the homosexual. This has shown that legislation and policy discussion, such as the Wolfenden Report, has still had an important effect upon the framing of the law.[47] Quite rightly, the assumption here is that once the law starts to name and describe activities, whether public or private, it invariably defines what the law will do. As such, this invites us to think about the function of law as either reflecting or shaping morality, according to the choices made by those who take part in its deliberations and judgements.

Like the historiography of blasphemy, the optimism of the reforms and permissive attitudes of the 1960s met with something of a backlash as the following decades dawned. Just as the Salman Rushdie affair introduced a note of pessimism to the previous generation's modernisation, the history of homosexuality and the law was also affected by the AIDS pandemic. Antony Grey's almost autobiographical work (as a campaigner through the period of Wolfenden and decriminalisation in 1967) is notable for how the tone of pure liberalisation alters within its last sections. Written before the liberalisation of the law in 1994 and 2001 was even a possibility, this work is notable, since it argued that a new agenda which stressed sexual education and health issues would potentially become as important as legal changes.[48]

In a counterpart of the defence of the unique British morality argument we saw in the area of blasphemy, Christie Davies has argued that prohibitions and legal sanctions against homosexuality should be seen as expressions of national identity.[49] These expressions were enforced by what he sees as religiously 'orthodox' societies. Davies suggests that these strongly religious societies were able to resist the tide of liberalisation for the longest. Thus his explanation of Scotland's comparative sluggishness in legalising homosexual behaviour is attributed to Scotland's later secularisation and its ability to organise religious sentiment around moral defence.[50] This, Davies also argues, explains the delay in bringing fringe legislative bodies (such as Jersey and the Isle of Man) into line with the mainland. In his discussion of Northern Ireland's final acceptance of homosexual law reform, alongside the Irish Republic, these two states faced what Davies has described as 'the final defeat of the moral periphery'.[51] When this did happen, as occurred with blasphemy in English law, it was the imperatives brought by European legal integration that unwound the special protection for conservative identity that these jurisdictions sought to preserve.[52]

4. Case Studies

a) Blasphemy

In 1883 George William Foote had been editor of the atheist newspaper the *Freethinker* for little over eighteen months. In this short time he had published a number of inflammatory articles and comic depictions of both Old and New Testament stories. These were a further incident of blasphemy as a form of free-speech campaign and Foote's writings and journalism revisited this historiography, placing his own contribution entirely within this.[53] Eventually prosecution was brought against an article entitled 'What shall I do to be damned', written by a regular contributor to the paper, William Heaford. Subsequent prosecutions were brought against the 1882 Christmas Number of the paper, which contained a comic cartoon life of Christ. These prosecutions were actively encouraged by the Home Secretary Sir William Harcourt when prompted by a significant flow of complaints to the Home Office.[54]

The actions of the Judge, Justice North, did not make the law a benign protective influence as the 1841 Royal Commission had portrayed it. North defined the law strictly noting denial of the truth of Christianity (a view dealt with more leniently by the 1841 Commission) alongside the more familiar prohibitions upon vulgarity, Justice North embarked upon the perennial issue of trying to define the concept of blasphemy for his own contemporary age in describing it as 'contempt, derision ... or ridicule'. The arguments against Foote were, in legal terms, relatively clear-cut – he was undoubtedly responsible for the *Freethinker's* output and it was almost impossible to argue that the material was not intentionally blasphemous. Nonetheless, Foote had important arguments to air about the supposed anachronism of the law, its restraint of free speech and finally how the law appeared to be partial in its application.[55] The last of these was a particular issue, since North's definition of the offence should have made all criticism of religion blasphemous. Foote argued that the rich and learned would be protected from prosecution whilst the laws actively encouraged prosecution of the street-corner orator, or the radical whose message could be construed as vulgar. On the very last point Foote expanded the cultural definition of blasphemy by suggesting that the vulgarity of the Salvation Army was as unacceptable as Christians found his own blasphemy.[56] The first case against Foote reached a standstill when the jury could not agree a verdict. This was swiftly rectified by a retrial a few days later in which a guilty verdict led to a 12- month prison sentence for Foote and lesser sentences for his compatriots.

One of the related cases against Foote resulting from the *Freethinker's* activities had been transferred to Queen's Bench, and this was heard by an infinitely more sympathetic judge, Justice John Duke Coleridge, who set aside the suit and pronounced upon the common-law offence of blasphemous libel, thereby redefining it. Coleridge noted how widespread and ubiquitous all religious discussion had become. He widened the conclusions of the 1841 Royal Commission to recognise the right of sober religious argument. Coleridge declared, for the first time, that the Hale judgement (and its attendant statute) had been eroded over time.[57] This declared that Christianity could no longer justifiably claim to be part and parcel of the law of the land. In theory this opened the door to a much more liberal treatment of blasphemy. Yet many judges, notably James Fitzjames Stephen, took a different view and criticised this judgement, since it represented a modernisation of a law which should really have been abolished.[58] Whilst the liberal judgement from Coleridge inevitably made life easier for Foote and his compatriots, it also rejuvenated the law and made it less anachronistic, thereby preserving it. The effect for the authorities, and Sir William Harcourt in particular, were scarcely what had been intended. The law had been liberalised and action against the *Freethinker* had merely drawn attention to it and its content.

b) Homosexuality

No other instance demonstrates the persistence of moral fear and the enduring reach of some species of paternalism than the case against Laskey, Jaggard and Brown, which was heard in the British and European courts in the mid-1990s.[59] The court case was a result of a prolonged police operation, the code name for which ('Operation Spanner') became the instantly recognisable media nickname for what had occurred. During 1987, by chance, the Essex constabulary came into possession of videotapes portraying a number of men inflicting serious assaults and injuries upon other men. In the context of an earlier panic about so-called 'snuff movies' (videotapes of individuals allegedly being murdered), the police believed the violence to be severe enough for them to consider they were potentially involved in a murder investigation. The resulting inquiry, and expenditure on the surveillance of the three suspects, eventually raised something of a public outcry. The videos portrayed a number of sadomasochistic acts between homosexual men. The genitals of the 'victims' were assaulted with fishhooks, sandpaper, hot wax and needles. Alongside this, they were subject to beatings, either by hand or with implements such as spiked belts, stinging nettles and a cat-o'-nine-tails. It was also noted at the time that this treatment resulted in the flow of blood and lasting scarring for the 'victims'.

After a raid, three men; Colin Laskey, Roland Jaggard and Anthony Brown, were charged with assault and wounding under Sections 20 and 47 of the (1861) Offences Against the Persons Act. Nonetheless, it was clear that all who had received such sadomasochistic treatment at the numerous 'sessions' were wholly willing participants, consenting to all that had occurred. The activities had been conducted in private amidst considerable organisation and provision for the ultimate safety of those consenting. Consequently, the liberal-minded press strongly questioned the unwarranted intrusion of the police, suspicious that these men were singled out because of an unsavoury association between homosexuality and sadomasochistic activity.

Laskey was sentenced to five years and six months for a range of offences which included aiding and abetting the keeping of a disorderly house and possessing an indecent photograph of a minor. Jaggard was sentenced to three years' imprisonment for aiding and abetting unlawful wounding and assault, causing actual bodily harm. Brown received a sentence totalling two years and nine months for aiding and abetting assault and occasioning actual bodily harm.

In the light of this challenge to privacy and to individual rights (and discrimination against a particular branch of homosexual lifestyles) the defendants appealed, resulting in a reduction of the original sentences. Nonetheless, the defendants then appealed to the European Court of Human Rights, asserting that the criminal proceedings instigated against them contravened Article 8 of the European Convention on Human Rights. This article enforced the sentiment that 'everyone has the right to respect for his private and family life, his home and his correspondence'.[60] The defendants argued that this right had been violated through the 'interference by a public authority' which was explicitly prohibited within Article 8. However legal debate hinged upon the phrase which followed this assertion, which qualified it by allowing such action when it was 'in accordance with the law and is necessary in a democratic society'. The Article also allowed such interference 'for the prevention of disorder or crime, for the protection of health or morals, or for the protection of the rights and freedoms of others'.[61]

The European Court eventually found in favour of the British government and, indeed, amplified the legal arguments it had relied upon, notably the notion of privacy. In a concurring opinion, Judge Pettiti noted that activities behind closed doors were not by definition private, citing the law's recognition of the crime of marital rape.[62] The defendants restated the consensual and private nature of their activities with like-minded individuals, suggesting the issue of moral corruption was a species of speculation. Part of their argument suggested

> that their case should be viewed as one involving matters of sexual expression, rather than violence. With due regard to this consideration, the line beyond which consent is no defence to physical injury should only be drawn at the level of intentional or reckless causing of serious disabling injury.[63]

The government's reply was that it was still entitled to punish acts of violence amounting to torture, irrespective of whether consent had been given to them or not. Similarly it was justified in taking action against this violence since it had a duty to protect individuals from potential danger which overrode issues of freedom, expression and consent. Such danger, it was contended, undermined 'the respect which human beings should confer upon each other'.[64]

The Court supported the argument offered by the British government, identifying its actions with what it termed 'pressing social need' and the legitimate use of the criminal law to prevent harm.[65] The right to the privacy of the defendants was overridden by the actions of the criminal law because the activities 'involved a significant degree of injury or wounding which could not be characterised as trifling or transient', nor was it as predictable as the defendants claimed.[66] Prejudice against homosexuals and homosexuality was also rejected since the nature of the extreme activities seemed sufficient motive for the State's procedure against them.

Thus the British government's paternalistic desire to protect citizens from the potentially dangerous consequences of their own actions was exonerated. Laskey, Jaggard and Brown were portrayed, as a result of this judgement, as hedonistic, irresponsible and potentially predatory moral pariahs, rather than individuals pursuing their own sexual freedoms. As the report's final words described it: 'The protection of private life means the protection of a person's intimacy and dignity, not the protection of his baseness or the promotion of criminal immoralism.'[67]

Despite this verdict, interesting dissenting arguments also emerged from the judges on the European Commission of Human Rights. Judge Loucaides was unconvinced that the British government had established the likelihood of lasting harm, nor that their activities were likely to get out of hand. These were covered, in any case, by existing provisions of the criminal law which would govern either the issue of consent or of serious injury. The argument that the State had acted to protect potential participants from AIDS was similarly dismissed by Judge Loucaides, who noted that the State permitted acts such as boxing (with its greater likelihood of blood contamination), not to mention forms of 'legal intercourse' which carried the same risk.

Interestingly, Loucaides focused closely upon the government's actions in the protection of morals. If this were true, he contended, then the protection of public morals should have informed the taking of action against Laskey, Jaggard and Brown rather than being an *ex post facto* justification for such actions. As Loucaides noted, the legal opinion behind this judgement potentially constituted a government snoopers' charter.[68]

The case against Laskey, Jaggard and Brown demonstrated how aspects of paternalism still informed the law and could grow in sophistication. Moreover, the verdicts emphasised that the European Court was ready to support individual states in their quest to preserve the peace and so-called moral integrity. Here the concentration upon breaches of the peace, of protecting the individual and the maintenance of order once again showed the capacity for modern methods of policing and intervention to inherit the logic and rationality central to the paternalism of earlier centuries.

5. Conclusion

In this chapter, we have seen that the gradual recognition of individual rights has been partly qualified by events and decisions in the court-room. At the start of our period, in the seventeenth and eighteenth centuries, governments policed public morals because this represented quick and cost-effective methods of preventing disorder. Such reactive strategies to police low-level moral lapses functioned as a species of 'Bloody Code lite'. In this, they display many of the same characteristics and assumptions as those intended to deal with more serious crimes. In the early eighteenth century, the moral lapses that were prominent at any given time were those accorded most attention by legislation and forms of moral policing. Analogous to the situation with the original 'Bloody Code', the campaign against moral lapses was intended to provide a deterrent whilst also calming the fears of those terrified by the consequences of social collapse. As the reasoning of the day suggested, it was minor moral failings which inexorably promoted major crime and disorder and affronts to the sanctity of the law. The nineteenth and twentieth centuries saw an agenda of civil rights and liberties increasingly erode the arguments for laws which policed morals. At times this looked like modernisation, but there were still elements within British society that resisted the pace and nature of change in this area. As we noted, the 'moral peripheries' stood out against such changes until the agenda of equality before the law was forced upon them by the logic of European legal integration. Yet, as the Laskey and Brown case demonstrates, this didn't necessarily favour the forces of libertarianism. Moreover, this chapter is a useful way to commence this volume, since placing moral crimes, and these two examples in particular, within their context reminds us that a long-term history of law and 'crime in context' is not always a simple story of modernisation and the coming of 'civilised' practices.

Notes

1. See R.B. Shoemaker (1992) 'Reforming the City: The Reformation of Manners Campaign in London, 1690–1738', in L. Davison, T. Hitchcock, T. Keirn and

R. Shoemaker (eds.), *Stilling the Grumbling Hive: The Response to Social and Economic Problems in England, 1689–1750* (New York: St. Martin's Press), 99–120; T. Isaacs (1982) 'The Anglican Hierarchy and the Reformation of Manners, 1688–1738' *Journal of Ecclesiastical History*, 33, 391–411.

2. See Shoemaker, 'Reforming the City', passim.

3. Ibid., Table 6.1, p. 105.

4. See A. Cabantous (2002) *Blasphemy: Impious Speech in the West* trans. Eric Rauth (New York: Columbia University Press), 49–79 and D.S. Nash (2007) *Blasphemy in the Christian World* (Oxford: Oxford University Press), 147–83.

5. The law in Scotland took a different direction. See G. Maher (1977) 'Blasphemy in Scots Law', *Scottish Law Times*, 257, 256–60.

6. In an 1838 case (*R* v. *Gathercole* (1838) 2 Lew CC 237, 116) an Anglican clergyman who had written libels about a nunnery was acquitted because it was wholly lawful to 'attack Judaism, Mohammedanism, or even any sect of the Christian religion, save the established religion of the country'. Attempts to have the law of blasphemous libel extended to cover the Islamic faith in the wake of the Salman Rushdie affair were rebuffed by the then Home Secretary John Patten.

7. Hypatia Bradlaugh-Bonner (1923) *Penalties Upon Opinion* (London: Watts & Co.), 37.

8. M.J.D. Roberts (1983) 'The Society for the Suppression of Vice and its early Critics, 1802–1812', *Historical Journal*, 26:19, 159–76.

9. (1818) *The Constable's Assistant: Being a Compendium of the Duties and Powers of Constables, and other Peace Officers* (London: Society for the Suppression of Vice), 23. The text is the same in the 1807 edition.

10. Ibid., 27–8.

11. See D. Eaton and H. D. Symonds (1793) *The Trial of Daniel Isaac Eaton: Before Lloyd Lord Kenyon, and a Special jury, in the Court of King's Bench, Guildhall, London, July the tenth, 1793; For Selling a Supposed Libel, A letter, Addressed to the Addressers by Thomas Paine* (London).

12. See J. Wiener (1983) *Radicalism and Freethought in Nineteenth Century Britain* (Westport, CT: Greenwood Press).

13. Quoted in Bradlaugh-Bonner, *Penalties*, 70.

14. T.J. Toohey (1987) 'Blasphemy in Nineteenth Century England: The Pooley Case and its Background', *Victorian Studies*, 30:3, 315–33.

15. Bradlaugh-Bonner, *Penalties*, 114.

16. Memo signed 'HB' *c.*May 1913 before the 15th of the month from National Archives file HO 45/106652, item 216120/86.

17. See D.S. Nash (1999) *Blasphemy in Britain: 1789–Present* (Aldershot: Ashgate), 181–2.

18. See ibid., especially Chapter 5.

19. N. Walter (1977) *Blasphemy in Britain: The Practice and Punishment of Blasphemy and the Trial of Gay News* (London: Rationalist Press Association).

20. See Nash, *Blasphemy in Britain*, Chapter 8.

21. A.D. Harvey (1978) 'Prosecutions for Sodomy in England at the beginning of the Nineteenth Century', *Historical Journal*, 21:4, 939–48, especially 941.

22. N.M. Goldsmith (1998) *The Worst of Crimes: Homosexuality and the Law in Eighteenth Century London* (Ashgate: Aldershot), 38.
23. Ibid., 36.
24. Ibid., 37.
25. Ibid., 34. However it should be noted that court martials occurred for the offence as a result of 22 George II, c.33, cl.29.
26. H.G. Cocks (2003) *Nameless Offences: Homosexual Desire in the Nineteenth Century* (London: I.B. Tauris), 32–4.
27. Harvey, 'Prosecutions for Sodomy', 939.
28. See A. McClaren (1997) *The Trials of Masculinity: Policing Sexual Boundaries 1870–1930* (Chicago and London: University of Chicago Press), 16–17.
29. For the Cleveland Street Scandal see H. Montgomery Hyde (1976) *The Cleveland Street Scandal* (New York: Coward, McCann & Geoghegan); Cocks, *Nameless Offences*, 144–54 and T. Aronson (1994) *Prince Eddie and the Homosexual Underworld* (London: John Murray).
30. J. Weeks (1989) *Sex, Politics and Society: The Regulation of Sexuality since 1800* (2nd edn, Harlow: Longman), 114.
31. M. Houlbrook (2005) *Queer London: Perils and Pleasures in the Sexual Metropolis 1918–1957* (Chicago: University of Chicago Press), 273.
32. For a discussion of Northern Ireland's separate history of homosexual law reform see C. Davies (2004) *The Strange Death of Moral Britain* (London: Transaction), 153–61.
33. For a useful text on this see St J.A. Robilliard (1984) *Religion and the Law: Religious Liberty in Modern English Law* (Manchester: Manchester University Press), 25–45. See also A. Bradney (1993) *Religions, Rights and Laws* (Leicester: Leicester University Press).
34. Bradlaugh-Bonner, *Penalties*, passim.
35. G.D. Nokes (1928) *A History of the Crime of Blasphemy* (London: Sweet & Maxwell), 107–9.
36. A. Calder-Marshall (1972) *Lewd, Blasphemous and Obscene* (London: Hutchinson).
37. R. Webster (1990) *A Brief History of Blasphemy: Liberalism, Censorship and 'The Satanic Verses'* (Southwold: Orwell Press).
38. L.W. Levy (1981) *Treason against God: A History of the Offense of Blasphemy* (New York: Schocken Books) and L.W. Levy (1993) *Blasphemy: Verbal Offense against the Sacred from Moses to Salman Rushdie* (New York: Knopf).
39. See Nash, *Blasphemy in Britain*; D.S. Nash (2007) *Blasphemy in the Christian World* (Oxford: Oxford University Press); D.S. Nash (2008) '"To Prostitute Morality, Libel Religion, and Undermine Government": Blasphemy and the Strange Persistence of Providence in Britain since the Seventeenth Century', *Journal of Religious History*, 32:4, 439–56; D.S. Nash and C. Bakalis (2007) 'Hate and the State: Historical Perspectives on Hate Crime and its Definition', *Liverpool Law Review*, 28, 349–75 and D.S. Nash (2007) 'Placing Blasphemy in Social History: Analyzing Theoretical Approaches to the History of Religious Crime', *Journal of Social History*, 41, 5–29.
40. Weeks, *Sex, Politics and Society*, 99–101.

41. Ibid., 103.
42. The Jeffrey Weeks analysis is also contested by S. Brady (2005) *Masculinity and Male Homosexuality in Britain, 1861–1913* (Basingstoke: Palgrave Macmillan).
43. H.G. Cocks, *Nameless Offences*, 199–200.
44. Ibid., 6–7.
45. W. Cohen (1996) *Sex Scandal: The Private Parts of Victorian Fiction* (Durham, NC: Duke University Press).
46. D. Selfe and V. Burke (1998) *Perspectives on Sex, Crime and Society* (London: Cavendish), 16–19.
47. L. Moran (1996) *The Homosexual(ity) of Law*, (London: Routledge).
48. A. Grey (1992) *Quest for Justice: Towards Homosexual Emancipation* (London: Sinclair Stevenson), Chapter 21.
49. See Davies, *Strange Death of Moral Britain*, 141.
50. Ibid., 152–3.
51. Ibid., 161.
52. Ibid.
53. See for example G.W. Foote (1886) *Prisoner for Blasphemy* (London); G.W. Foote (1882) *Blasphemy No Crime: The Whole Question Treated Historically, Legally, Theologically and Morally, with Special Reference to the Prosecution of the 'Freethinker'* (London: H.A. Kempe) and G.W. Foote (1889) *Defence of Free Speech, Being a Three Hours' Address to the Jury in the Court of Queen's Bench before Lord Coleridge, on April 24, 1883* (London: Pioneer Press).
54. See National Archives HO45 9536/49902.
55. *Daily Telegraph*, 6 March 1883.
56. See Nash, *Blasphemy in Britain*, 132–3.
57. E.H. Coleridge (1904) *Life and Correspondence of John Duke, Lord Coleridge* (London), 291.
58. J.F. Stephen (1884) 'The Law on Blasphemy and Blasphemous Libel', *Fortnightly Review*, March, 289–318.
59. There is a significant and useful repository of documents and comment at http://www.spannertrust.org/documents/spannerhistory.asp.
60. http://www.spannertrust.org/documents/eurofinal.asp.
61. Ibid.
62. Text of Case of Laskey, Jaggard and Brown v The United Kingdom Judgement, Strasbourg (February 1997) 109/1995/615/703–705. Concurring opinion of Judge Pettiti.
63. Ibid. paragraph 39.
64. Ibid., paragraph 40.
65. Ibid., paragraph 42.
66. Ibid., paragraph 45.
67. Ibid. Concurring opinion of Judge Pettiti.
68. Report of the European Commission of Human rights on the Spanner appeal. Dissenting opinion of Mr Loucaides.

2 Cruelty and Adultery: Offences against the Institution of Marriage

Joanne Bailey

1. Introduction

From the early to the modern period, cruelty (acts categorised as violence which were committed by husbands against wives) and adultery (extra-marital sex) have been considered as offences with grave consequences for church, government, courts, and communities, as well as for individuals themselves. This is because the English state has historically viewed harmonious, stable marital relationships as crucial to familial and household order, and in turn, as the bulwark against crime, immorality and disorder. Two main factors have been perceived to undermine marriage both as a public institution and as a personal relationship: acts categorised as cruelty and as adultery. As such they were two of the primary grounds for judicial separation and, in varying forms, divorce until the introduction of 'no-fault' divorce in 1969. Given their perceived risk to marriage and therefore society, they have been subject to informal and formal regulation over time. This chapter traces the regulation of both offences by the state through legislation, charts their changing representation in the print media, and presents the fundamental shifts in cultural attitudes that shaped both phenomena. Given the constraints of space no attempt will be made to measure the incidence of the offences, establish causality, or detail their conviction or punishment rates.[1]

2. Chronology

a) Cruelty

State and community understandings of what forms of physical force are legitimate and illegitimate are subject to redefinition over time. The same is true of men's violence against wives. At the start of the period concerned, husbands were popularly believed to have the right to moderately correct their disobedient wives.[2] One legal authority in print from 1736 to 1832 stated: 'The husband hath, by law, power and dominion over his wife, and may keep her by force within the bounds of duty, and may beat her, but not in a violent or cruel manner.'[3] Cruelty was thus a legal term applied to indicate the point at which discipline became battery. Though the degree of force permitted by husbands to moderately correct wives was not specified in legal handbooks, this was not a licence for indiscriminate violence.[4] There is no evidence for the legal existence of the 'rule of thumb', supposedly confirmed by Judge Buller in 1782, that husbands had the right to strike their wives with a stick no bigger than their thumb, though it certainly existed as a popular myth.[5] Furthermore, the Church and State attempted to regulate men's behaviour towards their dependants, acting to prevent tyranny or the abuse of privilege. Wives were able to sue for separation from their husbands on the grounds of cruelty from the church courts until 1857 and a number of secular legal remedies were available to wives. Violent husbands could be prosecuted through arbitration by a magistrate, for breach of the peace, which allowed the use of a recognisance (or surety) to bind over threatening and abusive individuals, and by indictment for assault.[6] Wives from rural and urban environments and from a range of social ranks made use of these forms of amelioration throughout the eighteenth and early nineteenth centuries.[7] The secular remedies were short term and, while a decree from the ecclesiastical courts allowed spouses to live apart, it did not permit the end of the union and the formation of a new one. This was unchanged following the 1857 Matrimonial Causes Act which removed matrimony from canon law to civil law. Cruelty continued to be a ground for judicial separation, but was only considered as one of the aggravated faults that a wife had to prove in addition to her husband's adultery in order to obtain divorce.[8]

It is not clear precisely when men's right to correct their wives disappeared as a legal concept. Ecclesiastical court testimony suggests that husbands themselves did not consistently use the plea of correction as a defence from the second half of the eighteenth century.[9] Divorce Court rulings about violence following 1857 indicate a flexible application.[10] After 1831 the concept of correction was not deployed in reports in *The Times* of wife murders tried at the assizes, although nineteenth-century working-class men continued to adhere to the notion.[11] By the later

1880s, law handbooks tended to assume that the law of moderate correction was an outdated doctrine.[12] Nonetheless, 1891 is usually seen as the point at which it was categorically rejected. In *Regina* v. *Jackson*, the Lord Chancellor ruled in Queen's Bench that husbands had no legal authority to seize or hold spouses against their will and declared that the authorities giving men the right to beat their wives were no longer the law of England.[13]

Cases of marital violence were judged on their own merits, thus acts which were deemed cruel were subject to changing definition over time. Early modern wives who sought to separate from violent husbands were required to prove that their husbands had committed repeated, life-threatening acts of physical violence against them.[14] Lord Stowell's statement on cruelty in *Evans* v. *Evans* (1790) is recognised as a landmark precedent in its observation that only acts which caused bodily harm should be categorised as cruelty, and that this should be 'grave and weighty'. Nonetheless, his comment that the 'apprehension' of harm also was to be taken into account allowed flexibility.[15] Stowell himself claimed four years later that 'words of menace intimating a malignant intention of doing bodily harm' also amounted to legal cruelty.[16] In practice, however, cruelty separation cases heard by ecclesiastical courts over the course of the second half of the eighteenth century indicate a greater willingness to include acts of violence that did not constitute life-threatening violence. Moreover, economic deprivation was recognised as an additional form of cruelty.[17] Eighteenth-century justices of the peace in and out of sessions also regularly issued recognisances against husbands who *threatened* violence against wives.[18] The Divorce Court used social class as one means to distinguish whether men's acts against their wives were cruel.[19] Nineteenth-century courts began to formally recognise occasions when husbands' behaviour damaged women's health without direct violence, notably, for example, through the transmission of venereal disease.[20] In 1897 the courts accepted mental cruelty as being of sufficient gravity to warrant divorce.[21] By the early twentieth century there were demands that definitions of cruelty encompass emotional, psychological and sexual abuse as well as physical.[22] Yet, though cruelty was permitted as sole grounds for divorce in the 1937 Matrimonial Causes Act, the existing legal concept of cruelty remained largely in place since it was decided to omit an elaborate definition from the legislation and leave this to the courts to interpret.[23] Domestic violence is currently defined by the government as 'Any incident of threatening behaviour, violence or abuse between adults who are or have been in a relationship together, or between family members, regardless of gender or sexuality' and a far wider range of acts are considered abusive.[24]

Changing attitudes towards wife beating were often linked to the broader culture of violence. Between 1550 and 1750 husbands' correction of wives was legitimate when it mirrored the state's use of corporal punishment to punish a wrong and was enacted with rational self-control, but not with anger.[25] Ideals of manhood and community pressures also served to act as checks upon men's abuse of their dominant position.[26] Acceptance of physical violence as a means of control diminished in the later eighteenth and early nineteenth centuries. State forms of physical punishment shifted away from public forms of humiliating corporal punishment to transportation and penal incarceration.[27] The courts sought to eradicate illegitimate forms of interpersonal violence through harsher sentencing for assault with a move to imprisonment over nominal fines.[28] In the same period men's violence against wives was less likely to be seen as legitimate chastisement and more likely to be seen as madness and brutality. Governments' hardening attitudes continued through the nineteenth century with new legislation to punish assault.[29] Several of the statutes passed to curb interpersonal violence also brought men who beat their wives under their aegis. Indeed it has been suggested that much of the legislation was prompted by increasing concern about violence against women.[30] Thus the 1828 Offences against the Person Act, which extended summary jurisdiction to common assault and battery, meant wife beaters could be tried and sentenced in magistrates' courts. In 1853 the Act for better prevention of aggravated Assaults on Women and Children allowed magistrates to impose a six-month sentence on convicted men.[31] In 1878 the Matrimonial Causes Act allowed the Magistrates' Court to grant separations to (working-class) wives whose husbands were convicted of assaulting them. In 1895, this was extended in the Summary Jurisdiction [Married Women] Act to allow women to plead 'persistent cruelty' in order to achieve separation, maintenance and child custody orders from magistrates' courts.[32] These acts were accompanied by very vocal condemnation of marital violence with calls in parliament for the introduction of flogging for wife beaters, contemporary feminist criticism of wife beating, and outrage in print.[33]

Although it is clear that state and society were collectively rejecting many forms of personal violence, a consequential retreat of wife beating behind 'closed doors' at the end of the eighteenth century is not evident.[34] Studies show that the location of wife beating does not follow a simple chronology of 'privatisation' from street to home. Class and socioeconomic status played their part, since those who lived in poor urban areas were likely to witness marital violence, given the overcrowded living conditions and flimsiness of the built environment. While higher-status dwellings were larger and more substantial, family members, servants and friends nonetheless witnessed and tried to limit elite marital violence.[35] It is clear, however, that professional 'third parties' were coming to be seen as responsible for dealing with marital violence. By 1750 it was up to the wife to prosecute a husband for cruelty, although individuals could theoretically prosecute a husband for breach of the peace against his wife. By the mid-nineteenth century a police force was in place which could intervene in marital violence, though its powers to act as prosecutors of wife beaters after 1853 were not often used.[36] Indeed the police were frequently criticised for their failure to intervene between violent husbands and their wives in the nineteenth and twentieth centuries. Bureaucratic social agencies also developed which intervened to regulate working-class family life.[37] It is unwise to see the expansion of nineteenth-century magistrates' courts' jurisdiction over working-class marital violence and separation simplistically as middle-class policing or regulation of working-class life, since nineteenth-century beaten wives, like their eighteenth-century counterparts, used such means themselves. Collectively, however, this process did move responsibility for intervening in marital violence, to some extent, from individuals to third parties.[38] State intervention also focused professional and public attention on 'new' kinds of family violence, such as child abuse, thereby marginalising violence against women.[39]

Nonetheless, wife beating remained in the public eye throughout the period, though the style and volume of reporting and literary treatment varied over time. Cases involving violent husbands were reported in the eighteenth-century press, from short accounts of wife beaters who came before local courts to notorious 'celebrity' cases that involved aristocrats.[40] Some cases were published as trial pamphlets and sold for entertainment. Detailed daily reporting of cases of working-class husbands' cruelty increased following the 1828 Aggravated Assault Act and stories of their middle-class counterparts entered the newspapers in greater numbers after the 1857 Matrimonial Causes Act.[41] This had two major consequences. First, it aided the politicisation of the issue of wife beating. Divorce reporting influenced both sensationalist and realist nineteenth-century fiction, which adopted the structure of divorce cases as they were reported in the press after 1857, and entered debates about women's subordination in marriage.[42] Press publicity was useful to feminists who condemned marital violence both in specialist print, in order to demand the vote and refute arguments that all men were inherently better suited for political citizenship and in generalist print, to seek improved legislative relief for abused wives. Frances Power Cobbe's 'Wife Torture in England' led directly to the 1878 Matrimonial Causes Act.[43] Print culture can thus be argued to have played a part in the policing of domestic conduct, since by reporting middle- and working-class cruelty cases it constructed 'a community in which marital conduct was never private'.[44]

The second major consequence was the role of print in maintaining and disseminating the circulation of class- and gender-specific stereotypes of marital violence. The perception that physical violence in the household was committed by working-class men developed in the later eighteenth century and was firmly in place by the mid-nineteenth century.[45] Though public reporting was never without examples of elite physical violence, the stereotype was established that middle-class husbands abused through mental emotional cruelty, while working-class men used their fists and feet. The causes of wife beating were thus closely associated with working-men's culture of fighting and drinking by law-enforcement agencies, social work agencies and the press in the twentieth century.[46] This stereotype was pervasive. Reporters, social reformers, feminists, politicians and magistrates framed wife beaters as 'degenerative working-class men who deserved punishment'.[47] Working-class people themselves may even have conceptualised their relationships in these terms; for many twentieth-century working-class wives a good husband was simply one who never raised a fist to her. Also typical of some Western societies' reports of wife abuse in the early twentieth century was their deployment of notions of racial evolution, with wife beating positioned as a remnant of more savage times.[48] Critics also adopted an 'imperial' language of slavery and deployed Orientalist metaphors when describing ill-treated wives, as well as comparing them with beaten dogs and horses.[49] Another discourse became available following the First World War which was rooted in the emergence of the eugenics movement, in the development of psychoanalysis and psychopathology in the 1920s, and in the discovery of the condition of 'shell-shock', or post-traumatic stress, displayed by returning soldiers.[50] It allowed a move away from a criminal model of wife beating to a 'psychological model of the violent husband'. The former needed punishment and the latter medical treatment.[51]

In the twenty-first century, the government continues to attempt to reduce domestic violence, recently formulating the *Domestic Violence National Action Plan* and giving the police and courts new extended powers to deal with it through the Domestic Violence, Crime and Victims Act 2004.[52] Despite more sophisticated understandings and the determination of the state and numerous agencies to stamp it out, one incident of domestic violence is reported to the police every minute, and on average two women are killed every week by a current or former male partner.[53]

b) Adultery

Attempts were made to regulate adultery throughout the period because it was considered an act that threatened marriage, property, law and society, and, at times, the nation itself. The inherent risks posed by adultery to the transmission and ownership of property are best indicated by the existence of the sexual double standard, which shaped attitudes well into the twentieth century. For much of our period, men's extramarital activities were less harshly condemned in legal and prescriptive texts than women's; though Christian morality always rejected male infidelity and wives did not necessarily passively accept their husbands' extramarital liaisons in practice.[54] This double standard was primarily justified by the threat posed by women's adultery to rightful inheritance by bringing another man's off-spring into the family.[55] It shaped the suing of adultery separations before the church courts and was laid down in statute in the 1857 Matrimonial Causes Act, which made adultery the sole grounds for divorce for men, while women had to prove both their husband's adultery and another aggravated fault.[56] The severity of this sexual double-standard came under attack by feminists and social purity campaigners from the 1870s and '80s who demanded that men adopt the same [high] standards of moral behaviour that women exhibited.[57] Indeed it was such conservative demands that influenced the passing of the 1923 Matrimonial Causes Act, which gave women the same rights as their husbands to sue for the sole grounds of adultery, rather than a desire to award women legal equality.[58] The sexual double standard did not disappear, however.[59] Until 'no-fault' divorce legislation was passed in 1969,[60] economic insecurity, and the potential loss of children and home, meant that adulterous women paid 'a higher emotional, material and social price for their transgression than men'.[61]

During periods of perceived social and cultural disruption, anxiety was often deflected onto the sphere of sexuality.[62] The period 1770 to 1809, for instance, saw sustained criticism of upper-class infidelity. Four bills were brought before parliament seeking harsher punishment of the guilty parties in adulterous affairs, which although unsuccessful, focussed attention on the corrosive effects of infidelity on law and property by the early nineteenth century.[63] This activity was triggered in part by the backdrop of a sense of national crisis due to revolutionary threat. In the social and political upheaval of the last quarter of the nineteenth century, personal and familial moral purity became a 'metaphor for a stable society'.[64] Extended periods of war were also perceived to destabilize marriage and the family due to concerns about sexual morality. For example, sexual licence was perceived to have increased during both the First and Second World Wars thanks to the widening possibility of extra-marital encounters.[65] State concern was further heightened post 1945 by the sharp increase in the divorce rate and by worries about population collapse, resulting in a political desire to re-establish marital stability.[66] State sponsorship of the marriage guidance movement, which presented itself as an organization working to strengthen marriage, was one of the means by which this was attempted.[67]

Given its significance, therefore, both Church and state have sought to regulate adultery, though the means by which they have done so has changed from direct forms to a 'new and indirect regulation of personal life'.[68] Sex outside of marriage was defined by the Christian church as a sin and a crime and was one of the offences prosecuted by ecclesiastical authorities who acted as society's moral guardians during the Elizabethan and Stuart period.[69] Disciplinary 'office' cases targeted parishioners'

extra-marital liaisons and punished guilty offenders with public peni-
tence in their parish church.[70] Such regulation generally, however, formed
a minority of incontinence cases and waned from the later seventeenth
century to largely disappear by the 1720s.[71] Some moral regulation was
taken up by local secular courts, such as the Quarter Sessions, but here
too prosecution for adultery declined by the 1730s.[72] Canon law also enabled spouses to seek separation from unfaithful spouses until the 1857
Matrimonial Causes Act when matrimonial litigation became a civil rather
than ecclesiastical concern.[73] Nonetheless, the Church retained influence
in the regulation of sexuality and was a crucial component in the debates
on marriage preceding major statutory change during the nineteenth and
twentieth centuries. Thus, for instance, the Oxford M.P. and divorce law
reform campaigner Alan Herbert was required to compromise with the
Church alongside Stanley Baldwin's government to successfully get the
1937 Matrimonial Causes Act passed.[74]

The nineteenth-century state continued to directly regulate extra-
marital sexuality through legislation on marriage and divorce, which
delineated boundaries of sexual transgressions and punished those who
crossed them.[75] Nevertheless, there was tension over the extent to which
sexual transgressions such as adultery should be a matter for public regulation or private conscience. Early modern society already placed great
emphasis upon an excellent personal reputation, which could be damaged
by rumours of infidelity with serious repercussions.[76] A gradual shift is
evident over the eighteenth century towards the promotion of self regulation through an emphasis upon individual self control and the deleteri-
ous impact of illicit sexuality upon other people.[77] The decline in direct
forms of policing adultery is not unproblematic evidence that extra marital
sex was more tolerated as time went on, since moral regulation continued but in other forms. In late seventeenth century London and some provincial towns, for example, middling-sort individuals formed Societies for
the Reformation of Manners which brought 'private' prosecutions against
adulterers, amongst other offences such as fornication and prostitution.[78]
Equally, although the Victorian state focused on targeting public immorality such as prostitution, voluntary organisations, such as the social
purity movement, undertook vocal and influential campaigns for higher
standards of individual morality.[79] The belief that social stability lay in
individual and public morality led to demands that members of the establishment had spotless private lives in order to be fit for public office. For
example, when Charles Dilke, the liberal MP was named as co-respondent
in the Crawford divorce case in 1885, and his personal sexual morality
was opened up to public view, W.T. Stead campaigned against him acting in public life until he could clear his name as a sexual adventurer.[80]
The conflation of personal morality and public life remained a feature of
twentieth-century British political life.[81]

The shift to seeing adultery as a matter for individual conscience has largely been achieved in the twentieth century with a rethinking of the basis of sexual morality. Human sexuality was redefined as a creative force by sexologists and psychoanalysts in the early twentieth century. Since the institution of marriage was still identified as the lynchpin of social order, and reconceptualised as a companionate relationship, emphasis was placed upon mutual sexual satisfaction within marriage during the inter-war years.[82] In 'harness[ing] sexuality to the cause of morality' through the promotion of sex as one of the primary conjugal bonds, it was increasingly illogical for churchmen to promulgate a negative equation of sex since this denigrated the married state.[83] Nonetheless, officials did not withdraw from the arena and churchmen, politicians and professionals thereafter exhorted husbands and wives to behave with honesty and decency to each other.[84] Furthermore, while twentieth-century governments did not initiate divorce reform legislation, since it was controversial and politically divisive, with most bills introduced by private members, nevertheless they retained influence at a safe distance.[85]

The period also saw shifts in perceptions of the consequences of adultery, from a sin against Christian morality to an act that broke social mores; though the framework of Christian morality remained significant and any liberalisation in attitudes was a complex phenomenon. From the late seventeenth century, the meanings of adultery fractured so that by the middle of the eighteenth century it was less a crime against morality than one against prevailing notions of polite social refinement. Print culture played an important part in this shift since it made discussions of adultery more public and led to 'more complex deliberations on the causes and consequences of infidelity'.[86] The complexities of human behaviour and emotion continued to be exposed in the second half of the eighteenth century as criminal conversation actions between husbands and their wives alleged lovers became widely reported. By the end of the eighteenth century adultery could be seen as a failure of 'moral sense', which while still rooted in Christian moral duty, was combined with the culture of sensibility's insistence upon sensitivity to the feelings of others.[87]

Accounts of adultery further proliferated in the second half of the nineteenth century, thanks to divorce reporting in the aftermath of the 1857 Matrimonial Causes Act.[88] The landslide in press reports of scandalous adulterous relationships included notorious cases such as the 1864 Codrington divorce trial, the 1885/1886 Crawford-Dilke case and the 1922 Russell divorce, as well as rather more mundane cases heard by the courts.[89] This stimulated official anxiety that publicity of adulterous acts could corrupt society.[90] Following the 1857 Matrimonial Causes Act the dominant view was that publicity would uphold public decency, serving to warn people of the shame and dishonour consequent upon committing marital offences.[91] By the early twentieth century, however, the fear that publicity encouraged immorality took precedence and the 1926 Judicial Proceedings Act was passed to prohibit press coverage of divorce cases.[92] Media representations in the twentieth century continued to invoke shame in treatments of infidelity, celebrating partners who rejected an affair [*Brief Encounter* (1945)] or 'punishing' the transgressive spouse [*Fatal Attraction* (1987)]. While adulterous behaviour in the late twentieth century is still seen as a marker of national health, condemnation is situated mostly within the personal relationship, defining it as a selfish, immature act and highlighting its dangers to the children of the marriage.[93]

Overall, it is clear that the regulation of adultery corresponds closely to notions of the purpose of the institution of marriage. When marriage was primarily understood to be a public institution for the furthering of dynasty, lineage and property, then it was the only legitimate site for sexuality. The period studied, however, saw the rise of a competing discourse wherein marriage was conceived of predominantly as a personal relationship. Such a transition is identifiable in the period from the Second World War to the 1970s. During the war and the 1950s, adultery was less likely to be seen as an act that should cause a marriage's demise since marriage was still primarily identified as an economic union that provided security for wives and children and promoted mutual companionship between spouses. By the late 1960s, however, the 'eroticization of marriage' in which love and mutual sexual satisfaction within the relationship were made central to its success, had led, somewhat ironically, to the act of adultery being perceived to be far more threatening to the marital relationship.[94]

3. Historiography

Several key themes and approaches have shaped the historical study of cruelty and adultery. Perhaps most obviously, both offences are of interest to historians of the law and social policy who explore them to trace institutional change in divorce law.[95] Their analysis is also influenced by models of social progress. Wife beating is situated within the overarching framework of Norbert Elias's theory of the 'civilizing process' which postulated an increase in state control, development of self control, and reduced tolerance of inter-personal violence.[96] This is considered to be reflected in the diminishing toleration of acts of physical violence against wives. Historians have drawn attention to the broader acceptance of the discipline of wives when the public physical punishment of those convicted of misdemeanours and felony was standard practice. As state forms of physical punishment either became less visible or were abandoned, so, it is suggested, husbands' violence against their wives was condemned and thus itself became less visible, retreating behind closed doors.[97] Such theses of chronological linear progress have been recently nuanced, as the notion of an unproblematic 'civilising process' has itself been challenged.[98] Thus, for example, an assumption that variable rates of prosecutions reflect incidence and attitudes is usually rejected.[99] Social historians of wife beating show that this form of violence has always had a 'public' element since the household in most social ranks was open to people from outside the family, such as servants.[100] There has also been a move towards spatial analyses which help us understand the production and perception of interpersonal violence and again confirm that wife beating did not become increasingly invisible.[101] Historians of adultery also situate their accounts in a context of modernisation.[102] Yet, again, this has gone on to be problematised. The presumption that attitudes towards adultery have become less critical thanks to processes of secularisation and the liberalisation of attitudes towards sexuality has been opened up to analysis, revealing a less clear chronological pattern.[103] Furthermore, the precise relationship between numbers of divorces for adultery, its incidence, and wider societal attitudes towards it has been shown to be questionable.[104]

Another important imperative directing the study of both marital violence and adultery is the insights they offer into gender relations. For historians of women and feminist historians the causes and prosecution of intimate violence expose patriarchal hierarchies.[105] Thus, for example, historians of marriage typically examine records relating to husbands' violence against wives to draw conclusions about the power relations within the marital relationship.[106] Arguments have become increasingly sophisticated. The traditional view that men's greater access to formal authority and legal and economic privileges has always translated into a marital relationship in which men acted as agents and women as subordinates, and, where violence existed, as victims continues to be developed. It is recognised that wives have held formal authority in the household over some dependents, which could place them in a relatively equitable position in the family hierarchy, as well as informal power where the domestic economy and decision making were concerned.[107] Thus a broader gender approach has begun to investigate other forms of domestic violence, exposing the subjection of other members of the family to violence, including, controversially, husbands themselves.[108] Historians of British feminism, reveal the ways in which wife beating has been a powerful symbol of female oppression and has, therefore, been deployed as a political weapon.[109] Feminist historians have been interested in adultery since its representation and punishment is shaped by the sexual double standard and understandings of women's sexuality. As with the other areas of study mentioned, this too has been shown to be a complex situation. Thus for example, the sexual double standard's universal application and linear change over time has been challenged.[110] Historians of twentieth-century attitudes towards adultery point out that there can be conflict between behaviour and attitudes towards that behaviour.[111] Thus while greater liberalisation in attitudes towards sexuality increased, and, possibly, the incidence of adultery became more commonplace, attitudes towards adultery became harsher. This was the consequence of raising the importance of the marital sexual relationship, since it was seen as fatally undermined by extra marital sex.[112]

Notably, in all these fields, scholarship since the beginning of the twenty-first century has moved to an interest in discourse as well as experience, exploring not only what was said, but how it was deployed by its protagonists.[113] Analysis of various forms of cultural media has revealed shifting attitudes and exposed the interconnections between them and state action. For example, the nineteenth- and early-twentieth century press is increasingly seen as a disseminator and maintainer of stereotypes and as a disciplinary force in itself, as are fiction and film in studies of the later twentieth century.[114] Such investigations also offer insights into the stereotypes that society attaches to the offences and offers explanations for their evolution. So, changing assumptions about the social rank, personality and pathology of the typical wife beater are laid bare.[115] Where beaten wives are concerned, historians have begun to consider the impact of violence upon them, though it is sociologists and legal experts who explore how far such categories as the 'battered wife syndrome' are useful.[116]

The remainder of this chapter turns to a handful of case studies that are intended to bring the abstract to life and illuminate some of the issues outlined above.

4. Case Studies

In 1831 Susey Smirthwaite sought a separation on the grounds of cruelty from her husband David Smirthwaite, a merchant. The couple, who lived in Wakefield, Yorkshire, were married in 1818. Like many beaten wives, Susey had waited several years before turning to York consistory court for aid. The libel that her proctor drew up for her catalogued the ill-treatment she suffered, which, in order to build up a picture of the 'cruel disposition' of David, ranged from unpredictable emotional terrorism to severe physical cruelty, to sexual immorality.[117] Thus we know that David cursed her in front of servants and visitors and used 'lewd and licentious' language to his female servants in her presence. In common with many cases involving couples from households with servants, this was intended to humiliate Susey; a strategy furthered by David's insistence that his wife do the work of a menial servant. David also prevented his wife from reading her religious books, tearing them from her hands and throwing them on the fire. To make her life even more unpleasant he forced her to listen to him reading aloud 'bad licentious and profane Books'. Next, the libel described David's physical violence. He threatened to flog and strike her; he repeatedly struck her, kicked her; pinched her arms and neck; and knocked her to the ground 'with his doubled fist'. The latter description suggests that in the 1830s it was still necessary to differentiate between violence as a corrective and uncontrolled act. Clearly, a punch with a closed fist, a kick, or use of a weapon were considered unprovoked, intolerable violence and differentiated from a slap with an open hand that may have been considered corrective discipline. Susey had a strong case on several grounds. She was able to demonstrate that David's violence had left her deaf and her neck permanently marked. She could also show that he rejected the central premise of the conjugal union by proving that he refused to sleep with her because of her 'scurvy' and, ironically, since he caused them, because her injuries rendered her 'not fit to lie with'.[118] Susey was successful and obtained a separation.

The divorce suit of *Stone* v. *Stone* was reported in the *Manchester Times* in May 1860. Mrs Stone had sought to divorce her husband, a clerk in India House, on the grounds of adultery, and cruelty. Without sufficient evidence to prove the adultery, her counsel limited his application to a judicial separation on the grounds of cruelty. The cruelty had begun almost immediately after the couple married in 1853. The report detailed the 'gross and systematic' acts of cruelty, which included punching, biting, kicking, and threats to stab and shoot her. As with many such cases, Mr Stone formulated his own particular terrorising, here 'seizing her hands and beating her face with them'. Again, a common feature was his increased violence during his wife's pregnancy. Equally depressingly familiar was the fact that although the police were called in several times, Mrs Stone did not proceed against her husband because he promised to behave better. The second half of the report, however, though still sympathetic to the wife, transforms the divorce into entertainment by adopting a lighter, mocking tone in reporting Mr Stone's defence. After each of his statements it inserts in brackets 'Laughter', 'Loud Laughter', 'A Laugh' to indicate the court's derision of his claims that he did not use his wife ill during her lying-in and gave her everything she wanted – 'Dublin stout, wine, and brandy, together with every comfort and attendance' – and that he permitted her a '"pet" doctor'. 'Great laughter' met his claim that he only boxed her ears and pulled her nose once and that 'He was in the habit of drawing his child about in a perambulator, and was considered quite a "model husband".' Mr Stone's attempt to harness ideals of domestic manliness failed miserably both in court and in the press and Mrs Stone was granted her separation with costs. It is possible to see the press acting in this example as a forum for the public humiliation of husbands who beat their wives.

Yet there was one type of wifely behaviour that was generally under-stood to justifiably lead to a husband's violence: her adultery. The strength and reach of this aspect of the sexual double standard is perhaps revealed by the press report of Leeds Magistrates Court's dealings with Joseph Scholefield in 1858. The newspaper opens the report by declaring that it is an 'old maxim of English law, that if a man detected his wife in the act of adultery, he would be justified in slaying her and her paramour', though in practice wealthy men sought money compensation; an action beyond the reach of working-class men like Joseph. Thus, as the report explained, Joseph took the alternative path after his wife left him to live with her seducer, Michael Delany, stripping his house and deserting her children in the process. Positioning him as the victim of theft, Joseph got a police-man to enter a public house in order to discover his wife and her lover in bed. When confronted by the policeman the woman denied being Joseph's wife, so he called Joseph into the room. Joseph then lost his temper and attacked the couple with a poker. The police officer stepped in and pre-vented him killing them. The following day, Joseph was brought before the magistrates charged with wounding Michael Delaney. The two magistrates immediately dismissed the case, informing him 'that there was no blame whatever resting upon him' and that 'You are rid of her, as she has been guilty of adultery.' They agreed that Joseph need not live with his wife, nor support her. Clearly sympathetic towards Joseph, the report supported his use of violence to restore his reputation, consistently using vocabulary which positioned his wife as provoking.[119]

William Burr's adultery separation suit which he brought before York consistory court in 1843 was fairly typical in many ways, including his wife's failure to defend herself. Like many such men, he claimed that he immediately separated from his wife, Ruth, as soon as he discovered in January 1848 that she was having an affair with his friend. This strength-ened his case by avoiding any possible plea that he condoned [in practice, forgave] his wife's infidelity. William's suspicions had been roused when he opened a letter directed to his wife, which turned out to be from Thomas Ramsden arranging to meet her at a train station. Such adultery suits turned on proving the adultery rather than providing lengthy descriptions of a spouse's character and behaviour during marriage, as cruelty separation cases did about the violent husband. Thus the letter was presented as evi-dence and witnesses were brought to prove that Ruth had met Thomas and that they had slept together in a pub in September and November 1847. William's business partner revealed that William had brought a criminal conversation action against Thomas Ramsden for financial dam-ages for the loss of his wife's services and that Thomas had not defended himself, but agreed to the verdict.[120] This action was reported in the law intelligence section of *Lloyd's Weekly London Newspaper*, which stressed that by suffering 'judgement by default', Thomas admitted the allegations. The plaintiff's and defendant's attorneys had agreed a verdict of £500.[121]

After 1858 London and provincial newspapers reported routinely on adultery divorces. Witness information that the respondent had had opportunity to commit adultery with the co-respondent was perfunctorily summarised in more mundane cases.[122] Higher-status adultery suits, however, were given far more detailed coverage, such as the report entitled 'Adultery and Divorce in High Life', which covered Henry Boddington Webster's attempt to divorce his wife. Much was made of the location of the adultery, which occurred while the couple took a yacht cruise in the Mediterranean over the autumn and winter of 1850, until Mr Webster discovered that Mrs Webster was adulterous and left the yacht at Naples in January 1851. The report lingered most on the statements of witnesses testifying to Mrs Webster's disordered dress and hair, on glimpses of Mr Wingfield arranging his trousers, and on the arrangement of cushions on a sofa following the couple's time alone in the cabin, until abruptly ending with the statement that the valet then 'entered into a minute description of the acts of adultery which were alleged to have taken place on this occasion, the details of which are not fit for publication'.[123] As Gail Savage comments, it was such lacunae which gave space to the readers' imagination that eventually led the state to perceive such divorce-court reporting as particularly dangerous.

5. Conclusion

Most legislation relating to the offences of adultery and cruelty aimed to uphold the stability of marriage, though the strategies and justifying arguments differed over time. In a society that conceptualises family life as the key to social order, any perception of national crisis can trigger concern and result in state-sponsored attempts to regulate those factors that threaten it, in this case the threats that the male abuse of power and illicit sexuality pose to marriage. As such, the regulation of adultery and excessive male violence was for the most part conservative in nature and sought to maintain social and gender hierarchies.[124] This extended into the twentieth century. Thus, as stated in a 1905 case, the Divorce courts believed their role was 'to promote virtue and morality and to discourage vice and immorality'.[125] A.P. Herbert presented the reforms of the 1937 Matrimonial Causes Act, which allowed respondents to obtain a divorce on the grounds of cruelty alone and desertion for three years, as a force for stability.[126] Similarly, the goal of the Royal Commission on Marriage and Divorce, 1951, was 'to promote healthy and happy married life and to safeguard the interests and well-being of children'.[127] Indeed the objective of most legal and social agencies was to achieve spousal reconciliation, whether through ecclesiastical or secular courts in the eighteenth century or through the police, magistrates and social welfare agencies in the nineteenth and twentieth. Although the 1969 Divorce Act claimed that it aimed to facilitate reconciliation between spouses and was not intended to undermine the institution of marriage, Jane Lewis observes that it represents a shift away from legislation that made the stability of marriage the main focus towards giving priority to the quality of marital relationships. Once the quality of the relationship was the deciding criterion in the success or failure of a marriage, then its stability as an institution was less easy to secure.[128]

Notes

1. For work focusing on causes of marital violence see: P. Ayers and J. Lambertz (1986) 'Marriage Relations, Money and Domestic Violence in Working-class Liverpool, 1919–39', in J. Lewis (ed.), *Labour and Love: Women's Experiences of Home and Family, 1850–1940* (Oxford: Blackwell) and E. Ross (1982) '"Fierce Questions and Taunts": Married Life in Working-class London, 1870–1914', *Feminist Studies*, 8:3, 575–602.
2. For legal statements about correction see M. Doggett (1992) *Marriage, Wife-beating and the Law in Victorian England* (London: Weidenfeld & Nicolson), 8–15.
3. M. Bacon (1807) *A New Abridgment of the Law* (7 vols., London), I, 457, cited in Doggett, *Wife-beating*, 10.
4. E. Foyster (2005) *Marital Violence: An English Family History 1660–1857* (Cambridge: Cambridge University Press), 40–6.
5. Doggett, *Wife-beating*, 6–8.
6. For examples of the use of these procedures see J. Bailey (2003) *Unquiet Lives: Marriage and Marriage Breakdown in England 1660–1800* (Cambridge: Cambridge University Press), 32–49.
7. See for instance J. Hurl-Eamon (2001) 'Domestic Violence Prosecuted: Women Binding over their Husbands for Assault at Westminster Quarter Sessions, 1685–1720', *Journal of Family History*, 26, 435–54; G. T. Smith (2007) 'Expanding the Compass of Domestic Violence in the Hanoverian Metropolis', *Journal of Social History*, 41:1, 31–54 and A. Clark (1992) 'Humanity or Justice? Wifebeating and the Law in the Eighteenth and Nineteenth Centuries', in C. Smart (ed.), *Regulating Womanhood: Historical Writings on Marriage, Motherhood and Sexuality* (London: Routledge), 186–206.
8. Other faults were desertion, bigamy, rape, sodomy, and bestiality; see S. Cretney (2003) *Family Law in the Twentieth Century: A History* (Oxford: Oxford University Press), 169.
9. Bailey, *Unquiet Lives*, 120–2.
10. A.J. Hammerton (1992) *Cruelty and Companionship: Conflict in Nineteenth-century Married Life* (London: Routledge), 124–5.

11. M.J. Wiener (2004) *Men of Blood: Violence, Manliness, and Criminal Justice in Victorian England* (Cambridge: Cambridge University Press), 174.
12. See Hammerton, *Cruelty and Companionship*, 118–33.
13. M.L. Shanley (1989) *Feminism, Marriage, and the Law in Victorian England* (London: I.B. Tauris), 181.
14. Bailey, *Unquiet Lives*, 124.
15. Cited in Foyster, *Marital Violence*, 42.
16. For Stowell's statement of the law see Hammerton, *Cruelty and Companionship*, 120–1.
17. Bailey, *Unquiet Lives*, 63–70; 124 and Foyster *Marital Violence*, 43–53.
18. Hurl-Eamon, 'Domestic Violence Prosecuted', 437–9.
19. Hammerton, *Cruelty and Companionship*, 127.
20. G. Savage (1990) '"The Wilful Communication of a Loathsome Disease": Marital Conflict and Venereal Disease in Victorian England', *Victorian Studies*, 34, 41–2.
21. *Russell* v. *Russell* discussed in Cretney, *Family Law*, 264.
22. J. Burnett (2000) 'Exposing "The Inner Life": The Women's Co-operative Guild's attitude to "Cruelty"', in S. D'Cruze (ed.), *Everyday Violence in Britain, 1850–1950: Gender and Class* (Harlow, Essex: Longman), 144–5.
23. Cretney, *Family Law*, 264.
24. Home Office website: http://www.homeoffice.gov.uk/crime-victims/reducing-crime/domestic-violence/. For list of acts considered abusive see the information at the Womensaid website: http://www.womensaid.org.uk/.
25. S. Amussen (1994) '"Being Stirred to Much Unquietness": Violence and Domestic Violence in Early Modern England', *Journal of Women's History*, 6:2, 82.
26. J. Bailey (2006) '"I Dye [sic] by Inches": Locating Wife Beating in the Concept of a Privatisation of Marriage and Violence in Eighteenth-century England', *Social History*, 31:3, 290–2.
27. P. King (1996) '"Punishing Assault": The Transformation of Attitudes in the English Courts', *Journal of Interdisciplinary History*, 27:1, 43.
28. King, '"Punishing assault"', passim; for the nineteenth century see Weiner, *Men of Blood*, Chapter 1.
29. Weiner, *Men of Blood*, 21–9.
30. Ibid., 38.
31. Doggett, *Wife-beating*, 106.
32. For an examination of some of the cases heard by magistrates, see G. Savage (2007) '"A State of Personal Danger": Domestic Violence in England, 1903–1922', in K. Watson (ed.), *Assaulting the Past: Violence and Civilization in Historical Context* (Cambridge: Cambridge Scholars Press), 269–85.
33. A. Clark (2000) 'Domesticity and the Problem of Wife beating in Nineteenth-century Britain: Working-class Culture, Law and Politics', in S. D'Cruze (ed.), *Everyday Violence in Britain, 1850–1950: Gender and Class* (Harlow: Longman), 31–2.
34. M. Hunt (1992) 'Wife Beating, Domesticity and Women's Independence in Eighteenth-century London', *Gender & History*, 4:1, 23 and R. Shoemaker (2001) 'Male Honour and the Decline of Public Violence in Eighteenth-century London, *Social History*, 26:2, 190–208.

35. Bailey, '"Dye [sic] by Inches"', passim; Foyster, *Marital Violence*, Chapter 4; S. D'Cruze (1998) *Crimes of Outrage: Sex, Violence and Victorian Working Women* (London: UCL Press), Chapter 4 and Savage, '"State of Personal Danger"', 275.
36. Foyster, *Marital Violence*, 220.
37. S. D'Cruze (2000) 'Unguarded Passions: Violence, History and the Everyday', in S. D'Cruze (ed.), *Everyday Violence in Britain, 1850–1950: Gender and Class* (Harlow: Longman), 10.
38. Foyster, *Marital Violence*, Chapter 5.
39. D'Cruze 'Unguarded Passions', 10.
40. For instance the reporting of the marital problems of the Countess of Strathmore, see Bailey, '"Dye [sic] by Inches"', 293.
41. L. Surridge (2005) *Bleak Houses: Marital Violence in Victorian Fiction* (Athens: Ohio University Press), 8–9. For local newspaper reports on domestic violence see D'Cruze, *Crimes of Outrage*, 78–80 and Chapter 8.
42. Surridge, *Bleak Houses*, Chapters 2–3, 5–6, 7–8.
43. See especially S. Hamilton (2001) 'Making History with Frances Power Cobbe: Victorian Feminism, Domestic Violence, and the Language of Imperialism', *Victorian Studies*, 437–60.
44. Surridge, *Bleak Houses*, 44–5 and 146.
45. Foyster, *Marital Violence*, 72–81.
46. J. Carter Wood (2004) *Violence and Crime in Nineteenth-century England: The Shadow of our Refinement* (London: Routledge).
47. E. Nelson (2007) 'Victims of War: The First World War, Returned Soldiers, and Understandings of Domestic Violence in Australia', *Journal of Women's History*, 19:4, 83–4.
48. Hamilton, 'Making History with Frances Power Cobbe', 442.
49. Ibid., 442–5 and Surridge, *Bleak Houses*, 9.
50. Nelson, 'Victims of War', passim and L. Jackson (2000) 'Women Professionals and the Regulation of Violence in Interwar Britain', in S. D'Cruze (ed.), *Everyday Violence in Britain, 1850–1950: Gender and Class* (Harlow: Longman), 122.
51. See Nelson, 'Victims of War', passim.
52. See the first reference at note 25 above.
53. For statistics see ibid. For recognition of the scope of the problem see the National Domestic Violence Charity Women's Aid at http://www.womensaid.org.uk/.
54. K. Thomas (1959) 'The Double Standard', *Journal of the History of Ideas*, 20:2, 195–216; D. Turner (2002) *Fashioning Adultery: Gender, Sex and Civility in England 1660–1740* (Cambridge: Cambridge University Press), Chapter 2 and Bailey, *Unquiet Lives*, 143–9.
55. Men's interest in their wives as a form of property was also considered to be diminished by her adultery; see A.S. Holmes (1995) 'The Double Standard in the English Divorce Laws, 1857–1923', *Law & Social Inquiry*, 20:2, 604–5.
56. Debate in parliament over the 1857 legislation indicates that a minority of members invoked a Christian framework to object to legal distinctions between provision for men and women; see Holmes, 'The Double Standard', 612.
57. K. Israel (1997) 'French Vices and British Liberties: Gender, Class and Narrative Competition in a Late Victorian Sex Scandal', *Social History*,

22:1, 10–25. For demand that wives should be able to sue for divorce on the grounds of adultery due to the implications of infidelity see G. Savage, '"Wilful Communication"', 39.

58. Holmes, 'The Double Standard', passim.
59. A de-facto adherence to it continued in the courts; see ibid., 616.
60. J. Lewis and P. Wallis (2000) 'Fault, Breakdown, and the Church of England's Involvement in the 1969 Divorce Law Reform', *Twentieth Century British History*, 11:3, 309.
61. C. Langhamer (2006) 'Adultery in Post-war England', *History Workshop Journal*, 62, 106–10 and C. Smart (1996) 'Good Wives and Moral Lives: Marriage and Divorce 1937–51' in C. Gledhill and G. Swanson (eds.), *Nationalising Femininity: Culture, Sexuality and British Cinema in the Second World War* (Manchester: Manchester University Press), passim.
62. J. Weeks (1989) *Sex, Politics and Society: The Regulation of Sexuality since 1800* (2nd edn, London: Longman), 92–3.
63. D. T. Andrew (1997) '"Adultery a-la-Mode": Privilege, the Law and Attitudes to Adultery 1770–1809', *Historical Association*, 82:265, 9–10, 17–18 and passim.
64. Weeks, *Sex, Politics and Society*, 87.
65. Ibid., 214 and L. Hall (2000) *Sex, Gender and Social Change in Britain since 1880* (Basingstoke: Macmillan), 92–3.
66. J. Lewis (1990) 'Public Institution and Private Relationship: Marriage and Marriage Guidance, 1920–1968', *Twentieth Century British History*, 1:3, 235 and Smart, 'Good Wives and Moral Lives', passim. For figures of divorce see Cretney, *Family Law*, 281–2.
67. Lewis, 'Public Institution and Private Relationship', 244–5 and 253–6.
68. Ibid., 262.
69. M. Ingram (1987) *Church Courts, Sex and Marriage in England, 1570–1640* (Cambridge: Cambridge University Press), 3.
70. Ibid., 53–5.
71. Ibid., 249 and Bailey, *Unquiet Lives*, 141.
72. Turner, *Fashioning Adultery*, 5.
73. Weeks, *Sex, Politics and Society*, 83.
74. S. Redmayne (1993) 'The Matrimonial Causes Act 1937: A Lesson in the Art of Compromise', *Oxford Journal of Legal Studies*, 13:2, 183–200 and J. Lewis and P. Wallis (2000) 'Fault, Breakdown', 309 and passim.
75. Cultural attention on heterosexual marital love helped label other forms of sexual activity as deviant; see Jennings, 'Sexuality', 295.
76. Ingram, *Church Courts, Sex and Marriage*, 250 and 257.
77. Turner, *Fashioning Adultery*, 199–200.
78. Ibid., 5–7. See also Chapter 1 in this volume.
79. Weeks, *Sex, Politics and Society*, Chapter 5.
80. Israel, 'French vices', 9.
81. L. Kipnis (1998) 'Adultery', *Critical Inquiry*, 24:2, 314–16.
82. Lewis 'Public Institution and Private Relationship', 237; Jennings, 'Sexuality', 295 and Weeks, *Sex, Politics and Society*, 200–1.
83. Weeks, *Sex, Politics and Society*, 212 and Lewis, 'Public Institution and Private Relationship', 237.
84. Lewis, 'Public Institution and Private Relationship', 234.

85. Redmayne, 'Matrimonial Causes Act 1937', 183–200.
86. Turner, *Fashioning Adultery*, 194.
87. Ibid., 194–6.
88. B. Leckie (1999) *Culture and Adultery: The Novel, the Newspaper, and the Law 1857-1914* (Philadelphia: University of Pennsylvania Press), 1, 18 and Chapter 2.
89. M. Vicinus (1997) 'Lesbian Perversity and Victorian Marriage: The 1864 Codrington Divorce Trial', *Journal of British Studies*, 36:1, 70–98; Israel, 'French Vices', 1–26 and G. Savage (1998) 'Erotic Stories and Public Decency: Newspaper Reporting of Divorce Proceedings in England', *Historical Journal*, 41:2, 511–28.
90. Vicinus, 'Lesbian Perversity', 71 and 75.
91. Savage, 'Erotic Stories and Public Decency', 514.
92. Ibid., 517–23.
93. Kipnis, 'Adultery', 292, 294 and 325–6.
94. M. Richards and J. Elliott (1991) 'Sex and Marriage in the 1960s and 1970s', in D. Clark (ed.), *Marriage, Domestic Life and Social Change: Writings for Jacqueline Burgoyne (1944–88)* (London: Routledge), 44, 47–8. See also quote from Langhamer, 'Adultery', 90.
95. G. Savage (1992) '"Intended only for the Husband": Gender, Class, and the Provision for Divorce in England, 1858–1868', in K. O. Garrigan (ed.), *Victorian Scandals: Representations of Gender and Class* (Athens: Ohio University Press); S. Wolfram (1985) 'Divorce in England 1700–1857', *Oxford Journal of Legal Studies*, 5:2, 155–86 and Lewis and Wallis, 'Fault, Breakdown', 308–32.
96. N. Elias (2000) *The Civilizing Process: Sociogenentic and Psychogenetic Investigations* [1939], trans. E. Jephcott (rev. edn., Oxford: Blackwell).
97. See Bailey, '"Dye [sic] by Inches"', 274–9.
98. For recent work addressing the 'civilizing process' see the chapters in Part 1 of K. Watson, *Assaulting the Past*, 20–101.
99. See N. Tomes, '"A torrent of abuse": Crimes of Violence between Working-class Men and Women in London 1840–1875', *Journal of Social History*, 11, 328–45 and Hammerton, *Cruelty and Companionship*, 39–43.
100. Foyster, *Marital Violence*, Chapter 4.
101. Bailey, '"Dye [sic] by Inches"', passim; D'Cruze, *Crimes of Outrage*, Chapter 4 and Savage, '"A state of personal danger"', passim.
102. See D. Turner (2005) 'Adulterous Kisses and the Meanings of Familiarity in Early-modern Britain' in K. Harvey (ed.), *The Kiss in History* (Manchester: Manchester University Press), 80–1.
103. Jennings, 'Sexuality', passim.
104. Langhamer, 'Adultery', 110.
105. E. Ross (1982) '"Fierce Questions and Taunts": Married Life in Working-class London, 1870–1914', *Feminist Studies*, 8:3, 575–602 and D'Cruze, *Crimes of Outrage*, Chapter 4.
106. Ayers and Lambertz, 'Marriage Relations', passim.
107. For further discussion see F. Dolan (2008) *Marriage and Violence, The Early Modern Legacy* (Philadelphia: University of Pennsylvania Press).
108. Smith, 'Expanding the Compass', passim.
109. Hamilton, 'Making History with Frances Power Cobbe', passim.

110. Turner, *Fashioning Adultery*, 61–2; Israel, 'French Vices', passim and Holmes, 'The Double Standard', passim.
111. Langhamer, 'Adultery', 87–8. For the relationship between marriage and the stance on sexual morality see Lewis, 'Public Institution and Private Relationship', passim.
112. Richards and Elliott, 'Sex and Marriage in the 1960s and 1970s', passim.
113. For example, see all the contributors to the special issue on domestic violence and editor's note (2007) *Journal of Women's History*, 19:4. For adultery see Leckie, *Culture and Adultery*, passim.
114. Surridge, *Bleak Houses*, passim and Smart, 'Good Wives', passim.
115. Foyster, *Marital Violence*, Chapter 5.
116. Dolan, *Marriage and Violence*, Chapter 2.
117. Borthwick Institute for Archives, Cons. CP 1831/5, article 4.
118. See Mary Morley's deposition, ibid.
119. *Leeds Mercury*, Saturday 2 January 1858.
120. Borthwick Institute for Archives, Cons. CP 1848/3.
121. *Lloyd's Weekly London Newspaper*, 28 February 1848.
122. For one example, see 'local divorce suit' in *Bristol Mercury and Daily Post*, Friday 21 February 1879.
123. *Lloyd's Weekly London Newspaper*, Sunday 27 July 1851.
124. Savage, 'Erotic Stories', 528.
125. *Constandinidi* v. *Constandinidi* and *Lance*, cited in Cretney, *Family Law*, 188.
126. Cretney, *Family Law*, 251.
127. Langhamer, 'Adultery', 95.
128. Lewis, 'Public Institution and Private Relationship', 233–63.

3 Desperate Measures or Cruel Intentions? Infanticide in Britain since 1600

Anne-Marie Kilday

1. Introduction

For over 400 years, British society has debated whether women who kill their offspring should be pitied or punished. The longevity of the crime of infanticide itself, as well as the divergent reactions to its perpetration, has resulted in the enduring persistence of child murder in historical and contemporary discussions of criminality, and female criminality in particular.[1] Infanticide (which in this chapter is taken to mean the murder of a new-born child)[2] is a rare example of a gender-specific crime where men were seldom involved.[3] As a result of this, historians, in particular, have been fascinated with the crime of infanticide, as by its very nature, it offers a unique insight into the female experience which is so often hidden from view. Apart from the criminal evidence itself, midwives and local women offered their 'expertise' in the courtroom and descriptions of pregnancy, birth and maternity (experiences most of the time hidden from men) were debated in the traditionally male-dominated sphere of legal practice.[4]

In addition to illuminating aspects of the hidden world of women, infanticide is also worthy of scholarly attention as it can demonstrate the capacity of some women to commit acts of independent criminality and even violent behaviour.[5] As these traits are seemingly unusual and uncharacteristic of the female sex, they upset the traditional notions of female identity so loudly espoused by social commentators in the eighteenth and nineteenth centuries. Historians have been interested to study not only how infanticidal women were treated and regarded by male authorities, but by other women too.[6] Were infanticidal women singled out for harsher or more shameful treatment because they had overstepped the boundaries of acceptable maternal or feminine behaviour? Or, alternatively, were these women regarded as unfortunate victims who had merely acted out of desperation in the context of precarious circumstances? Again, the debate over whether infanticidal women should be pitied or punished emerges as a focal point for historical, sociological and criminological discussions of this crime and its context.

A further reason why infanticide merits specific and closer attention in historical studies relates to the way in which it often acts as a prism onto wider social concerns. Attitudes towards this crime throughout history can act as a mirror to changes in opinion amongst social, legal, moral and religious commentators with regard to women, illegitimacy, marriage, motherhood and the value of infant life. The inexorable, volatile and enduring link between child murder, legal attitudes and public opinion has retained infanticide's powerful relevance over time, and has enabled this crime to act as a microcosm of social change.[7]

Certainly, infanticide is an exceptionally emotive crime. Not only is this due to the innocence and helplessness of the victims involved, but also because this type of criminality inverts the expected 'normal' protective relationship (based on maternal instinct) between a mother and her child. Yet, as has been indicated above, a study of infanticide involves much more than an analysis of a few instances of child killing. Consequently, this chapter illuminates as much about the context for the crime of infanticide as about the perpetration of the crime itself. The next section will outline the chronology of attitudes to newborn child murder since the early modern period. This will be followed by an outline of the historiography relating to infanticide, where three key themes will be identified and then explored in more detail through the analysis of several case studies.

2. Chronology

According to Laila Williamson:

Infanticide is a practice present-day westerners regard as a cruel and inhuman custom, resorted to by only a few desperate and primitive people living in harsh environments. We tend to think of it as an exceptional practice, to be found only among such peoples as the Eskimos and Australian Aborigines, who are far removed in both culture and geographical distance from us and our civilised ancestors. The truth is, however, quite different. Infanticide has been practiced on every continent and by people on every level of cultural complexity, from hunters and gatherers to highly developed civilisations, including our own ancestors. Rather than being an exception, then, it has been the rule.[8]

Even in the present day, accusations of infanticide are still being brought to our attention, albeit rarely, by the media. Examples such as the 2006 trial of Sabine Hilschenz[9] or the alleged case against Leah Andrew brought in 2008[10] demonstrate that the notion of newborn child murder truly is 'an enduring phenomenon in the history of humankind'.[11]

Attitudes towards the crime of infanticide have not remained consistent or straightforward throughout history. Cultural divisions, religious differences and social conditions have generated very different views on the committal of newborn child murder. For instance, infanticide was condoned in a variety of pre-Christian and non-Christian civilisations as a method of controlling population size, and in some Eastern societies, the practice was (and is) actively encouraged in order to manage the gender balance within the populace.[12] Yet evidence of a less tolerant attitude toward the act of child murder exists in abundance. Such opinion can be traced as far back as 4,000 years ago, with a collection of Babylonian laws known as 'The Code of Hummurabi' which provided that 'if a nurse or mother allowed a suckling to die in her hands and substituted another, her breast should be amputated'.[13] Closer to home, however, it was not until the late sixteenth century that most European states singled out infanticide for severe punishment.

The confluence of three contemporary concerns amongst the authorities of the day resulted in the instigation of Europe-wide moral and legislative opposition to child murder during the early modern period. The first of these was a determination to protect infant life. Religious and legal institutions were thus encouraged to be more proscriptive in their defence of 'innocent blood' at this time, by becoming more hostile to interference with the natural course of human generation.[14]

The second key concern with the nature of infanticide was that it demonstrated behaviour which openly contradicted normally understood and expected maternal feelings and was regarded as a wholly unnatural transgression; 'a crime at the base idea of which the human mind revolts'.[15] Infanticide was clearly seen as a crime against womanhood, and more particularly, a crime against perceptions of how women, and mothers in particular, were expected to behave. Women who contravened this norm and killed their newborns had turned their backs on humanity, civil society and their gender. During the eighteenth century in particular, women accused of infanticide were commonly given the appellation 'monster' or 'demon' in court indictments as a reflection of the abhorrence provoked by their crimes.[16] Clearly, in a supposedly more 'enlightened' society, and in order to protect notions of maternity and gendered normality, infanticide could not be tolerated.

The final aspect of contemporary thinking, and indeed the one which was the real concern of the moralists of the day, was the apparent need to control the sexual morality of the populace. A growth in vagrancy across Europe, from the seventeenth century onwards, resulted in the authorities becoming increasingly anxious about how sexual immorality and criminal behaviour could be effectively managed.[17] Initially at least, concerns were principally related to a distaste regarding the actual act of fornication. Over time, however, this anxiety was transferred to the frequent end product of casual and supposedly immoral sexual activity: illegitimacy.[18] The growing condemnation of illegitimacy across Britain and Europe during the early modern period was not based solely on fears of the spread of immorality, however. Economic factors also played a part. The Church and the authorities of the day did not want the financial burden of additional mouths to feed in a regularly strained and increasingly unpredictable economic climate, especially when this 'burden' had been 'conceived' through sinful fornication. Indeed, several historians have argued that the cost of illegitimacy rather than its incidence ultimately resulted in the statutory legal changes related to newborn child murder which appeared in the early decades of the seventeenth century.[19]

The English 'Act to Prevent the Destroying and Murthering of Bastard Children', passed in 1624,[20] was ratified unaltered in Ireland some eighty-three years later. The Scottish 'Act Anent the Murthering of Children'[21] came on to the statute books in 1690, and although clearly founded on its English equivalent, was far more stringent and detailed in its contents. Despite different nuances within the legislative provisions both north and south of the Tweed, by the end of the seventeenth century, juries were directed to capitally convict British women accused of infanticide regardless of whether there was any direct evidence of murder.[22] Three conditions needed to be met for a charge of infanticide to be laid. First, that the woman had concealed her pregnancy. Secondly, that she had given birth alone and not called for assistance at the point of delivery. Thirdly, that her child was either dead or missing.[23] The directives of the statutes clearly illustrate the presumption that if a woman had concealed her pregnancy, by implication, she must have killed her child. As a result, and in contrast to the practice in all other murder trials, the burden of proof was firmly placed on the accused woman. In addition, the legislative provision related to infanticide was only applicable to unmarried women; married women were typically tried under the normal rules that governed other forms of homicide.[24]

The immediate impact of the initial infanticide legislation was a rapid increase in conviction and execution rates for newborn child murder across Britain.[25] However, by the first third of the eighteenth century, attitudes to this crime and the individuals who perpetrated it had changed once more.

Despite the stern legal provision, the statutes were not being fully enforced on a regular basis after 1740, unless there was incontrovertible evidence of violence having been inflicted on the child. Deficiencies in the evidence presented to the courts, and uncertainties amongst the legal authorities about how to deal with infanticidal women, served to undermine the authority of the 1624 and 1690 Acts.[26] Forms of 'judicial leniency', such as allowing (what amounted to) dubious forms of defence evidence to mitigate individual cases and granting petitions for banishment to avoid trial, resulted in a low conviction rate in eighteenth-century England.[27] In consequence, proponents of reform argued that the legislation needed to be revised to include 'the more certain application of a suitable (that is, lesser) punishment [which] would more effectively discourage women from concealing and murdering their illegitimate children'.[28]

Lord Ellenborough's Act of 1803[29] replaced the English and Irish statutes and made infanticide trials subject to the same rules of evidence that pertained in all other homicide cases. In effect, as Mark Jackson explains, 'the prosecution once again had to establish that a dead child had been born alive rather than being able to rely merely on evidence of concealment to prove murder'.[30] To alleviate the issue of jury reluctance to convict on the capital charge, the new statute introduced the offence of concealment of birth (which carried a maximum sentence of two years' imprisonment) as an alternative option for the conviction of unmarried mothers.[31] It was not until 1828 that the concealment provision was extended to all mothers regardless of marital status, and not until 1861 that the legislation was amended to include men.[32] In Scotland, Lord Ellenborough's Act was instituted in 1809,[33] but the legislation allowed for imprisonment for up to three years, perhaps reflecting the long reach of the Scottish Church and its preoccupation with the maintenance of social and moral order.

Although legislative provision and judicial responses to infanticide largely stabilised after the mid-nineteenth century, public opinion regarding newborn child murder was still very much divided. This debate seems to have been fuelled by the growing use of medical testimony amongst defence teams in infanticide trials from the late Victorian period onwards.[34] Attempts to understand infanticidal women and potentially explain their actions were welcomed in some quarters and rejected in others. As a result, the question of whether such women should be sympathised with or condemned persisted into the modern era. The regular inclusion and acceptance of complex evidence relating to the mental health of the accused mother (most commonly related to the puerperal insanity plea), along with several high-profile cases, resulted in a further shift both in the meaning of the term infanticide and in attitudes towards its perpetration by the early twentieth century.[35] Infanticide became a separate offence, categorised as a species of manslaughter, rather than murder, in the Infanticide Acts of 1922 and 1938.[36] The latter Act defines infanticide as any wilful act or omission on the part of a mother which caused the death of her child under the age of twelve months, while the balance of her mind was disturbed by reason of her not having fully recovered from the effect of giving birth to the child or by reason of the effect of lactation.[37]

This legislation, save for a few minor amendments, remains in force across Britain today.

Although omnipresent in the annals of crime in Britain and beyond, in more recent years, infanticide cases have received a significant amount of attention from the press and media. A wave of prominent child murder trials and quashed convictions (such as those of Sally Clark, Angela Cannings and Trupti Patel), as well as scandals involving expert medical testimony, have all served to retain the prominence of infanticide in the public arena.[38] It is difficult to see how the fascination with infanticide and infanticidal women in particular will diminish over the forthcoming centuries, given the particularly emotive nature of the crime, and the fact that the attention afforded to this offence has been increasingly sensationalised over the course of more than four hundred years.

3. Historiography

A burgeoning historiography related to the history of infanticide has emerged since the late 1950s. The focus of interest in this crime has not remained static during that time, but rather it has been shaped by individual scholars and their particular interests.[39] The historiography of newborn child murder can be broadly grouped into four themes of scholarly interest: regional and national experiences; attitudes towards infanticide and infanticidal women; the literary and cultural context for infanticide; and finally, understanding the rationale for this type of crime. Each of these themes will be now examined in turn, in order to get a clearer picture of the historiographical framework for infanticide and to identify if any lacunae exist in this field of historical research.

Regional and national perspectives of infanticide have largely been written by social historians and, as such, they have tended to focus more directly on the nature of the crime itself and the characteristics of the criminals involved in its perpetration. A significant variety of quantitative studies have been carried out (at both a regional and a national level), using court indictments and newspaper reports, in order to count the number of individuals indicted for infanticide and to establish how prevalent this crime was in comparison with other offences.[40] This kind of data, although problematic due to the unknown number of *actual* crimes as compared to *reported* crimes, have also been used to examine the kind of woman involved in episodes of infanticide in order to generate a profile of the typical offender. Despite varying social contexts, and some anomalies in practice on occasion, most historians would agree that, throughout time, infanticide has been typically practised by young, unmarried females. In the early modern period, most of women indicted were also domestic servants.[41] This kind of evidence has enabled historians to build up a relatively detailed picture of infanticide and has allowed for a more nuanced understanding of this type of offence. One strand of research to recently emerge from this type of analysis has been a focus on the methodology used in the committal of infanticide and how this may well vary depending on the social, religious and cultural contexts involved.[42]

When writing about attitudes towards infanticidal women and their crimes, historians have tended to focus on the legal context for newborn child murder and how attitudes and responses within this context have changed over time. This particular branch of the historiography (alluded to in Section 2 of this chapter) has been devoted to changes in the legal definition of infanticide and how these changes have shaped the way in which offenders have been treated by the courts and the legal authorities.[43] Some scholars, however, have looked beyond the legal context, to examine wider societal attitudes to this crime. These historians are much more interested in how infanticidal women came to be regarded by society at large, when they had so flagrantly rejected or ignored the boundaries of acceptable maternal and gendered behaviour.[44]

This kind of contextual analysis is best affected by examining cultural and literary perspectives on infanticide, a theme of historiographical study which has only emerged in recent years. This scholarship uses a broad range of source material (poetry, literature, dying-speeches, sermons, ballads and other pamphlet literature) to illuminate how infanticidal women were regarded by wider society in a variety of cultural contexts.[45] Broadly speaking, sympathy for women who murdered their children appears to have increased over time, as society began to understand why some women behaved in this way. Certainly, the sentiment surrounding newborn child murder has grown to become more nuanced since the early modern era of blanket abhorrence and repulsion.

Attempts to understand why women commit infanticide are ubiquitous in historical studies of this offence. As infanticide appears to be the antithesis of what was regarded as 'normal' maternal or feminine behaviour, historians have been preoccupied with providing an explanation for the inversion of the gender stereotype. In addition, historians have argued that if we can come closer to an understanding of why women committed newborn child murder, we will inevitably be able to draw a more complete picture of the female experience, which has so often been hidden from view, especially during the pre-modern period.

Explanations for infanticide which appear in the historiography tend to concentrate on three causal factors: shame, economics and medical explanations related to temporary insanity. Shame or opprobrium has long been held as one of the key factors involved in newborn child murder, owing to the historical relationship between infanticide and illegitimacy. Indeed, over the centuries, many of the women indicted before the courts for this crime have testified that it was the avoidance of the shame of an illegitimate child, more than any other factor, which had motivated them to kill their offspring. This sentiment appears to have been more strongly felt in cultures where women were under greater moral scrutiny, either from their peers or from religious officials.[46]

Economic factors have also been investigated by historians as a rationale for infanticidal behaviour. Most of the scholarship on this particular causal factor has focused on the stark implications of poverty and economic hardship for young, single women who found themselves pregnant. In precarious economic circumstances, some women appear to have turned to infanticide to avoid the extra expense of another mouth to feed and to safeguard their financial futures.[47] Moreover, some communities appear to have tacitly condoned this course of action to avoid an increased burden on the parish purse.[48] Another form of financial management associated with child murder has been highlighted by the scholarship carried out on burial insurance clubs and baby farming, largely in relation to the nineteenth century.[49] In these instances, infanticide was committed for profit generation, rather than in an attempt to avoid financial ruin. More research needs to be carried out on the economic factors associated with infanticide in order to explore the crime's relationship with the economy of makeshifts and the degree to which newborn child murder can be correlated with regional variations in the management of poverty.

The most recent historiography related to infanticide has been dominated by medical explanations for the perpetration of this crime. Some analysis has related to the reliability of medical evidence used in court trials,[50] but in the main, the literature has concentrated on attempts to establish the mental health of the mothers accused.[51] The recent flurry of writing about the relationship between infanticide and mental instability is most readily explained by the clearly burgeoning linkage between the legal sphere and medical opinion after 1850. From that time onwards, changes in the legal definition of infanticide depended on advances in medical knowledge. The confluence of the fields of medicine and the law in relation to newborn child murder has opened up the study of infanticide to medical and legal historians, and has introduced a further layer of perspectives on this crime, that was simply not in existence 50 years ago.

What has been written with regard to the more modern period has concentrated on medical defences and motives rather than the other associated characteristics involved in the perpetration of newborn child murder,

such as rate of incidence, methodology, victimology and the offender profile. These are all aspects of this offence which have been more thoroughly
dealt with by historians of the early modern era. There is, therefore, a clear
imbalance in the writing on infanticide that needs to be addressed.[52] Studies
of the early period (pre-1850) exclude medical explanations for infanticide,
whereas studies of the more modern period (post-1850) exclude everything *but* medical explanations for infanticide. At present, and until further
research has been carried out, the historiographical framework of newborn
child murder is more complete for the pre-modern period, and as such, the
case studies selected for this chapter are located within that epoch.

The following case studies pick up and illuminate three of the most
dominant themes which emerge from the pre-modern historiography of
infanticide. These themes are: acknowledged similarities in the personal
characteristics of the defendants involved; regional and cultural variations
in the way the crime was committed; and, finally, different perspectives on
why infanticide was carried out in the first instance.

4. Case Studies

Martha Lankey from Stretton in Shropshire was indicted at the Assize
Court in 1825 for the murder of a 'female bastard child'.[53] Lankey had
been working as a servant at the house of Thomas Lester, and one evening
after playing cards with one of her fellow servants, she complained 'of
a pain in her bowels' and she was sent to bed. When the mistress of the
house went to check on Lankey, she found her lying in a bed which was
covered in blood. Lankey explained the mess by saying that she had been
using the 'pot' in bed and had spilt its contents over the sheets. The mistress then sent for the doctor. When the doctor arrived to examine Martha
Lankey, he found a fully mature dead female child under her bed which
had a piece of ribbon twisted around its neck. He wrapped the body in a
black petticoat, left the room, and summoned the authorities.

Three years previously, in 1822, Richard Summerfield from Montgomery in Shropshire was indicted 'on a violent suspicion of wilfully murdering a male child'.[54] Summerfield's lover, Ann Edwards, had told him
early on in her pregnancy that he was the father of her unborn, illegitimate child, but she explained to him that he needn't be afraid of the
consequences of their situation, because a few of her friends and family had offered to care for her and the baby upon and after her delivery.
Unfortunately, Ann Edwards's labour came on unexpectedly, whilst she
was in the company of Richard Summerfield. She gave birth to a fully
mature male child, and whilst incapacitated, Summerfield took the child
up and went away with it. He latterly confessed to Edwards that he had

drowned their child in a stream near to his home, but warned her that if she acknowledged the truth to anyone, 'he would murder her'. Ann Edwards went straight to the authorities and Summerfield was arrested.

The case against Martha Lankey is very typical of pre-1850 indictments for infanticide with regard to the characteristics of the offender involved. As we have already noted, historians have acknowledged that the archetypal infanticidal mother was – like Lankey – a young, unmarried, domestic servant, who had concealed her pregnancy and had given birth alone and in secret. This profile is typical amongst indictments for newborn child murder for two reasons. First, it is not that surprising that the vast majority of the women accused of infanticide were domestic servants. Most servant girls were of childbearing age and they worked in close proximity to men. Illegitimate pregnancy would be disastrous for domestic servants as they were usually only employed on the basis that they remained single and childless. The loss of reputation to a household employing an unmarried pregnant servant would rarely be tolerated; she would inevitably be dismissed without a reference. The pressure on such women to conceal their pregnancies and thereafter rid themselves of the cause of ruin to their character and economic livelihood in the form of their bastard offspring can be easily understood.[55]

The second explanation for the typicality of the offender profile is that this type of woman was more likely to be caught for this crime. Contemporary concerns with illegitimacy had resulted in the more intensive supervision of young women, especially in rural areas. Although concealment of pregnancy might be readily achieved within this scrutinised environment, the disposal of unwanted offspring would be far more difficult to hide. Arguably, this preoccupation with 'policing' morality and 'promoting' sexual restraint may have allowed other individuals (particularly older women, married women and men) to commit newborn child murder without drawing too much attention to themselves. Certainly, indictments such as that against Richard Summerfield are quite rare, and the nature of the early modern infanticide legislation largely prevented anyone *but* unmarried mothers being convicted of the offence. The incidence of infanticide across early modern Europe is relatively insubstantial, at least in comparison to violent crimes committed by men.[56] Arguably, however, the way the offence was defined during the pre-modern period has added another shadow to the 'dark figure' of unknown crime. The true extent of infanticide, both in terms of incidence and in terms of the range of individuals involved in its perpetration, is probably considerably more substantial and extensive that the current evidence suggests.

Jannet Shanks was indicted at the High Court of Justiciary in Edinburgh in 1710 accused of newborn child murder.[57] She was charged with having given birth to a fully mature child which she then dismembered with the aid of a flattening-iron and a bread knife. By her own confession Shanks then attempted to feed the remains of her dead child to her master's two pet dogs who resided beneath her bed. After a time, however, the dogs refused to eat further, and Shanks resorted to administering Epsom salts (a laxative) to the household pets. One of the dogs subsequently escaped from the room and deposited 'a piece of the child's flesh' in his masters' slippers and the authorities were sent for. Latterly, parts of the child's fingers as well as its lungs were discovered in a pail in Shanks's bedroom amidst 'a sea of blood and depravity never to be forgotten by those who were witness to it'.

Mary Lloyd was indicted at the Court of Great Session in Wales in 1782.[58] Lloyd, from Llangathen in Carmarthenshire, was charged with the infanticide of her own newborn female child. She had 'been with child by her reputed father, with whom she lay whilst her mother slept in the workshop'. Lloyd was charged that she did wilfully and with malice aforethought 'choak and strangle the said child about the neck with both of her hands, causing it to die instantly'. Upon investigation, the Welsh authorities discovered the bodies of two further newborn infants buried in the vegetable plot of the family garden.

When discussing the methodology of infanticide, historians have generally categorised the crime as non-violent.[59] According to Samuel Radbill's early generalisation, 'The methods used in infanticide have not changed much throughout history. Blood is rarely shed.'[60] Since then, historians have maintained the view that as was the case with Mary Lloyd, rather than adopting more overt forms of violence, asphyxia was the principal means of child murder. As Laura Gowing observes during the pre-modern period, infanticide was 'understood to be a crime not of violent activity but of passivity or neglect'.[61]

Yet, as is exemplified by the case of Jannet Shanks above, the violent methods used by those accused of infanticide in Scotland produce a profoundly different picture to that encountered elsewhere. There, bloodshed was the norm rather than the exception, and the women involved were regularly overtly brutal and ultra-violent when killing their offspring. Explanations for this anomaly are likely to have been caused by heightened social pressures within a staunch religious context. This may well have contributed to the more aggressive behaviour on the part of Scottish women.[62] Certainly, their actions pointedly shatter those conceptions of infanticidal women as pitiable, desperate 'victims' who killed with a conscience, and suggest that historians are still some way off from a comprehensive understanding of the national, regional and personal dynamics of this complex offence.

Jean Black was imprisoned in the Tolbooth in Perth (Scotland) in May 1762 accused of the murder of her newborn daughter.[63] Prior to her arrest, Black had been visited on no fewer than 16 separate occasions by Kirk Session Ministers (church officials) who believed that she was pregnant 'with a bastard child'. Black was unmarried and already had an older illegitimate son who lived with her. She steadfastly refused to admit that she was again with child. Instead, after her delivery, she 'took her daughter to the side of the water of Esk and there smashed the child to pieces with the heel of her boot and with some rocks she found nearby'. When asked by magistrates why she had committed this act upon her own child, Black said she had killed her daughter 'to avoid appearing once more before the Kirk Session (church court)'.

Elizabeth Lloyd, from Bedstone in southern England, was indicted at the Assize Court in 1827 charged with the murder of her newborn child.[64] After giving birth, she first attempted to burn the child 'in a fire between to faggots', but when this failed to completely destroy the body, she buried the remains in a nearby field and covered it with large stones. When interrogated by court officials why she had behaved in this manner, Lloyd said 'it was to avoid any questions or examinations about the child from parish officers'.[65]

Historians have already suggested a plethora of motives for newborn child murder, ranging from poverty, profit, insanity, alcoholism and abuse to fear, jealousy, revenge, shame and abandonment.[66] The very personal and individualistic nature of the crime makes it very difficult to draw general conclusions in this respect. However, as the cases of Jean Black and Elizabeth Lloyd show, shame and the avoidance of opprobrium appear to have been key factors for many women. This form of social pressure seems to have been more intense in communities where Church authority dominated alongside other judicial forms of scrutiny and discipline.

The need to avoid the social stigma of being considered 'of easy virtue' and of having produced an illegitimate child was the most common explanation given by women accused of newborn child murder when they were asked to explain their actions during the early modern period. The contemporary opprobrium associated with an illegitimate pregnancy, substantiated by moralistic and religious commentators alike, would seemingly not only tarnish the reputation of the woman directly involved and damage her prospects of a 'good' marriage, but would almost certainly affect the status of the rest of her family amongst the wider community in which she lived. This disgrace became manifest if a woman suspected of an illegitimate pregnancy was brought before church officials (either in private or in public). She might, on occasion, be asked to account for her condition, to name the man responsible and even make reparations before the parish to atone for her sins. Bearing this in mind, therefore, it is perhaps not surprising that the guilt and shame involved in an unmarried pregnancy are suggested as key incentives for women to terminate the life of the cause of such degradation. Some historians have even gone as far as to say that the nature of pre-modern church discipline was a direct cause of infanticide at that time, as women simply could not face the embarrassment of appearing before the church authorities.[67] However, this argument must be treated with some caution, as there appears to be clear regional distinctions in how illegitimacy was regarded.[68]

Some analysis of the significance of religious-based shame as a causal factor in episodes of infanticide has already been carried out in relation to pre-modern Scotland,[69] but Elizabeth Lloyd's case suggests that a similar rationale may have operated elsewhere too. The role of the Church in instances of newborn child murder needs further, careful and detailed investigation. More generally, the analysis of infanticide in the early modern period would benefit much from an exploration of contemporary medical opinion regarding childbirth and maternity, of the type so readily available to historians after 1850 and beyond. Thus far, this type of enquiry has been largely absent from historical studies of the pre-Victorian period.

5. Conclusion

The history of infanticide, as this chapter has shown, has aspects of both continuity and change. In general terms, the motives for and the methods used in newborn child murder have not changed much since 1600, despite modernisation and the supposed influence of the 'civilising process'.[70] Yet the way in which infanticidal mothers are regarded has changed, in that society now makes more of an effort to understand why women still perpetrate this offence. A continuation of this more tolerant perspective is of course important, if we want to minimise this crime in the future.

What studies of infanticide have shown is that regardless of the historical period, it is context that holds the key to an understanding of this crime as it can reflect nuances in how and why the offence was carried out. The context can also impact upon how the crime was regarded and how the perpetrator was treated. In this sense, context is taken to mean both the time and the place where the offence was committed.

The historical scholarship on infanticide has given us a reliable picture of this offence and its perpetration over time – but there is still a great deal to learn. For instance, we could still know more about the involvement of older women, married women and men in episodes of infanticide. Similarly, much more analysis of victimology are yet to be carried out. We have regional pictures of child murder, but as yet, few national pictures of infanticidal incidence. There needs to be a further exploration of episodes of infanticide over a longer time span in order to identify patterns in committal and trends in accusations. We need to better understand the differing legal context for this crime across different countries and how these attitudes changed over time. The emotional pressures single women were under, particularly in the early modern period, need to be investigated in more depth, and the extent to which the Churches' and their different confessional attitudes played an important part in instigating instances of infanticide needs to be determined. We need to more fully understand the effect that modernity had on women's lives, relationships and maternity, and we need to become more familiar with community-based reactions to child murder throughout history. We also need to more accurately measure how the women accused of this crime were treated and how this varied over time and across geography. Finally, we ought to know more about the specific actions and characteristics of infanticidal women in the modern period, in particular, the 150 years after 1850. Only when we have accomplished analysis in all of these areas will we be closer to determining whether infanticide in Britain since 1600 has been a 'desperate measure' or a 'cruel intention'.

Notes

1. For a sample of works that reflect the longevity of interest in the crime of infanticide see A.M. Kilday and K. Watson (2008) 'Infanticide, Religion and Community in the British Isles, 1720–1920: Introduction', *Family and Community History*, 11:2, 84–99; M. Jackson (ed.) (2002) *Infanticide: Historical Perspectives on Child Murder and Concealment, 1550–2000* (Aldershot: Ashgate); P.C. Hoffer and N.E.C. Hull (1984) *Murdering Mothers: Infanticide in England and New England, 1558–1803* (New York and London: New York University Press); L. Rose (1986) *The Massacre of the Innocents: Infanticide in Britain 1800–1939* (London: Routledge & Kegan Paul); W.L. Langer (1974) 'Infanticide: A Historical Survey', *History of Childhood Quarterly*, 1, 353–65; K. Wrightson (1982), 'Infanticide in European History', *Criminal Justice History*, 3, 1–20; R. Leboutte (1991) 'Offence Against the Family Order: Infanticide in Belgium from the Fifteenth through the Early Twentieth Centuries', *Journal of the History of Sexuality*, 2, 159–85; J. Thorn (ed.) (2003) *Writing British Infanticide: Child-Murder, Gender and Print, 1722–1859* (Newark: University of Delaware Press); J. McDonagh (2003) *Child Murder and British Culture 1720–1900* (Cambridge: Cambridge University Press); K.L. Moseley (1986) 'The History of Infanticide in Western Society', *Issues in Law and Medicine*, 1, 345–61 and S.X. Radbill (1968) 'A History of Child Abuse and Infanticide', in R.E. Helfer and C.H. Kempe (eds.), *The Battered Child* (Chicago: Chicago University Press), 3–17.
2. For more on the definitional aspects of this crime see M. Jackson (1996) *New-born Child Murder: Women, Illegitimacy and the Courts in Eighteenth-century England* (Manchester: Manchester University Press), 6–7.
3. For further discussion of the gender dynamics involved in this crime see A.M. Kilday (2007) *Women and Violent Crime in Enlightenment Scotland* (Woodbridge: Royal Historical Society), Chapter 4.

4. For further discussion see Kilday, *Women and Violent Crime*, 59–60.

5. See for instance the evidence presented in Kilday, *Women and Violent Crime*, 66–70 and in A.M. Kilday (2002) 'Maternal Monsters: Murdering Mothers in South-west Scotland, 1750–1815', in Y. Brown and R. Ferguson (eds.), *Twisted Sisters: Women, Crime and Deviance in Scotland since 1400* (East Linton: Tuckwell Press), 156–79.

6. See A.M. Kilday (2008) '"Monsters of the Vilest Kind": Infanticidal Women and Attitudes Towards their Criminality in Eighteenth Century Scotland', *Family and Community History*, 11:2, 100–15; Kilday, *Women and Violent Crime*, 60–3, 67; A.N. May (1995) '"She at First Denied It": Infanticide Trials at the Old Bailey', in V. Frith (ed.), *Women and History: Voices of Early Modern England* (Toronto: Coach House Press), 19–50; A.M. Kilday (forthcoming 2010) 'The Shame and Fame of Half-Hanggit Maggie: Attitudes to Child Murder in Early Modern Scotland', in D.S. Nash and A.M. Kilday (eds.), *Cultures of Shame: Punishing Moral Lapses in the West 1500–1900* (Basingstoke: Palgrave Macmillan) and D. Grey (2008) 'Discourses of Infanticide in England, 1880–1922' (PhD thesis, Roehampton University, University of Surrey).

7. See for instance Kilday, *Women and Violent Crime*, 59–63.

8. L. Williamson (1978) 'Infanticide: An Anthropological Analysis', in M. Kohl (ed.), *Infanticide and the Value of Infant Life* (New York: Prometheus Books), 61–75.

9. *Guardian*, 2 June 2006.

10. *Guardian*, 24 July 2008.

11. J. Kelly (1992) 'Infanticide in Eighteenth Century Ireland', *Irish Economic and Social History*, 19, 5.

12. See R.W. Malcolmson (1977) 'Infanticide in the Eighteenth Century', in J.S. Cockburn (ed.), *Crime in England, 1550–1800* (London: Methuen), 208; D.E. Mungello (2008) *Drowning Girls in China: Infanticide in China since 1650* (Oxford: Rowman & Littlefield) and R. Dube Bhatnagar, R. Dube and R. Dube (2005) *Female Infanticide in India: A Feminist Cultural History* (Albany: State University of New York Press).

13. Radbill, 'A History of Child Abuse and Infanticide', 13.

14. For further discussion see Kilday, *Women and Violent Crime*, 60–3 and Malcolmson, 'Infanticide in the Eighteenth Century', 208.

15. B. Henry (1994) *Dublin Hanged: Crime, Law Enforcement and Punishment in Late Eighteenth Century Dublin* (Dublin: Irish Academic Press), 38.

16. See for instance Malcolmson, 'Infanticide in the Eighteenth Century', 189–90 and especially M. Francus (1997) 'Monstrous Mothers, Monstrous Societies: Infanticide and the Rule of Law in Restoration and Eighteenth-century England', *Eighteenth-Century Life*, 21, 133–56.

17. See Kilday, *Women and Violent Crime*, 60–3; Hoffer and Hull, *Murdering Mothers*, 12 and the chapter by Nash in this volume.

18. See Kilday, *Women and Violent Crime*, 60–3 and J. Delumeau (1990) *Sin and Fear: The Emergence of a Western Guilt Culture 13th–18th Centuries*, trans. E. Nicholson (New York: St. Martin's Press).

19. For further discussion see Jackson, *New-born Child Murder*, 15 and Chapter 2, especially 37–47 and J.R. Ruff (2001) *Violence in Early Modern Europe 1500–1800* (Cambridge: Cambridge University Press), 151.

20. 'An Act to Prevent the Destroying and Murthering of Bastard Children', 1624, 21 Jac. I c. 27.

21. 'An Act anent the Murthering of Children', 1690, 1 Wm. & Mary. c. 20, s. 2.

22. For further discussion of the context in which this legislation was passed and the nuances between the provisions see Kilday and Watson, 'Infanticide, Religion and Community', 92–3; Kilday, *Women and Violent Crime*, 62; Jackson, *New-born Child Murder*, 29–59 and M. Jackson (2002) 'The Trial of Harriet Vooght: Continuity and Change in the History of Infanticide', in M. Jackson (ed.), *Infanticide: Historical Perspectives on Child Murder and Concealment, 1550–2000* (Aldershot: Aldgate), 1–17 passim.

23. See Kilday and Watson, 'Infanticide, Religion and Community', 92–3; Kilday, *Women and Violent Crime*, 62 and Jackson, *New-born Child Murder*, 29–59 passim.

24. See Kilday and Watson, 'Infanticide, Religion and Community', 93.

25. For evidence of this see J.A. Sharpe (1983) *Crime in Seventeenth-Century England: A County Study* (Cambridge: Cambridge University Press); J.M. Beattie (1986) *Crime and the Courts in England 1660–1800* (Oxford: Clarendon Press) and K. Wrightson (1975) 'Infanticide in Earlier Seventeenth-century England', *Local Population Studies*, 15, 10–22. Evidence from a current research project indicates that the same pattern of heightened judicial activity was also evidenced in Scotland after 1690. ['Infanticide in Northern Scotland 1720–1820', British Academy Small Research Grant (2007–9), ref. SG-45762.]

26. For further discussion see Kilday, *Women and Violent Crime*, 62; Jackson, *New-born Child Murder*, 29–59 and Jackson, 'The Trial of Harriet Vooght', 5–7.

27. See Kilday, *Women and Violent Crime*, 62; Jackson, *New-born Child Murder*, 29–59 and passim and Jackson, 'The Trial of Harriet Vooght', 4–6.

28. Jackson, 'The Trial of Harriet Vooght', 6.

29. 'An Act for the Further Prevention of Malicious Shooting, etc.', 1803, 43 Geo. III c. 58.

30. Jackson, 'The Trial of Harriet Vooght', 6.

31. See Kilday and Watson, 'Infanticide, Religion and Community', 93 and Jackson, 'The Trial of Harriet Vooght', 6–7.

32. 'An Act for Consolidating and Amending the Statutes in England Relative to Offences Against the Person', 1828, 9 Geo. IV c 31, s. 14 and 'An Act to Consolidate and Amend the Statute Law of England and Ireland Relating to Offences Against the Person', 1861, 24 & 25 Vict. C. 100, s. 60. For further discussion see Jackson, 'The Trial of Harriet Vooght', 7.

33. 'An Act for Repealing an Act of the Parliament of Scotland Relating to Child Murder, and for Making other Provisions in Lieu Thereof', 1809, 49 Geo. III c. 14, s. 3.

34. For further discussion of the growing use of medical testimony in infanticide trials from the mid-Victorian period see for instance Margaret L. Arnot (2000) 'Understanding Women Committing Newborn Child Murder in Victorian England', in S. D'Cruze (ed.), *Everyday Violence in Britain, 1850–1950: Gender and Class* (Harlow: Longman), 55–69; H. Marland (2004) *Dangerous Motherhood: Insanity and Childbirth in Victorian Britain*

(London: Palgrave Macmillan); P.M. Prior (2008) *Madness and Murder: Gender, Crime and Mental Disorder in Nineteenth-Century Ireland* (Dublin: Irish Academic Press), especially Chapter 5; T. Ward (1997) 'Law, Common Sense and the Authority of Science: Expert Witnesses and Criminal Insanity in England, c. 1840–1940', *Social and Legal Studies*, 6:3, 343–62; T. Ward (2002) 'Legislating for Human Nature: Legal Responses to infanticide, 1860–1938', in M. Jackson (ed.), *Infanticide: Historical perspectives on Child Murder and Concealment, 1550–2000* (Aldershot: Ashgate), 249–69 and Grey, 'Discourses of Infanticide', especially Chapters 3 and 4.

35. For further discussion see Jackson, 'The Trial of Harriet Vooght', 10 and Grey 'Discourses of Infanticide', especially Chapter 2.

36. Infanticide Act, 1922, 12 & 13 Geo. V c 18 and Infanticide Act, 1938, 1 & 2 Geo. VI c.36.

37. Jackson, 'The Trial of Harriet Vooght', 10–11.

38. For further discussion of these episodes see J. Batt (2004) *Stolen Innocence: A Mother's Fight for Justice – The Story of Sally Clark* (London: Ebury Press); A. Cannings [with M. Lloyd Davies] (2007) *Cherished: A Mother's Fight to Prove Her Innocence* (London: Sphere and the Little Brown Book Group); *The Times*, 30 April–27 June 2003 (for articles concerning the trial against Trupti Patel) and N. Marks (2003) 'An Expert Witness Falls from Grace', *British Medical Journal*, 12/07, 327 (7406), 110.

39. For a chronological study of the historiography of infanticide and child murder see Kilday and Watson, 'Infanticide, Religion and Community', 85–8.

40. For national studies of this type see for instance N. Woodward (2007) 'Infanticide in Wales 1730–1830', *Welsh History Review*, 23, 94–125; O. Ulbricht (1988) 'Infanticide in Eighteenth-Century Germany', in R.J. Evans (ed.), *The German Underworld: Deviants and Outcasts in German History* (London and New York: Routledge), 110–30; C. Rattigan (2008) "I Thought from her Appearance that she was in the Family Way": Detecting Infanticide Cases in Ireland, 1900–1921', *Family and Community History*, 11:2, 134–51; Kilday, *Women and Violent Crime*, Chapter 4; Kelly, 'Infanticide in Eighteenth Century Ireland', 5–26 and Leboutte, 'Offence Against the Family Order', 159–85. For regional studies of this type see for instance Jackson *New-born Child Murder*; E.C. Green (1999) 'Infanticide and Infant Abandonment in the New South: Richmond, Virginia, 1865–1915', *Journal of Family History*, 25, 187–211; J.M. Beattie (1986) *Crime and the Courts in England, 1660–1800* (Oxford: Clarendon Press), 113–24; Kilday, 'Maternal Monsters'; A. Rowlands (1997) "In Great Secrecy": The Crime of Infanticide in Rothenburg ob der Tauber, 1501–1618', *German History*, 15, 179–99; K. Ruggiero (1992) 'Honor, Maternity and the Disciplining of Women: Infanticide in Late Nineteenth-century Buenos Aires', *Hispanic American Historical Review*, 72, 353–73 and S. Wilson (1988) 'Infanticide, Child Abandonment and Female Honour in Nineteenth Century Corsica', *Comparative Studies in Society and History*, 30, 762–83.

41. For studies concerned with establishing an offender profile for infanticide see for instance Beattie, *Crime and the Courts*, 113–24; Kilday, *Women and Violent Crime*, Chapter 4; Hoffer and N.E.C. Hull (1984) *Murdering Mothers*, passim; A.R. Higginbotham (1989) "Sin of the Age": Infanticide

and Illegitimacy in Victorian London', *Victorian Studies*, 32, 319–37 and Kelly, 'Infanticide in Eighteenth Century Ireland', 5–26.

42. For studies concerned with methodology see for instance Kilday, *Women and Violent Crime*, Chapter 4; Radbill, 'A History of Child Abuse and Infanticide', 3–17; L. Gowing (1997) 'Secret Births and Infanticide in Seventeenth-century England', *Past and Present*, 156, 87–115; Malcolmson, 'Infanticide in the Eighteenth Century', 187–209 and R.H. Helmholtz (1975) 'Infanticide in the Province of Canterbury during the Fifteenth Century', *History of Childhood Quarterly*, 2, 379–90.

43. For studies concerned with the legal context of infanticide see for instance C. Damme (1978) 'Infanticide: The Worth of an Infant under Law', *Medical History*, 22, 1–24; Jackson, 'The Trial of Harriet Vooght', 1–17; Jackson, *New-born Child Murder*; S.M. Butler (2007) 'A Case of Indifference? Child Murder in later Medieval England', *Journal of Women's History*, 19, 69–82; Hoffer and Hull (1984) *Murdering Mothers*, passim; Arnot, 'Understanding Women', 55–69; Ward, 'Law, Common Sense and the Authority of Science', 343–62; Ward, 'Legislating for Human Nature', 249–69; Grey 'Discourses of Infanticide', Chapter 2 onwards; M.W. Piers (1978) *Infanticide: Past and Present* (New York: W.W. Norton) and Z.E. Rokeah (1990) 'Unnatural Child Death among Christians and Jews in Medieval England', *Journal of Psychohistory*, 18, 181–226.

44. See for instance Francus, 'Monstrous Mothers'; Kilday, 'The Shame and Fame of Half-Hanggit Maggie', passim and Kilday, '"Monsters of the Vilest Kind"', 100–15.

45. For studies concerned with the literary and cultural context of infanticide see for instance Thorn, *Writing British Infanticide*; McDonagh, *Child Murder and British Culture*; Kilday, 'The Shame and Fame of Half-Hanggit Maggie', passim; Kilday, '"Monsters of the Vilest Kind"', 100–15; A. Hunt (2006) 'Calculations and Concealments: Infanticide in Mid-nineteenth Century Britain', *Victorian Literature and Culture*, 34, 71–94; C.L. Krueger (1997) 'Literary Defenses and Medical Prosecutions: Representing Infanticide in Nineteenth-century Britain', *Victorian Studies*, 40, 271–94; D.A. Symonds (1997) *Weep Not For Me: Women, Ballads and Infanticide in Early Modern Scotland* (University Park: Pennsylvania State University Press); G. Walker (2003) 'Just Stories: Telling Tales of Infant Death in Early Modern England', in M. Mikesell and A. Seeff (eds.) *Culture and Change: Attending to Early Modern Women* (London: Associated University Presses), 98–115 and V. McMahon (2004) *Murder in Shakespeare's England* (London: Hambledon and London), Chapters 4, 8 and 9.

46. For studies concerned with the link between shame and infanticide see for instance Kilday, *Women and Violent Crime*, 75; Kilday, 'The Shame and Fame of Half-Hanggit Maggie', passim; Kilday, '"Monsters of the Vilest Kind"', 100–15 and Ulbricht, 'Infanticide in Eighteenth-Century Germany', 108.

47. For studies concerned with the relationship between economic and infanticide see for instance Kilday, *Women and Violent Crime*, 75; Higginbotham, "Sin of the Age", 319–37 and M. Daly and M. Wilson (1988) *Homicide* (New York: Aldine de Gruyter), 69.

48. See the references at note 19 above.

49. See for instance M.L. Arnot (1994) 'Infant Death, Child Care and the State: The Baby-farming Scandal and the First Infant Life Protection Legislation of 1872', *Continuity and Change*, 9:2, 271–311; O, Pollak (1950) *The Criminality of Women* (Philadelphia: University of Pennsylvania Pree) 19–20 and Rose, *The Massacre of the Innocents*, Chapters 15 and 16.

50. See for instance Jackson, *New-born Child Murder*, passim and T.R. Forbes (1985) *Surgeons at the Old Bailey: English Forensic Medicine to 1878* (New Haven and London: Yale University Press), 96–108.

51. For studies concerned with the mental health of infanticidal women see for instance the references at note 34 above and also Krueger; 'Literary Defenses and Medical Prosecutions', 271–94; M.L. Arnot (1994) 'Gender in Focus: Infanticide in England 1840–1880' (PhD thesis, University of Essex), especially Chapter 3; G.K. Behlmer (1979) 'Deadly Motherhood: Infanticide and Medical Opinion in Mid-Victorian England', *Journal of the History of Medicine and Allied Sciences*, 34, 403–27; T. Ward (1999) 'The Sad Subject of Infanticide: Law, Medicine and Child Murder, 1860–1938', *Social and Legal Studies*, 8, 163–80 and Rabin, D. (2002) 'Bodies of Evidence, States of Mind: Infanticide, Emotion and Sensibility in Eighteenth Century England', H. Marland (2002) 'Getting Away with Murder? Puerperal Insanity, Infanticide and the Defence Plea' as well as C. Quinn (2002) 'Images and Impulses: Representations of Puerperal Insanity and Infanticide in Late Victorian England', in M. Jackson (ed.), *Infanticide: Historical Perspectives on Child Murder and Concealment, 1550–2000* (Aldershot: Ashgate), 73–92, 168–92, 193–215.

52. It is hoped that future research will address this imbalance; see for instance A.M. Kilday (forthcoming 2010) *The Unforgivable Crime? A History of Infanticide in Britain* (Basingstoke: Palgrave Macmillan).

53. National Archives (NA) Assizes: Oxford Circuit – Criminal Depositions and Case Papers, ASSI6/1/1/Box: Case Against Martha Lankey (1825).

54. (NA) Assizes: Oxford Circuit – Criminal Depositions and Case Papers, ASSI6/1/1/Box: Case Against Richard Summerfield (1822).

55. For further discussion of the link between domestic service and infanticide in the existing historiography see Kilday, *Women and Violent Crime*, 70–3.

56. See Ibid., 63–6.

57. National Archives of Scotland (NAS) Justiciary Court Records (J.C.) 3/3: Case against Jannet Shanks (1710).

58. National Library of Wales (NLW) Records of Court of Great Session 4/475/1/64: Case against Mary Lloyd (1782).

59. For further discussion of the historiography related to the methodology of infanticide see Kilday, *Women and Violent Crime*, 66–70.

60. Radbill, 'A History of Child Abuse and Infanticide', 9.

61. Gowing, 'Secret Births and Infanticide', 106.

62. For further discussion see Kilday, *Women and Violent Crime*, Chapter 4 and the Conclusion.

63. NAS, J.C.3/3: Case against Jean Black (1762).

64. NA, Assizes: Oxford Circuit – Criminal Depositions and Case Papers, ASSI6/1/1/Box: Case Against Elizabeth Lloyd (1827).

65. Lloyd clearly indicated that in this instance, the 'parish officer' referred to was a church functionary and should not be confused with a Poor Law official.

66. For further discussion of the historiography relating to infanticidal motive see Kilday, *Women and Violent Crime*, Chapter 4, especially 73–8 and the Conclusion.

67. See for instance Kilday, *Women and Violent Crime*, 75; Ulbricht, 'Infanticide in Eighteenth-century Germany', 108 and R. Mitchison and L. Leneman (1989) *Sexuality and Social Control: Scotland 1660–1789* (Oxford: Blackwell), 136 and passim.

68. See Kilday, *Women and Violent Crime*, 70–7.

69. See for instance Kilday, *Women and Violent Crime*, Chapter 4 and the Conclusion; Kilday, '"Monsters of the Vilest Kind"', 100–15 and A.M. Kilday (forthcoming 2010) 'The Shame and Fame of Half-Hanggit Maggie', passim.

70. For further discussion of this see N. Elias (1994) *The Civilizing Process: The History of Manners and State Formation and Civilization*, trans. E. Jephcott (Oxford: Blackwell).

4 'Most Intimate Violations': Contextualising the Crime of Rape

Kim Stevenson

1. Introduction: A Problem of Truth

Apart from murder, the crime of rape is the most devastating in terms of its consequences and effect, and a much harder crime to prove, at least to the criminal law standard of beyond 'all reasonable doubt'. Sexual intercourse is a very personal and private activity. Where consent is contested, cases will inevitably turn on whom the jury believe; the complainant or the man accused. Predictably, cultural and gendered stereotypes will dominate. Because of the very intimate nature of rape, independent evidence is rarely available, making it difficult, if not impossible, for a court to establish exactly what happened. Rape therefore presents significant and enduring problems for the law. This is exacerbated by the fact that, as Foucault surmised, people rarely speak the 'truth' about sex. From Victorian times sex became shrouded in myth and secrecy, making the true incidence of rape impossible to ascertain. Everyday language became desexualised, making it difficult for both sexes, but women in particular, to speak about sex openly and in explicit terms, thereby compromising the truth of their narratives, especially in the public delivery of courtroom testimony. Constructing a historiography of rape is, therefore, a considerable challenge and one compounded by the absence of information in the historical record, as official statistics and documents are often incomplete or unreliable, adding to the mystique.

From a legal perspective, the meaning of rape and understandings of its effect and impact were determined by men. Female sexuality, at least until recently, has been largely constructed and understood from a masculine perspective, and this was reflected and reinforced in the law. Until the late twentieth century, law was enacted by the men of Parliament or determined by the male judges of the common law; women were prosecuted, represented and judged predominantly by men, including an all-male jury. Unsurprisingly, allegations of rape have often been treated by legal professionals with suspicion. Advocates have sought to apportion blame to the victim by looking for reasons to criticise her conduct and persona, shifting responsibility from the man accused to the victim herself, thus excusing his culpability. Women's voices were largely unheard and feminine engagement in shaping the law minimal.

Until 2000, when the Labour government undertook a long overdue review, the law relating to rape and other sexual offences had remained virtually unchanged since the mid-nineteenth century. David Blunkett, then Home Secretary, described it as 'archaic, incoherent and discriminatory'.[1] The Home Office consulted widely, ensuring a high level of female representation. Its report, *Setting the Boundaries,* was highly critical, concluding that the law was failing to protect women as it failed to recognise situations when women were not in fact consenting to sexual intercourse.[2] The subsequent Sexual Offences Act 2003 introduced, for the first time, a new legal definition of consent and, after much debate, it was also decided that rape should remain a gender-specific crime that only men can commit. But despite such legal reforms, and greater understanding and awareness of the impact of sexual violation, the influence of stereotypical myths and assumptions is still omnipresent. These are largely rooted within nineteenth-century societal norms associated with respectability. Even more disconcerting is the fact that the current conviction rate for rape is lower than at any period during the last 30 years, stubbornly remaining at no more than 5 per cent of the total number of complaints reported to the police (compared to nearly 30 per cent in the 1970s).[3] This chapter reviews the key legal responses to rape in the modern period and, by situating them within their social context. It presents three related historiographical themes supported by case studies focusing on the identification of rape in the historical record, the contested issue of consent, and the influence of respectability.

2. Chronology

a) A Crime against the Person?

Rape has always been constituted as a 'legal problem' both in terms of its definition and punishment, because initially it was perceived as a crime against property rather than a crime against the person. From Neolithic times, female sexuality, i.e. a woman's reproductive capacity, was utilised as a commodity that could be acquired, and controlled, by men. The sexual violation of another man's wife or daughter constituted a crime against the patriarchal male estate. The emphasis of rape was therefore more concerned with abduction than sexual violation per se (*violentis concubis*), as a woman's sexuality was primarily regarded as the property of her male protector. In medieval times, rape was an 'emendable' crime, meaning criminal proceedings could be avoided if compensation was paid. King Cnut declared that if a freeman took another freeman's wife he must pay full weregild, buy another wife for the injured husband, and deliver her to his house.[4] The Normans regarded sexual violation more seriously, making it a felony punishable by loss of limb or death. The complainant could redeem her defiler if she agreed to marry him, unless she was a virgin, in which case William the Conqueror decreed her defiler be castrated.[5] The Statute of Westminster I (1265) reduced the crime to a mere trespass against the person, allowing 40 days in which to lodge an appeal and a punishment of two years' imprisonment. This was swiftly reversed by the Statute of Westminster II (1285), which reinstated rape as a felony but with the privilege of 'benefit of the clergy', meaning that although the case would be heard in the secular courts, on conviction a death sentence could, in principle, be avoided. In 1576 Parliament restored full secular jurisdiction, making rape triable on indictment at the Assizes, and bringing back the death penalty. Presented with a stark choice of death or acquittal, many juries were reluctant to convict as they were unable to return an alternative verdict for a lesser charge.[6] This was acknowledged in 1765 by jurist Sir Matthew Hale in a statement that became highly influential to judges and jurors, not to mention prejudicial:

> It is true that rape is a most detestable crime and therefore ought feverly [severely] and impartially to be punished with death; *but it must be remembered that it is an accusation easily to be made and hard to be proved* – and harder to be defended by the party accused, tho – never so innocent.[7] (emphasis added)

In 1841, after the demise of the Bloody Code, the death sentence was withdrawn and commuted to a maximum life sentence.[8] In the mid-nineteenth century, very severe cases involving gang rapes were punished by transportation of between 10 and 25 years, depending on whether the prisoner was the main perpetrator or an accomplice.[9] By the 1870s, 5 years' imprisonment was the typical sentence for a single rape or group rape committed without excessive violence or force.[10] This was confirmed by Justice Mellors at Stafford Assizes in 1876, who said he would give 'the sentence he always inflicted when an offence was committed single handed and no more violence was used than was necessary for the object in view'.[11]

Thus the maximum sentence of life imprisonment was rarely imposed and remains so to the present day, as mirrored in the sentencing guidelines issued by the Sentencing Guidelines Council, confirming the rules established in the case of *Milberry* 2003.[12] The starting point is 5 years' imprisonment for a single rape, increasing to 8 years or more where there are aggravating factors, such as violence, the victim was specifically targeted, or a multiple rape; and 15 years for the repeated rape of the same victim. If the offender is a serious risk and danger to society, then lengthier custodial sentences may be justified.[13]

b) What is Rape?

Historically, Parliament has shown itself reluctant to deal with the crime of rape. The development of statute law is largely characterised by a complete absence of any associated political will to protect women from such sexual violation and a failure to construct any adequate definition. Relevant statutory provisions have been subsumed into much broader, contextual agendas rather than specific enactments directed at minimising rape. Moral panics about curbing and controlling prostitution were the main drivers behind two key statutes; the Criminal Law Amendment Act 1885 and the Sexual Offences Act 1956. The Sexual Offences Act 2003 stands out as an exception, enacted in response to overriding concerns about the problem of rape; but only because Parliament had left it so long to tackle the law that it had become indefensibly out of date.

The common law simply defined rape as the 'forced sexual intercourse of a woman against her will', illustrated in this typical charge against James Barrett, indicted at the Old Bailey in 1779: 'for feloniously committing a rape on the body of Ann Lowther, spinster, and carnally knowing her against her will'.[14] Similarly, in 1780, James Purse was indicted 'for that he, on the 16th of April, on Elizabeth Midwinter, spinster, feloniously did make an assault, against the will of her, the said Elizabeth, did ravish and carnally know'.[15] A more unusual charge was levied against John Briant in 1797 'for not having the fear of God before his eyes, but being moved and seduced by the instigation of the devil, on the 19th of July upon Jane Bell, spinster, did make an assault against her will, feloniously did ravish, and carnally know'.[16] All three were sentenced to death, but Barratt was later pardoned. These examples are some of the last cases available in the public record, as from 1796 onwards the Old Bailey started to suppress its publication of court transcripts of sexual offences on the grounds of 'immorality'.[17] As the common law failed to clarify what could constitute genuine consent as opposed to non-consent, the judiciary developed the principle that all sexual acts were consensual unless that consent had been vitiated (invalidated) by the use of threats, force or fraud on the part of the accused to obtain it. The onus was therefore on the victim to convince the court that she had done everything physically possible to avoid the violation; submission equalled consent, and it was not until 1982 that the Court of Appeal was prepared to acknowledge the possibility that submission is not genuine agreement.[18]

Rape was not made a statutory crime until the Offences against the Person Act 1861 attempted to codify the law on physical assaults, yet it barely featured in the Parliamentary debates. An earlier 1828 enactment[19] confirmed that 'whosoever shall be convicted of the crime of rape shall be guilty of a felony' and sentenced to penal servitude for life. It also removed the requirement of proof of 'emission of seed' to prove penetration. Sections 48–55 of the 1861 Act covered sexual offences, but mainly in the context of abduction and procuration, reflecting the emphasis on property rights. Section 48, the rape provision, simply restated the 1828 enactment. While detailed provisions were drafted for some fifty non-sexual offences in the Act, no attempt was made to formulate any statutory definition for rape, in particular the generally obligatory components of all crimes; the *actus reus* (guilty act) and *mens rea* (guilty mind). Some members of the judiciary expressed their concern at this lack of specification, 'gravely condemning' the proposed simplicity of the provision.[20] The *mens rea* concept of intent had been discussed in the leading case of *Camplin* 1845, and the *actus reus* elements of resistance and consent in *Hallett* 1841 and *Case* 1850,[21] but a number of judges were looking to Parliament to take the lead. Not only did this failure to clarify any specific legal meaning result in some highly controversial cases (see case study b) but it made the law uncertain, as many rapes were charged as indecent assault, carnal knowledge or assault with intent to ravish, making it difficult to identify true rapes in the historical record. It also meant that it was left to the non-elected, all-male judiciary to fill the gaps and develop the law.

An ideal, but missed, opportunity presented itself with the Criminal Law Amendment Act 1885. Moral concerns about the 'white slave trade' and the abduction of young English girls to continental brothels epitomised in Stead's article 'The Maiden Tribute of Modern Babylon' published in the *Pall Mall Gazette* precipitated the enactment.[22] This promoted significant debate in the House of Lords about the need to protect men from unwarranted 'feminine charms'. Lord Norton inquired: 'at what age should a girl be considered capable of consenting to her ruin, so as to exonerate the man from the guilt of criminal injury in taking advantage of her ignorance?'[23] The issue of men violating women was alluded to but not seriously considered. There was some debate about rape, but only in relation to the established common law principles of consent induced by fear, force or fraud. These were then formulated into the lesser offence under Section 3 of the Act of procuring (bringing about) the defilement of a woman by threats, false pretences or stupefaction, which carried a penalty of just 2 years' imprisonment.

One of the most controversial cases of the nineteenth century, *R* v. *Clarence* 1888 (see case study a) was to have a significant impact on liability for marital rape. The nine judges hearing the Crown Case appeared to resurrect and condone Hale's common-law statement made in 1736 (when marriage was indissoluble) that 'The husband cannot be guilty of a rape committed by himself upon his lawful wife, for by their mutual matrimonial consent and contract the wife hath given herself in this kind unto her husband, which she cannot retract.'[24]

Blackstone had already dismissed this interpretation that the marriage contract bestowed on a husband an 'irrevocable privilege' of implied consent from his wife to all acts of sexual intercourse.[25] Hale's statement appeared in 1822 in Archbold's *Criminal Pleading, Evidence and Practice*,[26] but hardly featured in the law until seized upon and 'fictionalised' by the judges in *Clarence*. The defendant in *Clarence* was not even charged with rape but with causing grievous bodily harm after infecting his wife with gonorrhoea, but the judges' reasoning that a husband cannot be guilty of raping his wife endured and was not overruled until 1991.

No further legal developments or significant changes were made during the first half of the twentieth century although, belatedly, the Punishment of Incest Act 1908 was enacted as a result of pressure from the National Vigilance Association and the National Society for the Prevention of Cruelty to Children (NSPCC). The next major piece of legislation was the Sexual Offences Act 1956. As its title suggests, this was the first subject-specific statute to address sexual offences, but apart from some new provisions to tackle prostitution, it was predominantly a consolidating Act. Disappointingly, the Act largely reproduced the provisions of the 1861 and 1885 enactments. The crime of rape was contained in Section 1, underlining its severity, but the wording remained unaltered. Twenty years later, and the futility of simply reproducing the 1861 provision became evident following public outrage concerning the case of *DPP* v. *Morgan* (see case study b). The lack of any formal expression of the requisite *mens rea* allowed the defendants to claim that they 'honestly and genuinely believed' Morgan's wife was consenting to intercourse when Morgan, who had invited his colleagues home to have sexual intercourse with her, knew she would not. The Sexual Offences (Amendment) Act 1976 amended Section 1 to cover culpability where defendants were 'reckless' as to whether the complainant had consented or not. A further concession substituted 'unlawful sexual intercourse' for the outdated term 'carnal knowledge'. However, this proved counter-productive as 'unlawful' was widely interpreted as meaning outside the bonds of marriage. thereby reinforcing the marital rape exemption; and restricted to vaginal intercourse (*per vaginum*) because of the assumption of marriage being primarily associated with procreation. It was not until the case of *R* v *R* in 1991 that the House of Lords finally overruled years of misogyny and declared the decision in

Clarence incorrect, ruling that a husband could no longer enjoy immunity from charges of marital rape (see case study a). Male-on-male rape was an even greater taboo and not formally criminalised until Section 142 of the Criminal Justice and Public Order Act 1994 removed the superfluous 'unlawful', indirectly extending rape to male victims and the *actus reus* of rape to include *per anum*.

Thus the law has shown itself to be far from exemplary in its treatment of rape, largely because it consistently failed to consider the societal context within which sexual relations operate. The Sexual Offences Act 2003 has, for the first time, provided a coherent legal definition for rape and broadened it to include forced fellatio. Section 1 provides that it will be rape where a person engages in penile penetration with another person without their consent. It is implicit that only a male can commit the offence but it may be committed against a male or female, by vagina, anus or mouth. The Act also introduced new offences of assault by penetration (Section 2), sexual assault (Section 3) and causing non-consensual sexual activity (Section 4). Section 74 provides the first statutory definition of consent where a person 'agrees by choice and has the freedom and capacity to make that choice', supplemented in Sections 75 and 76 by a list of circumstances where it will, or may, be presumed that consent is or is not present. Where the accused seeks to rely on the defence of consent, Section 1(2) requires that he must convince the court that he *reasonably believed* the complainant was in fact consenting. Consequently it took hundreds of years for the law to produce a workable definition for rape.

3. Historiography

Perhaps more than any other crime, the gendered impact of rape presupposes that the development of the law must be heavily influenced by the prevailing societal context and moral norms. But before any useful historiographical debate can be undertaken, an amount of reliable data and source material are necessary, so that rape crimes can at least be identified in the historical record. This is particularly problematic as, at first glance, public records are limited both quantitatively and qualitatively. This next section starts with the problem of identifying cases of rape and then examines the contested issues of consent and respectability.

a) Identification: The Invisibility of Rape

Rape is one of the most problematic crimes for any researcher to investigate, because of its most intimate violation. Official and public reluctance to discuss personal sexual matters, the humiliation and distress suffered by the victim, the deficiencies of language to describe intimate sexual detail and the 'disagreeable' nature of the subject potentially diminish the accuracy of any true record. Wiener found that rape was 'barely visible' in court indictments from the mid-sixteenth century to the end of the eighteenth century, and even at the Old Bailey there were just 203 indictments from 1730 to 1800.[27] As Anna Clark's leading work confirms, from 1796 the Old Bailey suppressed the publication of transcripts of sexual crimes and few rape depositions survive in the Assize records after 1830.[28] Conley and D'Cruze have also made significant inroads into understandings of rape for the first half of the nineteenth century through local studies of Kent and north-west England, but there is still much work to be done from 1850 onwards and the early part of the twentieth century.[29]

Case disposals can be tracked through court records, but these provide little in the way of detail of the specific violation or the factors that influenced acquittal or conviction. Gatrell's examination of the annual crime statistics is also basically quantitative; from 1856 to 1900 there is evidence that while most indices of violence declined, the number of committals to trial for sexual assaults increased, peaking in 1886–1890.[30] But this is a fairly broad category and supplies little contextual historiography. Gatrell attributes this increase as 'incidental' to the new offences of procuration and defilement enacted in the Criminal Law Amendment Act 1885, but other factors also need to be considered. The fluctuations and 'invisibilities' in the historical record suggested above do not represent the true incidence of rape for any of these periods, as many cases were simply never proceeded with. A woman who alleged rape endangered her respectability simply by the fact of having been the victim of a rape. She would need to instigate and possibly fund criminal proceedings herself; there was no state prosecutor until 1879 and prosecutory societies such as the Associated Society for the Protection of Women and Children were only really effective from the 1860s.[31] The social position of a complainant was also critical; servants, women employed 'in-house' and the destitute and dispossessed often had neither the means nor the knowledge to assert their complaints.

As crime statistics and disposals produce little in the way of qualitative data and court records and depositions are generally not available, are there any other alternatives to fill the gaps? One primary research source that has largely been overlooked is newsprint. Victorian newspaper coverage of the day-to-day aspects of the criminal justice system is vivid and detailed, permitting a more fully informed understanding of what happened in numbers of rape cases, especially in the lower courts. Such reports usefully illustrate the factors and influences that affected jury decisions and the arguments presented. More importantly, they were often written by barristers and so carry considerable legal integrity, making them a reliable source.[32] The word 'rape' rarely appeared in respectable discourse and was often avoided in the rhetoric of the press. Researchers need to be alert to the many euphemisms used to desexualise reports of rape. Newspaper bylines and references to the commission of an 'outrage' or 'moral outrage' often indicate a non-consensual sexual offence. Defendants were alleged to have 'effected their purpose', 'committed the outrage', 'completed the offence', 'ravished' or 'violated the person'. Complainants 'fainted', 'suffered ill-health', 'their person was bruised' or 'their injuries were consistent with the attack complained of'. Consequently, nineteenth century newspapers, such as *The Times*, *Daily Telegraph* and *News of the World*, if carefully read and interpreted, can reveal much about the social and legal history of Victorian rape.

Another issue that has disguised many cases of actual rape, particularly in the summary courts, is the ambiguity of the charge preferred. Allegations of rape were charged as 'attempted rape', 'assault with intent to commit a felony, or intent to ravish', 'criminal assault', 'indecent assault' or 'unlawful carnal knowledge'. This was because the substance of the charge was usually expressed in the complainant's own words or the prosecuting counsel's interpretation of what she told him. Many victims, particularly young girls, neither understood what had happened to them, nor were able to effectively articulate or verbalise it; as respectable ladies they were not supposed to possess any sexual knowledge or understanding. Moreover, any distinction between rape and the even vaguer offence of indecent assault is even more blurred. In 1867 the Home Office was forced to seek guidance from the law officers for the most appropriate charge under the Offences against the Person Act 1861 where an indecent assault was committed but without violence: Was it an indecent assault (Section 52; 2 years' imprisonment)? A common assault (Section 42; 2 months' imprisonment)? Or an aggravated assault (Section 43; 6 months' imprisonment)? The Attorney General and the Solicitor General advised an aggravated assault, thereby indirectly disguising what was actually a sexual offence in the historical record.[33] The lack of definition is typified in an example from Conley, who cites an explanation given to the jury by Mr Justice Brett in 1875: 'I cannot lay down the law as to what is or is not an indecent assault beyond saying that it is what all right-minded men, men of sound and wholesome feelings would say was indecent.'[34] Typically this takes no account of the views of any right-minded women.

b) Without her consent

Rape cases inevitably become contested over the problematic issue of consent, not least because the act of intercourse usually occurred in the absence of witnesses, and medical evidence generally confirmed that intercourse took place but not necessarily whether it was non-consensual. It was therefore incumbent on the complainant to convince the court that she did not in fact consent; there was no requirement on the accused to prove that it was reasonable in the circumstances for him to believe that she had consented. If a woman was found to be 'unchaste', consent was automatically presumed and the myth developed, reinforced by the common law, that a prostitute could never be raped. The enduring influence of such stereotypical norms is demonstrated in more recent history. In 1991 Justice Harman asked a female witness: 'I always thought there were three kinds of women, wives, whores and mistresses. Which are you?'[35] He later claimed he had been joking. Another crass example was uttered by Judge Wild at Cambridge Crown Court in 1982: 'women who say no do not always mean no. It is not just a question of saying no, it is a question of how she says it. If she doesn't want it she only has to keep her legs shut and she would not get it without force and there would be marks of force being used.'[36]

And in 1990 Judge Raymond Dean told an Old Bailey jury, which subsequently acquitted a 39-year-old man of rape: 'As the gentlemen on the jury will understand, when a woman says "no" she doesn't always mean it.'[37] As a result, the modern judiciary is now required to undertake specialist training before hearing rape cases.

To avoid such imputations, complainants needed to prove that any act of intercourse was against their will. The case of *Hallett* confirmed that juries could be directed to consider whether she had made every physical resistance she possibly could, as illustrated in the following two examples reported in *The Times*. In 1876 at the Central Criminal Court, Joseph Tidy, a 19-year-old labourer, was accused of raping Susan Mann, aged 15, while she was out walking. Witnesses who intervened confirmed that she had blood on her neck where he had knuckled her to the ground. The surgeon stated that her underclothing was bloodstained and disarranged and that 'what had been done must have been done with great muscular force'. Yet despite such evidence of violence, the defence counsel argued that the natural resistance expected of Susan to protect her chastity 'left much doubt'. The jury agreed, and acquitted Tidy.[38] In another case that year at Hereford, Elizabeth Dale refused George Goodwin's demand for a kiss and, as he attempted to ravish her, she 'resisted to her uttermost', screaming 'Mother', 'murder', and 'Lord Jesus, let me die'. Goodwin was found guilty and sentenced to the maximum sentence of 2 years, suggesting that Elizabeth's invocation of religious protection demonstrated that his acts were not only against her will but also against God's.[39]

Of course, any suggestion that a woman was intoxicated would automatically negate consent, but what if the accused had deliberately induced her to take alcohol, or the modern equivalent, the date-rape drug Rohypnol? In *R* v *Camplin* 1845, Camplin had given a 13-year-old girl alcohol with the intention, he said, of merely 'exciting her'. He argued that he had not used any force, which normally should be countered by her imposing her physical will in response, so therefore he should not be held liable. Probably because of the age of the victim, the court was not persuaded that evidence of force was necessary in these circumstances to prove that rape had occurred. The 13 judges held that rape could be committed 'without her consent' rather than 'against her will',[40] but in practice the latter still prevailed. For example, in 1856 Mr Justice Willes commented that there was 'some doubt entertained whether the offence of rape could be committed upon the person of a woman who had rendered herself perfectly insensible through drink'.[41] The responsibility of the victim when under the influence of alcohol was addressed very recently in the case of *R* v. *Bree* 2007 where the Court of Appeal unanimously held that despite having drank substantial amounts of alcohol, provided the victim was still capable of agreeing to have intercourse, it would not be rape.[42]

c) Respectability: Protecting her honour

The leading jurist of the nineteenth century, Fitzjames Stephen, asserted that in relation to the legal status of women 'submission and protection are correlative', meaning that provided a woman conformed to society's expected standards of respectability, public opinion and the law would protect her.[43] To an extent this was true, but it was not always practically feasible or possible for every woman to absolutely discharge their side of the 'respectability contract'. A woman's submissive position in society was heavily reliant on maintaining her honour, reputation and feminine dependence, financially and otherwise, on her male protector, be he husband or father. Many women, particularly working women, needed to assert their independence and free themselves from such masculine protection, but in so doing risked jeopardising their respectability. The advent of the railways provided not only the means of independent travel for women but a potentially ideal locale for those intent on perpetrating sexual violation in the darkened carriages and tunnels. Women gained greater physical mobility but voluntarily placed themselves in a potentially dangerous situation, breaking the terms of this social contract. Would the law still protect them if they were then sexually assaulted or attacked? Women, who tried to escape from their carriage, often clinging on to outside windows and doors for dear life, were more likely to have their complaints taken seriously as they had risked their lives to protect their modesty.

Respectable women would of course 'fight to the death' to protect their honour and ideally display the requisite bruises, but rarely was the evidence always so clear-cut. In the courtroom the competing strengths of respectability claimed by the male defendant and female complainant determined the outcome of many cases. Juries would usually find in favour of the party who demonstrated the most powerful conformity with the respectability code. Unsurprisingly, few men of status were convicted of rape and deference to male respectability was highly influential. Respectable gentlemen could call on any number of equally respectable witnesses to testify as to their reputation, profession and general 'honourableness'. Women, on the other hand, found it much more difficult to provide such sponsors. Charges could be dismissed simply because it was presumed impossible that a gentleman would have resorted to such sexual violation. A rapist would only lose his respectability on conviction, and only then if handed a sentence with hard labour requiring him to serve with common criminals. A woman could lose her respectability simply by the fact of having been raped, as surely she must have broken the code to have put herself in a position of risk in the first place? Doubt could easily be cast on her respectability before she even entered the courtroom, based on the geographical location of the attack; respectable women simply did not go out in public unaccompanied by their guardians and protectors. Again, the enduring effects of such views are evident in more recent history. Judge Bertrand Richards commented in 1982 that a woman 'was guilty of contributory negligence' because she had been raped when hitchhiking home: 'It is the height of imprudence for any girl to hitchhike at night. That is plain, it isn't really worth stating, she is in the true sense asking for it.'[44]

Appearance and demeanour were key stereotypical tropes employed to affirm or diminish respectability. Descriptors in the press of either defendant or victim possessing a 'respectable appearance' indicated the person more deserving of winning the case. Complainants were expected to appear 'modest' and 'innocent' both in terms of their looks and behaviour; to be pretty, appropriately dressed and coy. Women regarded as ungainly or 'less pleasing on the eye' tended to be associated with immoral behaviour, especially if there was any suspicion of coarseness or alcohol. Men of a 'gentlemanly appearance' or in a position of power could more easily establish their respectability; the nature of the defendant's profession and his employment record was highly influential. Even where found guilty, his respectable status could mitigate any sentence imposed, reducing its length or removing the need for hard labour. The conduct and behaviour of the complainant after any violation were also examined closely. Victims were expected to report such incidents immediately; any delay could have a detrimental effect on her case, as it might then be presumed that she was making a false allegation to cover up any immoral act that she genuinely consented to. Yet despite the difficulties faced by complainants in the courtroom and the highly stereotypical expectations to be met, numbers of women were successful in seeing their violators convicted. But if found to have compromised their respectability in any way, then it was likely that their attacker would walk free, even if it was evident to all that he was in fact responsible.

4. Case Studies

a) An 'irrevocable privilege': Summary and Extracts from the Case of *R v. Clarence* (1888) 22 QBD 23

In 1888 Charles James Clarence was tried at the Central Criminal Court in London upon two indictments:

1) Unlawfully and maliciously inflicting grievous bodily harm (GBH) upon his wife Selina Clarence contrary to section 20 Offences Against the Person Act 1861 and
2) Assaulting her occasioning actual bodily harm (ABH) contrary to section 47 of the same Act.

On 20 December 1887, Clarence, who knew that he had contracted gonorrhoea from a prostitute, had 'connection' (sexual intercourse) with his wife Selina. She had no knowledge of his disease and, if she had been aware of it, she would not have submitted to the intercourse. The trial judge directed the jury that if all of the requisite elements of the two offences were proven on the facts as presented, then they should convict Clarence, irrespective of the fact that the prosecutrix was his wife. The jury found Clarence guilty on both counts. However, because there were concerns about whether Clarence should have been convicted of the two assaults on his wife, the Recorder of London referred the case to the 13 most senior judges in the land to determine whether the conviction should stand. Clarence was unrepresented and so a barrister, Forrest Fulton, was instructed by the Solicitor to the Treasury to present the case for the defence. Fulton argued that Clarence did not 'unlawfully' inflict GBH on his wife as the act of sexual intercourse was not unlawful because they were married. He cited Hale's proposition that a husband cannot be guilty of rape on his wife in support, though acknowledged that if the conviction was confirmed, Selina would be entitled to a judicial separation. In respect of the second count, he argued that there could be no assault of ABH because 'If coition, as between husband and wife, cannot constitute rape, it follows that coition cannot as between them constitute an assault by the husband.' Fulton concluded that 'If the conviction is right, it appears to follow that any man who is accused by a prostitute of having defrauded or infected her may be prosecuted for an indecent assault, if not for rape.'[45]

The Crown had deliberately charged GBH and ABH as there were no precedents establishing that the failure to disclose a venereal disease could vitiate consent to sexual intercourse and it is unlikely that any complaint of rape would have succeeded. The defence purposefully shifted the emphasis away from offences against the person and highlighted the case as one of sexual propriety. The cleverly chosen charges were dismissed as misguided as there was no physical assault because there was no 'unlawful sexual violation'; Selina was Clarence's legally contracted property. And on a narrow legal point there was no 'infliction' of GBH as sexual congress cannot physically 'inflict' harm in the same way as a knife or weapon. The case is fascinating, as the judgements discuss the wider facets of Victorian sexuality, including prostitution, consent and seduction. The judges generally failed to acknowledge that a husband's unfettered sexual access to his wife could cause harm. The nine majority judges determined that no crime had been committed at common law; in effect decriminalising rape within marriage, despite the lack of any existing precedents supporting this perspective other than Hale's controversial statement.

From the extracts of the majority judgments led by Fitzjames Stephen, it was clear that he did not adhere to his promise that if women were respectable and submissive the law would protect them. Justice Smith stated:

> At marriage the wife consents to the husband exercising the marital right. The consent then given is not confined to a husband when sound in body, for I suppose no-one would assert that a husband was guilty of an offence because he exercised such right when afflicted with some complaint of which he was then ignorant. Until the consent given at marriage be revoked, how can it be said that the husband in exercising his marital right has assaulted his wife? In the present case at the time the incriminated act was committed, the consent given at marriage stood unrevoked. Then how was it an assault? The utmost the Crown can say is that the wife would have withdrawn her consent if she had known what her husband knew, or, in other words, that the husband is guilty of a crime, viz., an assault because he did not inform the wife of what he then knew.[46]

Justice Stephen added:

> I think that the act of infection is not an assault at all ... Infection is a kind of poisoning. It is the application of an animal poison, and poisoning, as already shewn is not an assault. Apart, however, from this, is the man's concealment of the fact that he was infected; such a fraud as vitiated the wife's consent to his exercise of marital rights, and converted the act of connection into an assault. It seems to me that the proposition that fraud vitiates consent in criminal matters is not true if taken to apply in the fullest sense of the word, and without qualification. It is too short to be true, as a mathematical formula is true. If we apply it in that sense to the present case, it is difficult to say the prisoner was not guilty of rape, for the definition of rape is having connection with a woman without her consent, and if fraud

vitiates consents, every case in which a man infects a woman or commits bigamy, the second wife being ignorant of the first marriage, is also a case of rape. Many seductions would be rapes and so might acts of prostitution procured by fraud, as for instance by promises not intended to be fulfilled. These illustrations appear to shew clearly that the maxim that fraud vitiates consent is too general to be applied to these matters if it were absolutely true.[47]

From the extracts from the dissenting judges led by Hawkins, it was clear that the minority judges agreed that Clarence had caused his wife GBH and ABH but refused to consider the conceptual leap to rape. Also they were unwilling to acknowledge Hale's proposition as having any substance in law and agreed that a wife does not have to consent to every act of marital intercourse under every circumstance, particularly if it will leave her injured. Hawkins stated:

> my judgement is not based upon the doctrine that fraud vitiates consent, because I do not think that doctrine applies in the case of sexual communion between husband and wife. The sexual communion between them is by virtue of the *irrevocable privilege conferred once and for all on the husband* at the time of the marriage, and not by virtue of a consent given upon each set of communion, as is the case between unmarried persons. My judgement is based on the fact that the wrongful act charged against the prisoner was not involved in or sanctioned by his marital privilege and for which no consent was ever given at all. For this reason it is unnecessary to discuss or express any opinion upon the various cases cited during the argument relating to connection obtained by fraud, and I accordingly abstain from doing so.[48]

The case of *Clarence* was used to reinforce the position that marital rape was unlawful, and was not reviewed until *R v. R* 1991, when the House of Lords considered a number of appeals based on test cases where husbands had been convicted of rape, mainly with other offences of violence.[49] In October 1989 R's wife left the matrimonial home with their 4-year-old son and moved in with her parents. She commenced divorce proceedings, but 3 weeks later R forced his way into her parents' house while they were out and attempted to have sexual intercourse with her against her will, squeezing her neck with both hands. In July 1990 he was convicted of attempted rape and assault occasioning ABH, and sentenced to 3 years' imprisonment for the attempted rape and 18 months to run concurrent for the assault. R appealed on the grounds that the trial judge had made a mistake in law in ruling that a man could rape his wife when her consent had not been revoked by a court order or agreement. The prosecution argued that Hale's statement that a wife cannot withdraw her consent had never been formally recognised in case law and was doubted by the dissenting judges in *Clarence*. In the Court of Appeal, Lord Chief Justice Lane, agreeing with the trial judge, dismissed the appeal on the grounds that Hale's proposition was inconsistent with the proper relationship between husband and wife, 'a rapist remains a rapist irrespective of their relationship'. R then appealed to the House of Lords, where all five judges were unanimous in holding that the rule that a wife was deemed to have consented irrevocably to sexual intercourse was nothing more than a 'common-law fiction'. They also said that the word 'unlawful' in Section 1(1) of the Sexual Offences Act 1956 was of mere 'surplussage' and should be ignored.

R then took his case to the European Court of Human Rights in *S.W. v. UK; C.R. v. UK* (1995),[50] arguing that this removal of marital immunity violated Article 7.1 of the European Convention on Human Rights because it operated retrospectively and did not apply in 1990. The European Court unanimously held that 'there was an evident evolution' in the criminal law through judicial interpretation 'which was consistent with the very essence of the offence'. The court confirmed that 'the abandonment of the unacceptable idea of a husband being immune against prosecution for the rape of his wife was in conformity not only with a civilised concept of marriage but also, and above all, with the fundamental objectives of the Convention, the very essence of which was respect for human dignity and freedom'.

b) Honest or Reasonable Consent? Summary and Extracts from the Case of *DPP v. Morgan* [1976] AC 182

On 24 January 1974 at Stafford Crown Court Robert McDonald, Robert McLarty and Michael Parker were convicted as principals for the rape of Daphne Ethel Morgan, and together with William Morgan – Daphne's husband – all four were convicted as accessories in that they aided and abetted the rape. Morgan could not be charged with rape because of the principle in *Clarence* that husbands could only be charged with aiding and abetting rape. The defendants were allowed to appeal to the House of Lords as a matter of general public importance. McDonald, McLarty and Parker claimed that they honestly believed that Daphne had consented to sexual intercourse.

On 15 August 1973 Morgan, a senior NCO in the RAF, invited three junior colleagues to his home, suggesting they have sexual intercourse with his wife. The three were 'at first incredulous but were persuaded that Morgan's invitation was intended seriously when he told them stories of his wife's sexual aberrations and provided them with contraceptive sheaths to wear'.[51] They claimed Morgan had said to expect 'some show of resistance on his wife's part', but assured them that she would feign reluctance and refuse consent for her own pleasure. Daphne testified that while she was asleep her husband woke her and, with the other men, 'part dragged, part carried' her to another bedroom. Each took it in turn to have sexual intercourse while the others restrained her, covering her face and holding her limbs. Daphne struggled and screamed for her son to ring the police and repeatedly called out to her husband to tell the men to stop. Judge Jones advised the jury that they must be satisfied that each defendant intended to have sexual intercourse without consent. If they wished to rely on the defence of belief in consent, that belief must be honestly and reasonably held. The jury found the defendants guilty, as they did not consider the belief to be both honest and reasonable. Morgan and his associates contended that their honest belief in consent was sufficient; it need not be reasonable. By a majority (Lords Hailsham, Cross, Simon) of 3:2 (Lords Simon, Edmund-Davies dissenting), the House of Lords held that where a person genuinely believes that a woman was consenting, even though the jury considered that belief to be unreasonable, he could not be convicted of rape. The defendants therefore 'won' the point of law but the court applied the proviso under Section 2 of the Criminal Appeal Act 1968, which meant that no miscarriage of justice had occurred and so they were not released from custody.

This case illustrates the difficulties where there is no statutory definition of rape, particularly as regards the requisite *mens rea* and the meaning of consent: Section 1 of the Sexual Offences Act 1956 simply prescribed that it was an offence 'for a man to have sexual intercourse with a woman who does not consent'. Nor was there any guidance in the common law other than Justice Denman's stereotypical echoes in R v. *Flattery* 1877;[52] 'There may be cases where a woman does not consent in fact, but in which her conduct is such that the man reasonably believes she does ... [especially] where the resistance is so slight.' Lord Edmund-Davies specifically refers to the difficulty 'with the Victorian, rape cases' and their outdated rulings,[53] and Lord Simon intimates that amendments to the 1956 Act are needed for clarification. The jury, as in many rape cases, were left with a stark choice of two incompatible stories. The men admitted they had been drinking beforehand and that some degree of struggle had taken place but asserted that Mrs Morgan not only consented but 'actively co-operated and enjoyed what was being done'. Lord Hailsham therefore determined that ultimately the jury must decide which they believed; 'a violent and unmistakeable rape of a singularly unpleasant kind or active co-operation in a sexual orgy'.[54]

The decision, which was largely misunderstood by the media and the police, was misconstrued as a Rapist's Charter and thought to allow certain defendants to get off rape. Parliament responded immediately and enacted the Sexual Offences (Amendment) Act 1976: Section1(1) provided that: a man commits rape if he has unlawful sexual intercourse with a woman *who at the time does not consent and he knows that she does not consent or is reckless* as to whether she consents (emphasis added). The defendants were certainly reckless as to whether Daphne consented, but lingering concerns remained about whether such belief must also be reasonable. Section 1(1) of the Sexual Offences Act 2003 finally clarified the position: rape is committed where the defendant 'does not reasonably believe that the victim consents'. Section 1(2) reinforces this, by adding 'whether a belief is reasonable is to be determined having regard to all the circumstances including any steps taken by the defendant to ascertain whether she consented'. Therefore the onus is now on any man charged with rape to ensure that he did all that he reasonably could to ensure the other person was in fact consenting.

5. Conclusion

This chapter has highlighted some of the problems and consequences where historically, the law has failed to provide an adequate definition for the crime of rape. Without a formal framework classifying the nature and circumstances that constitute the unlawful act, it has been left to the unelected and traditionally all-male judiciary to determine who can commit rape and to formulate the meaning of consent and sexual assault. Indefensibly, until as recently as the 1990s and beginning of the twenty-first century, husbands enjoyed immunity, male rape was not illegal, submission could constitute consent and the nature of non-consensual sexual intercourse was significantly circumscribed. Parliament, in enacting the Sexual Offences Act 2003, eventually acknowledged that the law was unworkable, unfair and gender-biased. But despite such advances and clarification to legally define rape more comprehensively, the problem of low conviction rates remains endemic. The Ministry of Justice is attempting to address this 'justice gap' by deploying specialist rape prosecutors and units. But if the historiography of rape can tell us anything, it is that law can never operate successfully in isolation from its social context. From an historical perspective, it is not surprising that the Ministry of Justice has finally identified that one of the key factors likely to influence the outcome of any contested rape case is the stereotypical attitudes of not just legal professionals but lay jurors. While initiatives are currently being undertaken to increase awareness and understandings of rape mythology, it is disappointing that these are only now being considered when the historical evidence is so compelling.

Notes

1. D. Blunkett (2002) *Protecting the Public* (London: Home Office Consultation Paper Cmnd.5668), Foreword.
2. Home Office (2000) *Setting the Boundaries: Reforming the Law on Sexual Offences* (London: Home Office Communications Directorate).
3. L. Kelly, J. Lovett and L. Regan (2005) *A Gap or a Chasm: Attrition in Reported Rape Cases* (Home Office Research Study 293, Home Office Development and Statistics Directorate) and Her Majesty's Inspector of Constabulary and Her Majesty's Crown Prosecution Service (2007) *Without Consent*, see http://inspectorates.homeoffice.gov.uk/hmic/inspections/themat ic/wc-thematic/.
4. See F. Attenborough (1922) *The Laws of the Earliest Kings* (Cambridge: Cambridge University Press), 71.
5. H. Bracton (1922) *On the Laws and Customs of England*, ed. and trans. G. Woodbine (Oxford: Oxford University Press), 414.
6. M. Wiener (2004) *Men of Blood, Violence, Manliness and Criminal Justice in Victorian England* (Cambridge: Cambridge University Press), 87.
7. M. Hale (1936) *Pleas of the Crown*, 1 (London: Professional Books), 635.
8. 4 & 5 Vic c.38 Punishment of Death Abolition Act 1841.
9. See K. Stevenson (forthcoming 2009) '"She Got Past Knowing Herself and Did not Know How Many There Were": Uncovering the Gendered Brutality of Gang Rapes in Victorian England', *Nottingham Law Journal*, 1.
10. Ibid.
11. *The Times*, 27 November 1876.
12. *R v. Milberry* [2003] 2 Criminal Appeal Reports(S) 31.
13. Sentencing Guidelines Council see http://www.sentencing-guidelines.gov.uk/guidelines/council/final.
14. Proceedings of the Old Bailey Ref: t17790707-49.
15. Proceedings of the Old Bailey Ref: t17800510-57.
16. Proceedings of the Old Bailey Ref: t17970920-12.
17. See A. Clark (1987) *Women's Silence, Men's Violence: Sexual Assault in England 1770–1845* (London: Pandora Press).
18. *R v Olugboja* [1982] QB 320.
19. 9 Geo IV, c.31 An Act for consolidating and amending the Statutes in England relative to Offences against the Person.
20. (1854) 'The Judges on Codification,' *Edinburgh Review*, 99, 573.
21. *Camplin* (1845) 1 Cox CC 311; *Hallett* (1841) 9 C&P 748 and *Case* (1850) 1 Den 580.
22. *Pall Mall Gazette*, 4 July 1885.
23. HL 1883 [280] 1391.
24. Hale, *Pleas of the Crown*, 629.
25. W. Blackstone (1826) *Blackstone's Commentaries* (1769), Vol. 4, 16th. edn. (London: Cadell, Butterworth & Son), 215.
26. J. F. Archbold (1822) *Criminal Pleading, Evidence and Practice* (London, Sweet & Maxwell), 259.
27. Wiener, *Men of Blood*, 77–8.
28. See Clark, *Women's Silence, Men's Violence*, passim.

29. See S. D'Cruze (1998) *Crimes of Moral Outrage* (London: UCL Press) and C. Conley (1991) *The Unwritten Law: Criminal Justice in Victorian Kent* (Oxford: Oxford University Press).

30. V. Gatrell et al. (1980) *Crime and the Law: The Social History of Crime in Western Europe since 1500* (London: Europa), 289.

31. K. Stevenson (2004) 'Fulfilling Their Mission: The Intervention of Voluntary Societies in Cases of Sexual Assault in the Victorian Criminal Process', *Crime, History & Societies*, 8:1, 93–110.

32. See J. Rowbotham and K. Stevenson (2003) 'Causing a Sensation: Media and Legal Representations of Bad Behaviour', in J. Rowbotham and K. Stevenson (eds.), *Behaving Badly: Social Panics and Moral Outrage – Victorian and Modern Parallels* (Aldershot: Ashgate), 31–46.

33. National Archive HO119/118.

34. Conley, *The Unwritten Law*, 83.

35. G. Slapper, 'The Law Explored: Ethnic Minorities and the Judiciary', *The Times*, 4 July 2007.

36. Cited in E. Carrabine et al. (2004) *Criminology: A Sociological Introduction* (London: Routledge), 116.

37. *The Independent*, 12 April 1990.

38. *The Times*, 25 November 1876.

39. *The Times*, 29 July 1876.

40. *R v. Camplin* (1845) 1 Cox CC 311.

41. *The Times*, 6 December 1856.

42. *R v. Bree* [2007] EWCA Crim 256.

43. F. Stephen (1873) *Liberty Equality, Fraternity* (London: Smith, Elder & Co), 209.

44. Cited in Carrabine et al., *Criminology*, 116.

45. *R v. Clarence* (1888) 22 QBD 23 at 25.

46. Ibid., 37.

47. Ibid., 42–3.

48. Ibid., 53.

49. *R v. R* [1992] 1 AC 599.

50. Respectively Case No 47/1994/494/576; Case No 48/1994/495/577.

51. *DDP v. Morgan* [1976] AC 182, p. 186.

52. *R v. Flattery* (1877) 2 QBD 410 at 414.

53. Ibid., 238.

54. Ibid., 207.

5 Murder and Fatality: The Changing Face of Homicide

Shani D'Cruze

1. Introduction

The rates of lethal violence in English society have changed significantly since the Middle Ages. Viewed historically, fatal violence is best interpreted as an aspect of social interaction. Despite major changes in historical context and in the recorded incidence of homicide, patterns or 'scenarios' of killing seem far more durable over time. Therefore, we should ask whether the development of modernity meant alterations in behaviour so that people have less often resorted to extreme violence. Similarly, to what extent have historical changes in criminal justice and social regulation more widely served to inhibit extreme violence?

2. Chronology

Historians have estimated that in the thirteenth and fourteenth centuries there were something like 24 homicides per 100,000 population. By the mid-sixteenth century homicide rates were between 3 and 9 per 100,000 population and in the mid-nineteenth century the rate was about 1.8. The lowest English national rate was 0.6 per 100,000 population, recorded in the 1960s. Thereafter homicide levels have risen. National figures for 2001 show 891 homicides amongst a population of 58,789,194, or a rate of 1.52 per 100,000. Given the difficulties of interpreting historical sources, such figures are always only estimates. Nevertheless, there is a clear, broad trend of a secular decline in the homicide statistics to the mid-twentieth century, followed by a rise. Furthermore, allowing for unevenness in timing, similar trends are evident across Western Europe.[1]

Despite media emphasis on killings by strangers, it is in fact far more common that killer and victim are known to each other. Home Office statistics for the years between 1997 and 2001 include 17 per cent of homicides where there had been a prior sexual relationship between killer and victim, and another 14 per cent were other domestic killings. A further 22 per cent were confrontational male-versus-male homicides.[2] Drawing on 2003–4 figures, the most common perpetrator of homicide was white (in 78 per cent of cases), male (90 per cent), and a young adult (between 21 and 40 in 63 per cent of cases). In 70 per cent of such cases the victim was either related to, or an acquaintance of, the killer. Of these, 98 per cent of killings were of one single victim and 54 per cent arose from a quarrel or with the killer in a violent rage.[3] A recent survey of 786 men serving life sentences for murder in British prisons further showed that such men were likely to have been socially disadvantaged and to have had previous criminal convictions.[4] Today, homicide is a largely masculine practice, a component of cultures of violence either in confrontation with other men, or as an attempt to exert control at home. This is not to ignore the fact that women also kill; they do so, but in significantly smaller numbers and more frequently in a domestic setting. Criminological work has also suggested that homicides tend to be associated with social situations where individuals perceive their options to be heavily constrained, because of social disadvantage, or because prevailing cultures of violence seem to dictate that violence should escalate in a specific social encounter.[5] How do such findings about murder and homicide in the twenty-first century compare with earlier periods?

In London in 1783, John Clarke, known as Mad Tom, had spent the day drinking with Thomas Johnson. Both were journeymen shoemakers, working for wages. Eventually, Clarke became jealous, thinking that Johnson had been alone with Clarke's common-law wife Nan Goodman, a fish-seller. Clarke complained of this to neighbours, plunging his knife into a table top to emphasize his point. That evening he fetched Johnson out of a public house, and plunged the knife into Johnson's belly. Johnson died two days later. Clarke, who claimed to have no recollection of the events because he was drunk, was found guilty and hanged.[6] In Liverpool in 1896 two labourers, Robert Devine and John Donolly, had quarrelled all day. Eventually Devine challenged Donolly: 'If you want to fight me, come now and fight fair.' In the ensuing contest Devine was fatally stabbed in the neck.[7] In 1992 Jan Christofides was playing pool in a crowded pub. A fight broke out with Peter Maffey, who, Christofides said, had insulted him. Christofides hit Maffey over the head with a pool cue. Maffey, having also been punched and probably kicked by another individual,

Michael Lyons, collapsed outside the pub and died a few weeks later of a pulmonary embolism. Christofides was found guilty of murder but his third appeal was finally upheld in 2001 on the grounds of technical difficulties arising from the original trial.[8]

Each example shows violence embedded in cultures of men's leisure and drink with fatality arising through escalating aggressive confrontation. Violence addressed an affront to honour through insult, challenge or (alleged) appropriation of a sexual partner. In the 1896 example, the semi-formal ritual of the 'fair fight' is clear and was sufficient to reduce the murder charge to manslaughter. Elements of challenge and response are also, if less clearly, evident in the cases against both Clarke and Christofides. This frequent pattern runs historically parallel to violence born of victimisation, of individuals perceived as 'not us'. Racially motivated violence, for example, has a long history.[9] In the 1993 murder of Stephen Lawrence, not only was the original motivation for violence racist, but also the subsequent handling of the enquiry demonstrated what has come to be termed 'institutional racism' within the Metropolitan Police (see Chapter 8).

Equivalent occurrences can be found in domestic or intimate homicide. In 1791, Edward Pritchard, a master farrier of Smithfield in London, was heard by neighbours beating his wife over two successive evenings. He said she had been drinking, though no other witnesses confirmed this. On the second evening neighbours found her lying in the stables, badly bruised and with her skull fractured. She died a few hours later, saying that it was Pritchard who had murdered her. He was hanged for murder, though he claimed she had been hurt falling downstairs.[10] Millworker Mark Fiddler had, by 1875, spent several years drinking and quarrelling with his young wife Dorothy, who also worked in the mills. He sold their furniture and Dorothy had to take separate lodgings. One night Mark kept her out talking till late. As she finally returned to her lodgings, he cut her throat and left her to die in her landlady's arms. He, too, was hanged for her murder.[11] In September 2007, police inspector Gary Weddell was on bail, charged with the murder of his wife, Sandra. In January 2008 Weddell killed his mother-in-law with a shotgun and then committed suicide. It seemed that he believed she was taking his three children to live in New Zealand.[12] All these cases involve men's extreme violence either to exert or (as the Fiddler and Weddell cases make particularly clear) to try to regain power and control over their family and domestic life. They have been selected to underline that domestic violence and the murder of intimates has never been exclusively a practice of the socially marginal. The well-documented connections between non-lethal domestic violence and the killing of intimates are clear in the Fiddler and Pritchard cases.

The similarities across two centuries in such scenarios of violence (to use Polk's term) is striking, and have informed social psychological analyses which see homicide as an intrinsic feature of human behaviour.[13] Historical analysis, however, tries to understand such behaviour in its historical context. Eighteenth-century households, for example, also commonly contained servants and apprentices who might be subject to domestic violence in the same way as wives and children.[14] The changing incidence in recorded homicide and the changing treatment of fatal violence by the criminal justice system also alter the social and criminological significance of apparently similar violent behaviour at different periods.

There have been comparable kinds of enduring patterns in the killing of infants and young children, the most frequent scenario of fatal violence committed by women (see Chapter 3). We will return to killings of adults by women when reviewing the criminal justice system's response to fatal violence. However, some mention is needed of more exceptional murderers and of the historical persistence even in patterns of serial killing, or of murder by children. Serial or multiple killers, or the murderers of strangers, have loomed larger in cultural perceptions of murder than their numbers perhaps warrant, certainly since the nineteenth century. The modern typology of the serial murderer arose out of moral panics in North America during the 1970s and 1980s, when one estimate suggested that over a quarter of murder victims were killed by a small number of psychopathic killers.[15] Contemporary British examples which fit the model included Peter Sutcliffe (the Yorkshire Ripper) and Dennis Nilsen, each of whom committed numbers of psychologically delusional, sexually motivated murders.[16] There are also far older historical instances. The Victorian poisoner Thomas Neil Cream's killings were an expression of power similar to that of modern medical murderers such as Harold Shipman and Beverley Allitt.[17] The 1888 'Jack the Ripper' murders of prostitutes in the East End of London have never been solved, and the continuing mystery has attracted numerous and often less plausible theories ever since. Both at the time and subsequently, 'Jack' became a powerful symbol of the sexual and physical dangers inherent in the modern metropolis.[18]

Other especially disturbing modern cases have involved killings by young children, notably the 1993 murder of 2-year-old James Bulger by two 10-year-old boys.[19] Yet the murder of children by children has a far longer history. The killing of two very young children in 1968 by 11-year-old Mary Bell and her friend Norma is the example most frequently compared with the Bulger murder, but there have been others. The 1861 killing of toddler George Burgess bears a striking resemblance to the Bulger case. Such killings, normally committed by more than one child and often involving a good deal of cruelty, apparently represent the extremes of violent play. Historically, such cases have received uneven treatment by the criminal justice system.[20]

3. Historiography

a) A Civilising Process?

Many historians have associated the long-term decline in homicide rates with a decline in non-lethal violence. The dominant explanation links the growth of the state with changes in behaviour.[21] The idea of a 'civilising process' was originally formulated by Norbert Elias, who suggested that the development of comparatively centralised states in Western Europe since the later medieval period reduced the autonomy of feudal aristocracies. These controlled territory through both law and the command of numerous armed retainers. Aristocracies displaced their physical and military aggressiveness into competition for the goods accompanying elite status. Elite social groups demonstrated their dominance, not least through masculine identities which regulated and ritualised interpersonal violence through codes of honour (for example, duelling) and feminine identities which were normatively non-violent. Over centuries, so this argument runs, the combination of a more developed system of criminal justice and later policing, and the association of 'civilised' behaviour with high status, led to the ever-wider social diffusion of non-violent or at least less violent behaviour.[22]

This paradigm has been elaborated and refined. Pitt argues that in periods where the authority of the state weakens, interpersonal violence may rise; shown for example by the significant increase in Cheshire homicide levels before the English Civil War.[23] Wiener has interpreted the increasing attention of the Victorian criminal justice system to serious violence as a 'civilising offensive' chiefly directed against men's interpersonal violence.[24] Social groups that based claims to status not least on their 'civilised' conduct distanced themselves from the interpersonal violence of the mob, something that has been argued both for public male versus male cultures of insult and violence in eighteenth-century London, as well as for the middle class as a whole during the early and mid-nineteenth century.[25] Abstention from violence was also frequently used to demonstrate the superiority of British national identity.[26]

Whilst it is in many ways a very plausible explanatory framework for the recorded decline in homicide rates, there are several ways in which the civilising process paradigm has been criticised.[27] It is difficult to substantiate historically the precise linkages between the coercive pressures of criminal justice and policing, the dominance of cultures that privilege reticence and 'politeness' and the psychological internalisation of inhibition; there is plenty of evidence that cultures of violence that produce both fatal and non-fatal outcomes have had continued historical currency amongst men in particular, up to the present. Furthermore, the extent, if not the general trend of the historical decline in homicide has itself been debated.

Historians argue that homicide was a fairly accurate index of violence in society. However, for a number of reasons, this assumption may be unsafe.[28] For example, the level of unlawful fatality in society is related to the effectiveness of medical treatment for injury. Over time, access to effective medical treatment has become more widely available, and has arguably had a large, if unquantifiable effect in depressing modern homicide rates.[29]

The criminal justice process itself has shaped how fatal violence has been recognised as a criminal offence. Since the medieval period, coroners have been the officers of the Crown charged with investigating or recording suspicious deaths.[30] However, the coroner's inquest was subject to community or institutional pressures that helped shape its decisions. Sharpe finds eighteenth-century instances which hint that the local community took initiatives over whether a coroner should be called in the first place. Emmerichs has found that suspiciously few nineteenth-century London coroners' inquests resulted in prosecutions for murder. In 1842 the Westminster coroner held over 300 inquests but took medical evidence in only 18 cases and ordered only 4 post mortems. Overall, many inquests were superficial and often settled for neutral verdicts such as 'found dead'. Before the 1860s, Quarter Sessions had control over which cases came to inquest and were anxious to cap costs. Until 1883 JPs had some level of control over coroners' salaries.[31] Victorian coroners' courts were actively filtering out suspicious deaths and arguably reduced homicide figures.

Howard Taylor questions even more comprehensively whether nineteenth- and twentieth-century homicide figures are an accurate reflection of unlawful killing. To quote Taylor's key finding:

> Between 1900 and 1909 there were 1,500 murders, giving an average of exactly 150 per year for that decade. There were also 150 murders in 1923 and 1924. The range of the figures is just as remarkable. In only five of the 104 years between 1862 and 1966 were there either fewer than 120 murders or more than 179, i.e. the number of murders was kept within a tight band of 20 per cent (30 murders) on either side of the average of 150.[32]

Taylor suggests that the rationing of resources (murder investigations and trials are expensive) have served to cap the numbers of deaths treated as murder. A number of modern cases suggest such possibilities. Carol Park was listed as a missing person for 30 years after she disappeared in 1976. Her husband Gordon Park was found guilty of murder only in 2005, almost thirty years after he killed her and dumped her body in Coniston Water.[33]

In summary, much of the historiography of violence has followed an explanatory framework that links the growth of the state and the coercive effect of criminal justice with changes in violent behaviour and consequent reductions in unlawful killing. But there have been qualifications to this thesis, not least because of the intrinsic uncertainties of homicide statistics as an index of violent behaviour, or even of historical levels of fatal violence. The extent and nature of recorded homicide have been in part products of the action (or inaction) of the criminal justice system itself. How, then, have historians viewed the changing criminal justice process over time?

b) Fatality, the Law and Criminal Justice

In the early modern period, mortality and morbidity levels were high and people of all ages could die suddenly. Malcolm Gaskill argues that there was no widespread framework of rational, scientific knowledge to identify the precise etiology of disease or injury. Consequently, homicide was harder to detect. Supernatural explanations for sudden or otherwise inexplicable deaths had widespread currency and were institutionalised within the criminal justice system. Witchcraft was then a capital felony. Tests such as the renewed bleeding of a corpse at the touch of the murderer had credibility in court.[34] Early modern conceptions of legal proof differed from modern rules of evidence. Garthine Walker finds that the prime purpose of the law was to uphold social order, and this meant recognising hierarchies which operated by class, gender and age. The jury assessed the guilt of an accused person mostly in relation to their social position, so rumour and opinion were relevant as well as fact. Social hierarchy conveyed authority over subordinates, and violence was an acceptable means to enforce that authority. Killing became unlawful where violence had exceeded its legitimate use, and the degree of a killer's culpability depended on how far that line had been overreached.[35]

By the end of the sixteenth century, manslaughter and murder had been distinguished as separate categories. The classic specification, still the starting point for the law at the turn of the twenty-first century, was Lord Chief Justice Coke's seventeenth-century definition of murder as killing with 'malice aforethought'; that is, the intention to kill or commit serious bodily harm. Both assize judges' charges to juries and popular pamphlet literature distinguished the murderer as a particularly heinous offender. Nevertheless, Garthine Walker has found that in seventeenth-century Cheshire, only just over a quarter of men tried for murder were found guilty.[36] The rest were 'either acquitted, pardoned after verdicts of death by misfortune or self-defence or – most common of all – were branded after they were found guilty of a reduced charge of manslaughter': typically a killing arising from male-versus-male confrontation.[37] Men were also entitled to use forms of violence to order their households although none in this sample who beat their wives to death were convicted of murder. Men were expected to defend and maintain their reputation through violence; manslaughter was interpreted as instances where such violence was miscalculated.[38]

Women made up one-fifth of those tried for unlawful killing in seventeenth-century Cheshire and most frequently killed people from within their own domestic circle.[39] Female sexuality was held to be intrinsically disorderly and could both explain women's transgressions and sometimes make them more threatening. Proportionately more accusations against women than men were dismissed at the pre-trial stages. However, once found guilty of homicide, women were far more likely to hang than men; manslaughter was not a criminal offence applicable to women. Where servants killed their masters, or wives their husbands, the threat to social hierarchies was particularly stark. Between 1351 and 1826 such killers committed the offence of petty treason, for which the penalty was burning at the stake. Early modern law treated men's fatal violence as intrinsically different from that of women, producing uneven treatment not only between men and women *per se*, but between different gendered scenarios of killing.[40] Historians have found that such unevenness recurred, even as new attitudes towards legal proof and new kinds of evidence came to inform the trial process.

By the 1720s, the 'fact-like fictions' developed by the law were becoming generalised to other areas of culture – replacing the use of supernatural sign and community reputation as determinants of proof.[41] The legal system was still readily used (and influenced) by those who brought prosecutions and sought redress for a range of ills but by 1800, people did so through adopting the objective discourses of evidence and through the mediation of legal and other professionals. By the 1780s, lawyers for both prosecution and defence were frequently present in court.[42] As Douglas Hay and others have argued, the purpose of criminal justice was less to restore consensual social order and more to discipline individuals who had transgressed the social hierarchies that the institutions of the law embodied.[43] By the later eighteenth century, more of the criminal law was increasingly governed by statute and punishments became more severe.

Early in the nineteenth century, however, it became clear that severe sentences did not reduce crime. The population was growing fast during the early stages of industrialisation and standards of living for many working people were worsening.[44] The spectacle of public execution and the risk of riot from the large crowds that assembled were worrying to the state. Transportation to Australia provided an alternative penal measure whilst prison reformers were advocating penitentiary sentences to combine punishment with rehabilitation.[45] Martin Wiener has outlined a series of judicial changes which, he argues, amounted to a 'civilising offensive' targeted mostly at male violence. From 1803, the statute law on violence was progressively extended. A series of laws, in particular the Offences against the Person Acts (OAPA) of 1837 and 1861, wrote tougher penal responses to violence into black-letter law. Magistrates in the lower courts were given increasing scope to try petty violence without a jury. Prison sentences were used for a wider range of serious violence and manslaughter. Defences of provocation were progressively narrowed when claimed by male defendants, especially those that killed other men.[46] Fatalities caused by culpable negligence were more firmly incorporated into the law on manslaughter. The extent of criminal responsibility for murder was clarified through the restrictive M'Naughten Rules on insanity. Only late in the nineteenth century did insanity defences achieve limited headway in mitigating sentence, if not verdict, for some male homicide defendants. However, from the 1840s, capital punishment was effectively reserved for murder and high treason, a situation formally confirmed in the 1861 OAPA. Neonaticide had effectively ceased to attract capital penalties.[47]

Consequently, adult murder became more clearly distinguished from other kinds of serious violence, and murder trials loomed larger in public consciousness, helped by the development of the press. Trials lasted longer due to the larger role of defence and prosecution counsel. The practice of cross-examining witnesses, and the more focused attention to evidence, including forensic evidence, heightened the drama of the courtroom. Developments in forensic medicine and toxicology made 'secret' murder more possible to detect and expert witnesses became a more regular feature in trials for fatal violence.[48]

The manner and appearance of the accused as well as the circumstances of the case achieved a higher cultural visibility in the Victorian period. Murder trials became significant cultural as well as judicial events, where social norms (particularly gender and class) were tested against the specific events and individuals involved in a fatality and retold in melodramatic press narratives. Historians interested in violence and the history of gender have argued that where defendants had maintained normative social and gender roles, punishment tended to be mitigated.[49] Hence, even though juries were now expected to reach verdicts on the evidence with the legal direction of the judge, rather than on the assessments of reputation, they still often took strong views as to the *kind* of person they saw in the dock. Either through their verdict (to the annoyance of judges keen to enforce the more stringent Victorian law) or through recommendations to mercy, juries continued to make *ad hoc* assessments as to gradations of culpability. In a number of murder cases there was comparative sympathy for women on trial for adult homicide (particularly for killing objectionable husbands and lovers) who could present properly submissive feminine demeanours. Nevertheless, uncongenial women killers were readily hung.[50]

The first half of the twentieth century saw the combination of a strongly rehabilitative tendency in overall penal policy and very low murder rates. The mechanisms of appeal and reprieve by the Home Secretary meant that between 1900 and 1949, 40.3 per cent of convicted male murderers and as many as 90.8 per cent of sentenced women avoided the gallows, though there were around thirteen executions each year.[51] Unsurprisingly, there was pronounced press and public interest in sensational murders, many of which involved domestic or intimate relationships. For example, May of 1924 had seen widespread and detailed press coverage of both the Vaquier case, and the so-called 'Bungalow Crime'. Vaquier had poisoned the land-lord of a public house in Byfleet, Essex, following an affair with his glam-orous wife, Mrs Jones. Patrick Mahon (35 and married) had murdered and dismembered the body of his mistress Emily Kaye (37 and single) at an Eastbourne holiday bungalow.[52]

Women on trial for murder who had endured a violent or sexually importunate partner continued to receive sympathy from the criminal justice system. In 1922, Mme Fahmy shot and killed her husband Ali Bey Fahmy at the Savoy Hotel in London. He was an aristocratic Egyptian. She was French, and had had something of a chequered past life. She was acquitted, more or less against the evidence. Mme Fahmy successfully pre-sented herself as a victim; because the public and the court accepted that an 'Oriental' such as Fahmy might well be capable of bestial violence and perverse sexuality anathema to white society.[53] In contrast, sexually trans-gressive women could find their criminal culpability taken for granted. Edith Thompson was hanged in 1922 as was her lover, Freddie Bywaters, for the murder of her husband. Edith took no part in the killing, but the prosecution argued a conspiracy to murder between them. By selective and partial readings in court from her highly coloured letters to Bywaters, it was accepted without any forensic evidence that Edith had tried to poison her husband.[54]

Amidst a low homicide rate overall, the preponderance of domestic and intimate murders, which seemed not to be amenable to deterrence, added weight to the vocal, minority, middle-class movement calling for the aboli-tion of hanging. After the Second World War several contentious capital sentences, particularly those of Timothy Evans, Derek Bentley and Ruth Ellis, reinforced parliamentary opinion against capital punishment. The Homicide Act of 1957, amongst other provisions, introduced a partial defence to murder of diminished responsibility and capital punishment for murder was finally abolished in 1965 (see Chapter 9). As post-war crime rates began to rise, killers such as John Christie, the serial murder of marginal women, and George Haigh, the so-called 'acid-bath' murderer, appeared more predatory. The A6 murder of 1961, this chapter's case study, exemplified 'mindless' post-war violence, though doubts about this conviction increased the pressures for abolition.[55] The murders of children by Ian Brady and Myra Hindley, which might have reduced parliamentary sympathy for abolition, came to trial in 1966 after capital punishment had been repealed. Nevertheless, as the statistics show, the killing of intimates and acquaintances were the vast majority of homicides throughout the post-war decades.

Not all killing is unlawful (the police might lawfully kill a dangerous suspect) and not all unlawful killing is murder. Since 1922, English criminal homicide statistics have included manslaughter and infanticide (see Chapter 3) but do not include assisting a suicide (a separate crime since 1961) nor causing death by dangerous driving (recorded separately from 1956 onwards). The criminal responsibility of corporations for homicide has been covered by dedicated legislation only since 2007. Murder has long been – and remains – very much a matter of interpersonal violence and in modern society continues to be understood in terms of individual culpability.

Since 1965 a life sentence has been mandatory for murder. Despite the recommendation of the Nathan Committee of the House of Lords (1989), governments have not altered the law to allow judges full discretion on sentences for murder (as they have for all other offences). In some recent instances, Home Secretaries have increased the sentence tariff stipulated by the judge, for example in the Bulger murder. The legislative response to this case was also, in 1998, to set aside the presumption of *doli incapax* (incapable of harm) by which children over the age of criminal responsibility (currently 10 but younger in the past) yet under 14 were presumed not to understand the seriousness of their criminal acts unless positive evidence to the contrary was produced.[56] Feminist criminologists in the 1970s and 1980s pointed out the comparatively light sentences given to certain men who killed their wives in comparison to several women who killed abusive husbands or partners. Such killings did not fit the established partial defence of provocation which required *immediate* retaliatory violence (an example of how models of male-versus-male confrontation have continued to structure the law on homicide). Public campaigns and reconsideration by the Appeal Court eventually established the acceptance of 'slow-burn' provocation as a partial defence. In the 1990s, as Chapter 3 shows, several women were also jailed for killing their infant children on the basis of since discredited expert scientific opinion, in cases now recognised as miscarriages of justice.[57]

Viewed in the long term, therefore, as homicide became statistically rarer, so penalties became comparatively more severe in comparison with the eighteenth century, when capital punishment was used for a far wider range of offences. Since the repeal of the death penalty for murder, and especially since the 1980s, as murder rates have increased, sentencing severity has been tightened through the mechanism of the sentence tariff. Furthermore, the criminal justice process has become rather tougher on a-typical murderers in high-profile cases.

Historically, some cases of murder have attracted little attention from the media. However, other cases have become celebrated either because as a criminal case they have been complicated, contested or inconclusive, or because they expressed some anxiety in the prevailing social imaginary. The case study that follows became notorious on both these counts.[58] Occurring at a date when recorded homicide rates were at their lowest, the A6 murder demonstrated behaviour that was far from 'civilised'. This violence might be explained as individual psychopathology, but nevertheless can be shown to be hooked into patterns of masculine violence that were historically located and also connected with more enduring social uses of violence. Forensic and identification evidence have been pitted together in this case, exemplifying how mid-twentieth century conceptions of identity played a part in shaping the plausibility of different kinds of evidence, in assessing the likely culpability of the defendant, and indeed in opening the way towards late modern ideas about the victimology of (criminal) fatal violence.

4. Case Study

The trial and execution of James Hanratty in 1962 was notorious at the time and has returned to public attention on several occasions since. The crime itself was a particularly shocking, gratuitously violent murder and rape of two strangers. Atypical of the general patterns of modern homicide, the event focused post-war anxieties about violent crime. The evidence at trial was circumstantial and depended heavily on identification from the surviving victim. There were irregularities in the police investigation and a lack of disclosure of evidence to the court. Hanratty protested his innocence throughout, and before he was executed another man had confessed to the crime. On the other hand, Hanratty changed his alibi while the trial was in progress and was an admitted petty criminal who had served a 5-year sentence for car theft. He was tried at a time when the abolition of capital punishment was on the political agenda and there was sufficient uncertainty to make the conviction worrying in some quarters. The Hanratty family's subsequent campaigning has been endorsed by journalists and celebrities, including John Lennon. A review in 1974 upheld the verdict but in 1999 the Criminal Cases Review Commission referred it back to the Appeal Court. The latest appeal in 2002 upheld the conviction, on the basis of new DNA evidence which matched samples from Hanratty's exhumed body with that of material from the crime scene. The defence submitted that these tests were inconclusive because of the possibilities of contamination, and Hanratty's supporters still maintain his innocence.[59]

On an August evening in 1961 Michael Gregsten and Valerie Storey were sitting in a Morris Minor car parked in a Bedfordshire cornfield; they were having an affair. Valerie Storey was single and Gregsten was married with two young children. They were threatened by a man with a gun who compelled Gregsten to allow him into the back seat of the car and then commandeered both the couple and the vehicle in a bizarre and apparently aimless night drive around West London and the Home Counties. The gunman claimed to be on the run and desperate. During the night he shot Gregsten twice in the head at point blank range. Valerie Storey was later forced into the back of the car and raped. As morning approached she was made to demonstrate how to drive the car and to drag Gregsten's body onto the side of the road. She was then shot several times and left for dead while the gunman drove away. Three witnesses testified to seeing the Morris Minor being driven erratically in London the following morning, and one of them identified Hanratty as the driver. The car was found abandoned in London and the gun was recovered from a hiding place under the upstairs back seat of a 36A bus.

The police first arrested Peter Alphon, following information from the manager of the downmarket Vienna Hotel in Maida Vale, north London, that Alphon had remained locked in his room there for five days following the murder. Alphon was released when Valerie Storey failed to pick him out from an identity parade, but later rearrested and charged with threatening another woman with a gun (an incident in which he claimed to be the A6 murderer). However, the police had excluded Alphon and there were few other clear leads, until the manager of the Vienna Hotel again intervened, having found two cartridge cases on a chair in a basement bedroom of the hotel last occupied by a James Ryan. This man had stayed in the hotel during the period Alphon was also there. Ryan turned out to be Hanratty's alias. He was arrested in Blackpool on 11 October and was identified by Valerie Storey. This identity parade became controversial first, because Storey had asked the men to speak (the gunman had had a distinctive London accent) and secondly, because Hanratty appeared with unnaturally bright orange hair. He had had his hair dyed black and later bleached in the preceding weeks.

Hanratty's defence at first seemed to have a fairly plausible alibi. He had gone to Liverpool on the morning of the murder, allegedly to sell some stolen property, and was identified asking directions in a sweetshop in Scotland Road that afternoon. His whereabouts on the evening of the 22nd (when the car hijacking began) remained unclear, but during the trial he claimed to have taken a bus to the north Welsh resort town of Rhyl, still looking for someone to buy the stolen jewellery. He did not know the address where he said he had stayed for two nights (22 and 23 August 1961), but described it fully, especially an attic bedroom with a green bath. The defence produced the landlady of 'Ingledene' guest house, who recalled a young man with a London accent, but she proved a poor witness in court and her evidence was discounted. In the late 1960s, journalist Paul Foot interviewed 14 people who claimed to have seen Hanratty in Rhyl on 23 August.[60]

The role of Peter Alphon has long complicated the Hanratty case. He wrote to the *Daily Express* in 1962 recommending Hanratty for a reprieve and also to the Home Office confessing to the crime. He repeated this confession to the media in Paris a few years later. Alphon also knew Hanratty's friends, the France family. Carol France (the daughter) had dyed Hanratty's hair so inexpertly. Charles France (the father) gave evidence of Hanratty's habit of disposing of unwanted stolen goods under the upstairs back seat of London buses. Alphon later claimed that France had been involved in the planting of the gun and Hanratty's handkerchief on the bus, and also in placing the cartridge cases in the Vienna Hotel. France committed suicide shortly before Hanratty was hanged. Alphon also claimed that he was paid £5,000 by Michael Gregsten's wife to frighten Gregsten and Storey and break up their affair.

It is not my purpose here to retry Hanratty, but to use the available information to illustrate two themes of this chapter, first the importance of unlawful killing in relation to wider scenarios of violence, secondly as an example of the contested nature of legal proof in the modern era. The A6 murder bears plausible relation to wider cultures of crime and violence in London at that period. Hanratty was in many ways a marginal figure, of poor educational attainment, despite his respectable working-class family. He was operating at the fringes of metropolitan criminal networks where the biggest and most successful players enforced their control of illegal and semi-legal business activity through the ready and sometimes gratuitous use of violence, including firearms. The late 1950s and early 1960s were the heyday of powerful and colourful crime organisations, especially that of the Kray Twins in the East End and the Richardson brothers south of the river. The Metropolitan Police had been criticised from the 1950s for inefficiency and corruption and were unable to control organised crime.[61] Hanratty was by no means in the criminal big-time. Nevertheless on his release from a prison sentence in March 1961 he had tried to buy a gun in order to 'do some stick-ups'. [62] If we follow the Appeal Court in concluding that the new DNA evidence means that Alphon was not the A6 killer, his subsequent actions in claiming to be the murderer and doing exactly the kind of 'stick-ups' that Hanratty had apparently contemplated demonstrate something of gun crime's dubious glamour at the fringes of the London 'underworld' (see Chapter 6). The A6 murder also reflected cultures of masculine aggression in that it combined sexual and physical violence. Sexual violence has been widely argued to be foremost a demonstration of power. Indeed, the whole A6 episode can be read as the brutal and miscalculated social enactment of the aggressive and hence powerful masculine identity that was dominant in the cultures of criminal violence prevailing in and around London during that period.

The Hanratty case has proved a quintessentially modern episode in the history of criminal justice, not least because of its handling of evidence. As we have suggested, the authority of factual and scientific evidence in the modern courtroom had a long historical evolution. In the twenty-first century, cutting-edge forensic evidence made a dramatic intervention in the Hanratty case. It is unusual for the modern Appeal Court to allow fresh prosecution evidence, a decision which in itself underlines the extent of the doubts about the original verdict. In the 2002 appeal, the DNA evidence was able to sweep away all the other evidential uncertainties and questions about the conduct of the original police prosecution which, had they been fully explored in 1962, might have produced a not-guilty verdict or a commutation of the capital sentence.

DNA profiling is not, however, foolproof. Earlier tests in the 1990s had been inconclusive. The recent tests produced a profile match only through the use of a new technique, PCR, whereby DNA molecules are split and replicated to obtain a sufficient quantity to produce a sample. The cycle of replication was undertaken 34 times in this instance.[63] Consequently, even a tiny amount of contaminant could produce a false profile. The materials in question, though separately bagged, travelled to and from the courtroom in 1962 in the same box. The cloth fragment from Valerie Storey's knickers was lost for 30 years and was found attached to a file, wrapped but in an unsealed envelope. The file also contained a broken glass vial whose original contents were supposed to have been a wash from Hanratty's trousers that could be assumed to have contained his DNA. However, only two DNA profiles were found on the knickers. The 1962 tests had identified semen and in 2002 the only male DNA profile to account for it was a statistically convincing match to that from Hanratty's corpse.

Even after the 2002 appeal, longstanding pro-Hanratty campaigner Paul Foot still distrusted the DNA profile, preferring the identification evidence he had obtained that supported Hanratty's Rhyl alibi.[64] In the 1962 trial, both sides relied on (conflicting) identification evidence. The plausibility of identification evidence depends on modern ideas about truth telling, about the witnesses' capacity for visual recognition and also about the unique distinctiveness of individuals.[65] The power of the evidence in court depends on the witnesses' certainty, though as Michael Sherrard, Hanratty's defence barrister, pointed out: 'The witness may be perfectly honest, absolutely convinced that he or she has identified the right man or woman and you're not going to be able to cross-examine them to show that they're lying ... (because) ... they're not lying, they're telling the truth as they see it.'[66] Valerie Storey's identification of Hanratty was the key piece of evidence. As she expressed it in an interview much later: 'My evidence was unshakable because I was telling the truth.'[67] In 2002 the forensic evidence

underlines her certainty. In 1962, however, a good deal of her plausibility depended on her demeanour and her status as the surviving victim,
both in the courtroom itself and more widely through the media. She had
given her evidence from a wheelchair, and the press were keen to publish
pictures. Newspapers repeatedly juxtaposed a picture of her in a bathing
suit with the image of her arriving in court on a stretcher. The proliferat-
ing visual as well as textual representation of victims along with accused
or convicted offenders in the public media underline both their modern
individuality and also their roles in the melodramatic moral narratives that
modern popular culture relies on to make sense of sensational murder.[68]

5. Conclusion

Recently there have been attempts to pay more attention to the victims of
crime in the criminal justice process, most notably the idea of restorative
justice.[69] Of course, homicide leaves the victim dead, but the concept of
secondary victimisation has been developed to take into account the wider
harm that killing does. It took a long struggle for Duwayne Brooks, who
was with Stephen Lawrence when he was murdered, to be officially compensated for the police's treatment of him (see Chapter 8). Since the later
1990s, a number of victim support groups have campaigned. Politicising
their identity as victims provides mutual emotional support but, as Rock
argues, such intense investment in grief as a self-defining identity has also
had negative effects for bereaved individuals.[70] In the 1990s, one group
extended the concept of secondary victimisation to the families of serious
criminal offenders;[71] the A6 murder has certainly deeply coloured the subsequent history of the Hanratty family.

The early modern murderer was vilified because murder profoundly disturbed social order. Unlawful killing which could be accommodated within
accepted hierarchies was differently categorised at law: such killers were
not by definition murderers. In the twenty-first century, unlawful killing
has become an aspect of modern (or post-modern) identity politics. Current
focus on the cultural identity of the victim, primary or secondary, emphasises harm to the individual and to families, rather than to social order as a
whole. Murder is an exceptional social action, still experienced by comparatively few people, which for the most part follows enduring patterns arising out of cultures of interpersonal violence. However, the proliferation
of various media by the twenty-first century amplifies the representations
of murder, and circulates starkly different moral narratives that emphasise
evil and deviance. These have escaped from the 'fact-based fictions' that
became characteristic of the modernising criminal justice system by the
nineteenth century and which still formally underpin the rules of evidence.

Notes

1. See for instance M. Eisner (2001) 'Modernization, Self-control and Lethal Violence: The Long-term Dynamics of European Homicide Rates in Theoretical Perspective', *British Journal of Criminology*, 41, 618–38, at 623 and J.S. Cockburn (1991) 'Patterns of Violence in English Society: Homicide in Kent 1560–1985', *Past and Present*, 130, 70–106, at 77. Population figures from http.//www.statistics.gov.uk/cci/nugget.asp?id=185.
2. S. D'Cruze et al. (2006) *Murder: Social and Historical Approaches to Understanding Murder and Murderers* (Cullompton: Willan), 17 summarising F. Brookman (2005) *Understanding Homicide* (London: Sage), 312–15.
3. Law Commission (2005) *A New Homicide Act for England and Wales? A Consultation Paper*, 325 at www.lawcom.gov.uk/docs/cp177_web.pdf.
4. See R.E. Dobash et al. (2002) *Research Findings: ESRC Violence Research Programme* (Manchester: Manchester University).
5. K. Polk (1995) 'Lethal Violence as a Form of Masculine Conflict-resolution', *Australian and New Zealand Journal of Criminology*, 28, 93–115.
6. The Proceedings of the Old Bailey (hereafter OBSP), Ref: t17831210-4, John Clarke, killing: murder, 10 December 1783, viewed at http://www.hrionline.ac.uk/oldbailey/html_units/1780s/t17831210-4.html and (1783) *The Last Dying Words, and Confession of John Clarke, who was Executed this Morning for the Wilful Murder of Thomas Johnson* viewed at Eighteenth-Century Collections Online, http://galenet.galegroup.com/.
7. See J. Archer (2000) '"Men Behaving Badly"? Masculinity and the Uses of Violence, 1850–1900' in S. D'Cruze (ed.), *Everyday Violence in Britain c1850–c. 1950: Gender and Class*, (Harlow: Pearson), 44 and *Liverpool Mercury*, 1 August 1896.
8. Appeal Court Judgement, EWCA Crim 906, 2001, 1–5, viewed at http://www.ccrc.gov.uk/cases/case_referred.asp.
9. Archer, '"Men Behaving Badly"?', 44–5.
10. See OBSP, t17910413-19, Edward Pritchard, killing : murder, 13 April 1791, http://www.hrionline.ac.uk/oldbailey/html_units/1790s/t17910413-19.html.
11. See S. D'Cruze (1998) *Crimes of Outrage: Sex, Violence and Victorian Working Women* (London: UCL Press), 28.
12. *Daily Telegraph*, 15 January 2008, 9 and *Daily Telegraph*, 16 January 2008, 1.
13. K. Polk (1994) *When Men Kill: Scenarios of Masculine Violence*, (Cambridge: Cambridge University Press); M. Daly and M. Wilson (1988) Homicide (New York: Aldine de Gruyter) and Brookman, *Understanding Homicide*, 81.
14. See Cockburn, 'Patterns of Violence', passim.
15. P. Jenkins (1994) *Using Murder: The Social Construction of Serial Homicide*, (Edison NJ: Aldine Transaction), 65–8.
16. See for instance B. Masters (1985) *Killing for Company* (London: Cape) and K. Ramsland (2004) *Dennis Nilsen*, http://www.crimelibrary.com/serial_killers/predators/ nilsen.html.
17. See A. Mclaren (1993) *A Prescription for Murder: The Victorian Serial Killings of Dr. Thomas Neill Cream*, (Chicago and London: University of Chicago Press); http://www.the-shipman-inquiry.org.uk/ and N. Davies (1993)

Murder on Ward Four: The Story of Bev Allitt and the Most Terrifying Crime since the Moors Murders, (London: Chatto & Windus).

18. J.R. Walkowitz (1992) *City of Dreadful Delight: Narratives of Sexual Danger in late-Victorian London* (London: Virago).

19. C. Hay (1996) 'Mobilization through Interpretation: James Bulger and the Construction of a Moral Panic', *Social and Legal Studies*, 4, 197–223.

20. See S. D'Cruze et al., *Murder*, Chapter 4; G. Sereny (1972) *The Case of Mary Bell: A Portrait of a Child who Murdered* (London: Pimlico) and J. Rowbotham et al. (2003) 'Children of Misfortune: Parallels in the Cases of Child Murderers Thompson and Venables, Barratt and Bradley', *Howard Journal*, 42, 107–22.

21. See T.R. Gurr (1981) 'Historical Trends in Violent Crime: A Critical Review of the Evidence', *Crime and Justice: An Annual Review of Research*, 3, 295–353 and the debate in *Past & Present* between Lawrence Stone (1983) 'Interpersonal Violence in English Society, 1300–1980', 101, 22–33 and Jim A. Sharpe (1985) 'The History of Violence in England: Some Observations, 103, 206–15. See also L. Stone (1985) 'The History of Violence in England: Some Observations: A Rejoinder', *Past & Present*, 108, 216–24 and M. Eisner (2003) 'Long-term Trends in Violent Crime', *Crime and Justice: An Annual Review of Research*, 30, 83–142.

22. See N. Elias (1994) *The Civilizing Process: The History of Manners and State Formation and Civilization*, trans. E. Jephcott (Oxford: Blackwell).

23. J.A. Sharpe (1999) *Crime in Early Modern England; 1550–1750* (Harlow: Longman), 86–7.

24. See M.J. Wiener (2004) *Men of Blood: Violence, Manliness and Criminal Justice in Victorian England* (Cambridge: Cambridge University Press).

25. See R. Shoemaker (2001) 'Male Honour and the Decline of Public Violence in 18th-century London', *Social History*, 26, 190–208 and J. Carter Wood (2003) 'It's a Small World After All? Reflections on Violence in Comparative Perspectives', in B. Godfrey, C. Emsley and G. Dunstall (eds.), *Comparative Histories of Crime* (Cullompton: Willan), 36–52.

26. See J. Carter Wood (2004) *Violence and Crime in Nineteenth Century England: The Shadow of our Refinement* (London and New York: Routledge).

27. Discussions of the Elias thesis include P. Spierenburg (2001) 'Violence and the Civilizing Process: Does it Work?', *Crime, Histoire et Sociétés*, 5, 87–105 and E. Avdela et al. (2009) 'Introduction: De-Centring Violence History', in E. Avdela et al. (eds.), *Crime, Violence and the Modern State: Europe 1780–2000* (Ceridigion: Edwin Mellen).

28. Brookman, *Understanding Homicide*, 19–23.

29. Cockburn, 'Patterns of Violence', 101–2.

30. I.A. Burney (2000) *Bodies of Evidence: Medicine and the Politics of the English Inquest, 1830–1926* (Baltimore and London: Johns Hopkins University Press).

31. See for instance M.B. Emmerichs (2001) 'Getting Away with Murder: Homicide and the Coroners in Nineteenth-century London', *Social Science History*, 25, 1, 94–100, at 97 and especially J.A. Sharpe (2007) 'The State and Criminal Violence in the Eighteenth Century: The Evidence of

Cheshire Coroners' Inquests', paper delivered to Crime Violence and the Modern State conference, University of Crete, March.

32. H. Taylor (1998) 'Rationing Crime: The Political Economy of Criminal Statistics since the 1850s', *Economic History Review*, 51, 569–90, at 585.

33. D'Cruze et al., *Murder*, 110–13.

34. See M. Gaskill (2003) *Crime and Mentalities in Early Modern England* (Cambridge: Cambridge University Press).

35. G. Walker (2003) *Crime, Gender and Social Order in Early Modern England* (Cambridge: Cambridge University Press).

36. Ibid., 135.

37. Ibid.

38. Ibid., 118, 121, 140, 145–6.

39. Ibid., 135.

40. Ibid., 135–6.

41. See for instance Barbara Shapiro (2000) *A Culture of Fact: England, 1550–1720* (Ithaca: Cornell University Press), 32 and 206.

42. Gaskill, *Crime and Mentalities*, 279–80 and P.J.R. King (2006) *Crime and Law in England 1750–1840* (Cambridge: Cambridge University Press).

43. D. Hay et al. (1975) *Albion's Fatal Tree: Crime and Society in Eighteenth-century England* (Harmondsworth: Penguin).

44. See J. Humphries (2004) 'Standards of Living and Quality of Life', in C. Williams (ed.), *The Blackwell Companion to the Nineteenth Century* (Oxford: Blackwell), 287–304.

45. V.A.C. Gatrell (1994) *The Hanging Tree: Execution and the English People 1770–1868* (Oxford: Oxford University Press).

46. See J. Horder (1992) *Provocation and Responsibility* (Oxford: Oxford University Press) and Wiener, *Men of Blood*, passim.

47. See Wiener, *Men of Blood*, passim.

48. See G. Robb and N. Erber (eds.) (1999) *Disorder in the Court: Trials and Sexual Conflict at the Turn of the Century* (Basingstoke: Macmillan).

49. See for instance A. Ballinger (2007) 'Masculinity in the Dock: Legal Responses to Male Violence and Female Retaliation in England and Wales, 1900 to 1965', *Social Legal Studies*, 16, 459–81 and S. D'Cruze and L. Jackson (eds.) (2009) *Women, Crime and Justice Since 1660* (Basingstoke: Palgrave Macmillan), Chapters 7 and 9.

50. See G. Frost (2004) '"She is but a woman": Kitty Byron and the English Edwardian Criminal Justice System', in S. D'Cruze and A. Rao (eds.), *Violence, Vulnerability and Embodiment, Gender and History* [Special Issue], 16, 538–60 and A. Ballinger (2000) *Dead Woman Walking: Executed Women in England and Wales, 1900–1955*, (Dartmouth: Ashgate).

51. See J.B. Christoph (1962) *Capital Punishment and British Politics: The British Movement to Abolish the Death Penalty* (London: Allen & Unwin).

52. See, *Daily Mail*, 10 May 1924, 7, 9–10.

53. L. Bland (2000) 'The Trial of Madame Fahmy: Orientalism, Violence, Sexual Perversity and the Fear of Miscegenation', in S. D'Cruze (ed.), *Everyday Violence in Britain c.1850–c. 1950: Gender and Class* (Harlow: Pearson), 185–97.

54. See Ballinger, *Dead Woman Walking* and J.G. Hall and G.D. Smith (1997) *R. v Bywaters and Thompson* (Chichester: Barry Rose Law Publications).

55. See Lord Russell of Liverpool (1965) *Deadman's Hill: Was Hanratty Guilty?*, (London: Secker & Warburg) and L. Blom-Cooper (1968) *The A6 Murder: Regina v. James Hanratty – The Semblance of Truth* (Harmondsworth: Penguin).

56. D'Cruze et al., *Murder*, 88–92.

57. See for instance J. Radford and D.E. Russell (1992) *Femicide: Politics of Woman Killing* (Buckingham: Open University Press); M. Hester et al. (1996) *Women, Violence, and Male Power: Feminist Activism, Research, and Practice* (Buckingham: Open University Press); Law Commission (2003) *Partial Defences to Murder: A Consultation Paper* at http://www.lawcom.gov.uk/docs/cp173.pdf; Ibrams 1981 74 Cr App Rep 154; Thornton 1992 All ER 306, Crim LR 54 SBC 483 and Ahluwalia 1992 4 All ER 889 1993 Crim LR 63.

58. What follows is a necessarily brief outline of a very complex case. Readers wanting to explore further will find abundant primary and secondary material in the references below.

59. Investigations of the A6 murder include Lord Russell of Liverpool, *Deadman's Hill*; Blom-Cooper, *The A6 Murder*; Paul Foot (1973) *Who Killed Hanratty?* (London: Jonathan Cape) and Bob Woffinden (1997) *Hanratty: The Final Verdict* (London: Macmillan). Woffinden and Foot argue Hanratty's innocence. Leonard Miller (2001) *Shadows of Deadman's Hill: A New Analysis of the A6 Murder* (London: Zoilus Press) thinks him guilty. The evidence is fairly fully reviewed in the 2002 Appeal Court Judgement [2002] EWCA Crim 1141 of 10 May 2002, available at http://www.ccrc.gov.ukcases/case_referred.asp.

60. Foot, *Who Killed Hanratty?*, passim.

61. C. Emsley (1996) *The English Police: A Political and Social History* (2nd edn., London: Longman), Chapter 7.

62. [2002] EWCA Crim 1141; no 52.

63. *Horizon: The A6 murder*, BBC Two, 9.00 pm, Thursday 16 May 2002, programme transcript, http://www.bbc.co.uk/science/horizon/2001/a6murder trans.shtml.

64. P. Foot, *Guardian*, 13 May 2002.

65. A. Welsh (1992) *Strong Representations: Narrative and Circumstantial Evidence in England* (Baltimore, MD: John Hopkins University Press).

66. *Horizon:* programme transcript; see note 63 above.

67. See Fiona Barton, *Mail on Sunday*, 28 April 2002, 45.

68. M. Peelo and K. Soothill (2000) 'The Place of Public Narratives in Reproducing Social Order', *Theoretical Criminology*, 4, 131–48 and C. Valier (2002) 'Punishment, Border Crossings and the Powers of Horror', *Theoretical Criminology*, 6, 319–37.

69. R. Mawby and S. Walklate (1994) *Critical Victimology: International Perspectives* (London: Sage).

70. P. Rock (1998) *After Homicide* (Oxford: Clarendon).

71. G. Howarth and P. Rock (2000) 'Aftermath and the Construction of Victimization: "The Other Victims of Crime"', *Howard Journal*, 39, 58–78.

6 Criminality, Deviance and the Underworld since 1750

Heather Shore

1. Introduction

The underworld is a nebulous concept, not easy to capture and record. Whilst scholarly understandings recognise that crime and deviance are subject to networks, organisation and subcultures, the historical underworld has become obscured by cultural production. How to define the underworld is a problem. Thus it is not a 'thing' or a place; nor is it a set of practices, nor simply a literary construction. Our problems with definition lie in two broad areas. First, the underworld suggests something covert. The criminals who are associated with the underworld are those who are generally caught and have become involved in the criminal justice machinery. Yet a great deal of organised crime is undetectable, and certainly invisible to all but those most closely involved.[1] As historians we can only hope to capture fragments of this covert world in its overlapping with the various branches of criminal justice. Secondly, the historical underworld has become defined by a series of vignettes. These are the stories of real life criminals and detectives that have shaped and continue to shape how we see the underworld. In many ways they are a set of myths, far removed from the original events or personalities involved. The Victorian 'underworld' is vicariously lived through the writings of the middle-class social investigators who recorded the lives of the criminal and dangerous classes, and through the gaslit lens of Whitechapel, circa 1888. Similarly the early twentieth-century underworld culturally belongs to the drugs, bohemia, and razor-gangs of the inter-war period. Later, in the new world order of the post-war, *Fabian of the Yard* played to the new television medium of the 1950s, and 'gangland' flourished with the Kray Twins and the Great Train Robbery emerging as the front-page news of the 1960s.[2] Thus the focus for the historian of the underworld and organised crime is in the nature of relationships: the relationships between criminals and police; between criminals, law enforcers and historical media; between police, media and the public; between families, community and immigrant networks. The historian of the underworld thus charts the relationships between those highly visible accounts of the underworld and the 'routine' crime investigated by historians of petty crime, property crime and violence: police and court records; the records of the home office; trial and press reports. Indeed, many of the criminals are the same; at the very least they shared lives – the street, the public house and the workplace.

Ultimately, there are many models of the underworld. On the one hand is the world of criminality outside the basic structures of the criminal justice system. Thus it is the interactions and processes that create criminals and deviancy.[3] On the other hand is a highly organised world, with systems, structures and hierarchies. This paradigm of the professional underworld continues to dominate political and media representations of organised crime. However, the underclass is also periodically popular in public opinion about crime. This chapter aims to investigate some of these models and representations, and hopefully, in the process, to produce a more nuanced account of the meaning of the underworld. Section 2 will take a chronological approach, and consider a number of key-points which, arguably, have shaped historical understandings of organised crime and the underworld. Section 3 will explore the methodologies and approaches which have been used by both historians and criminologists. Section 4 will illustrate these approaches with reference to a selection of case-studies.

2. Chronology of Organised Crime

Perhaps the most useful way to organise a chronological overview of the historical underworld is to consider it in definitional contexts. Key terminology which is employed includes: gangs and gangland, organised crime, professional criminals and underworld. Other than references to gangs, none of these terms are used prior to the late nineteenth and early twentieth centuries, and others considerably later.[4] Certainly, as the early modern literature suggests, ways of referring to the criminal milieu were present historically. However it was the coming of urban infrastructures, particularly those associated with policing, the press and the maintenance of public order, which impart a degree of credibility to this terminology.

For criminologists, Jonathan Wild marks the first widely known example of criminal activity, with a recognisable element of organisation.

Wild came into prominence on the wave of crime which periodically surfaced in London between 1680 and 1720, and shaped both official and public ideas about crime both during the 1710s and 1720s, and after his execution in 1725.[5] The historical character of Wild is so interesting because he has arguably become a symbol for our knowledge about the history of crime, of policing and of writing about crime. Thus Wild was allegedly involved in a number of illegal enterprises, including fencing stolen goods, organising and running criminal gangs and extortion, as well as corruption in his public career as a thief-taker. Wild's ascendancy coincided with the peak of criminal biography. These hack-written accounts of criminal lives, often hurriedly produced for the scaffold audience, were an extremely popular form of cheap literature throughout the eighteenth century, although by the 1760s popular demand for this type of literature was waning.[6] In many ways publications such as the Old Bailey Sessions Papers, the Ordinary of Newgate's Account and the Last Dying Speeches of Criminals reflected contemporary fears about urban crime. Hence, they contained largely stereotypical portrayals of criminals and often had a didactic purpose. The highwayman was perhaps the most notorious and most romantic figure to emerge from this literature. Even by the mid-Victorian period the highwayman, long banished from the heaths and byways, predominated in juvenile literature.[7]

In its more mundane guise highway robbery was taken seriously by the authorities, and those caught were very likely to end up on the gallows. In many ways this is because highway robbery was associated with recidivism, and it was recidivists, or at least 'known' offenders who were most likely to be executed in the eighteenth century. Such 'known' criminals were frequently portrayed as being allied to a criminal gang. Whilst references to gangs can be found in pre-modernity, during the eighteenth century the emergence of a vociferous magistracy in London who were vocally engaged on a war upon crime focused attention on the proliferation of gangs in the metropolis. Henry Fielding boasted about his gang-busting activities in mid-eighteenth-century London, stating that under his remit at the Bow Street Office, he 'undertook to demolish the reigning gangs, and to put the civil policy into such order, that no gangs should ever be able, for the future, to form themselves into bodies, or at least to remain any time formidable to the public'.[8] However, one of the most notorious cases involving an organised criminal gang in this period would again expose the blurred boundaries between criminal activity and law enforcement in this period. Thus the MacDaniel gang, who were active about the time that Fielding was writing, involved a number of thief-takers who perverted justice by manipulating the rewards system.[9]

By the later eighteenth century policing initiatives to combat organised crime were being proposed by John Fielding.[10] Fielding was convinced that some sort of clearing-house for information was the best way to control criminal gangs. He published his General Preventative Plan in 1772–3 (developed with a grant of £400 from the Treasury), using the *Hue and Cry* as a way of publicising 'informations' from around the country.[11] Nevertheless, the gathering of criminal intelligence seems to have been somewhat marginalised in the police reforms of the 1790s onwards, which arguably focused much more on prevention, with a focus on physical presence and visibility, rather than detection.[12] Whilst at grassroots level, the police were concerned with breaking criminal networks and particularly with policing the various flash-houses and disreputable public houses which were felt to encourage crime, more publicly the focus seemed to be on petty street crime and the maintenance of public order.[13]

During the nineteenth century, concepts of criminal organisation moved away from the picaresque to be influenced by a new set of discourses. The most important of these was the emergence of a class discourse, and particularly the discussion of class in relationship to skills and categorisation. In the context of crime and criminality, the class discourse would take its most obvious shape with the evolution of the concept of the 'criminal class'. However, earlier ideas about the nature of class and crime proliferated and were publicised through social investigation. Arguably, these investigations built upon the mass of enquiry into policing and law enforcement that took place in the years prior to 1829. Hence it was the increasing organisation of law enforcement that in many ways led to the public belief in a criminal underworld or criminal class. The police had been central in the process of stigmatising certain areas as criminal milieu. During the early nineteenth century a number of schemes for policing the metropolis by both insiders in the criminal justice system, and by what might be called amateur reformers, were being suggested.[14] These schemes were strongly centred on identification, surveillance and supervision of criminal districts in London, echoing Fielding's scheme of the previous century. For example the Select Committee on Police in the Metropolis of 1816 extensively examined police surveillance of the flash-houses.[15] However, it was not until the establishment of the metropolitan police that such schemes were to become a more realistic strategy. The consequent increase in policing activity clearly aided in the redefinition of both criminal and poor space in London.

Whilst criminal intelligence was not to develop a great deal over the following decades, the raft of government investigation into law enforcement did much to sharpen public fears about the underworld in the early nineteenth century.[16] By the 1830s and 1840s, when a new generation of social investigators were treading the streets of London, a more specific spatial map of the underworld seemed to be evolving. As well as those areas which were already established as being a problem, such as St. Giles (with its large Irish population) and the Haymarket (notorious for street prostitution); the rookeries of Westminster (near Tothill Fields prison),

Field Lane and Saffron Hill and areas around the docks and to the east of the city were frequently evoked.[17] Of course all these areas had long been synonymous with plebeian and working-class lives. However, the criminal milieu was irresistible to Victorian social commentators. From the mid-nineteenth century the metropolis was apparently awash with social investigators, urban explorers, proto-anthropologists and missionaries. These texts, which have been heavily relied upon by orthodox historians of the Victorian underworld, provided a moral gazetteer for the armchair traveller of London's criminal rookeries and enclaves.[18] More importantly, they were to influence the emergent notion of a criminal class. This was an idea that was closely tied to new ways of understanding crime, poverty and delinquency in the nineteenth century. Established concepts fused with the emergence of class discourses, then scientific and ethnic discourses, to produce an increasingly confused and often unrealistic understanding of crime by the end of the century. Moreover, the notion of the criminal class was to be supported with the legal recognition of the recidivist within the categorisation of the habitual criminal from the 1860s.

The early twentieth century underworld was increasingly made visible due to a combination of police work, press coverage and wider cultural influences which shaped the public perception of gangsters. For example, during the late nineteenth and early twentieth centuries there was a proliferation of police biography. This was partly as a result of the growing professionalisation of the detective departments with the reformation of the Criminal Investigation Department in 1877, and the formation of the Flying Squad from 1919, which was to be essentially concerned with the detection and prevention of organised crime.

During the interwar period criminal organisation seems to have become more visibly intertwined with the various economies which structured British life. In particular, what might broadly be conceived as the leisure industry provided a lucrative field for would-be criminal entrepreneurs. Betting and gambling and subsequently, the protection industry, were key fields of operations for versions of organised crime. Thus various groups fought for dominance of the racecourses of the Midlands and the South-East of England throughout the 1920s and 1930s. Another institution which increasingly came to be the focus of press concern during the interwar period was the nightclub. Nightclubs, particularly those of the metropolis, were graphically described by contemporary commentators as a space for any number of illegalities. Through a series of highly sensationalised accounts concerns about drinking, prostitution, drugs and promiscuity (particularly that which might lead to miscegenation) were mediated.

The Second World War, arguably, consolidated these overlapping sets of illegalities into something more recognisably akin to late modern organised crime. The interwar period had seen the expansion of sex traffic, and increased police vigilance of the organised sex trade. The history of the 'underworld' from the 1940s became much more characterised by home-grown 'villains', the emergence of the gangland which was to peak perhaps most visibly in the 1960s with the ascendancy of Ronald and Reginald Kray, and the emergence of large-scale armed robberies, represented in particular by the events of the Great Train Robbery of 1963. Despite the dominance of metropolitan actors, in the post-war drama of 'gangland', the tentacles spread across the nation. For example Glasgow was known for its turf wars throughout the later twentieth century, arguably peak-ing in the 1980s in the 'ice cream wars', fought in Glasgow and beyond.[19] In late-modernity, practitioner and academic have refocused to reflect the globalisation of organised crime, alongside the growing links with politi-cal terrorism. For example, there is evidence that as early as the 1980s, the IRA was using the proceeds of drug trafficking in Northern Ireland to fund its activities.[20] Indeed, such is the lack of agreement between criminolo-gists about what constitutes organised crime, that the 'disorganised crime' thesis has increasingly gained in popularity.[21]

3. Historiography

From a historical point of view, there have been few serious scholarly attempts which try to understand how crime works outside the straight-forward mechanisms which we know from our knowledge of the criminal justice system. Popular histories have tended to dominate the field, along-side literary analysis of crime texts in the eighteenth and nineteenth centu-ries, and criminological and psychological studies in the twentieth century. Moreover, the chronological history of the underworld and historiography are closely intertwined. Historians have rarely tried to conceptualise or overview the underworld, and so their analysis and descriptions have tended to focus on fairly self-contained historical periods.[22] Historians have also overwhelmingly tended to focus on the metropolitan underworld. Moreover, in much of the writing on forms of criminal organisation, there remains a tension between the activities of the authorities and the iden-tification and control of specific offenders (or types of offender) on the one hand, and the promulgation of mythologies and typographies through criminal biography, confessions and trial reports on the other. Studies by Gerald Howson, John Beattie, and for an earlier period, John McMullan, have greatly enhanced our understanding of the relationship between met-ropolitan networks and urban, parochial authorities.[23] Indeed Ruth Paley's research on the McDaniel Gang illuminated the flexibility and abuses of what was a highly discretionary system of law enforcement.[24] The rela-tionship between myth and reality in the eighteenth-century underworld has also been explored by historians of highway robbery, such as James Sharpe, Robert Shoemaker, and Gillian Spraggs.[25] In his recent survey of the highwayman, Sharpe points to two pertinent issues:

> The first is the nature of legend, of how it gets created and perpetuated, an issue that also leads us into contemplating the nature of fame. The second is the relationship between history and legend, and, by extension, of how the two operate in our modern culture, and how we draw on them to imagine the past.[26]

For historians of the nineteenth century, imagination and speculation have been the predominant means of constructing narratives of the underworld. The most prevalent accounts of the historical underworld have tended to come from more 'orthodox' historians of crime, who have read developments in criminal justice as essentially humane and progressive. For such writers as J.J. Tobias, Kellow Chesney and Donald Thomas, there is a clear sense of division between the underworld and 'upper world'. Such texts are essentially descriptive and reliant on the most familiar and most accessible primary texts.[27] For example, Donald Thomas's 1998 monograph, *The Victorian Underworld*, was narrowly based on published work by Henry Mayhew and John Binny, and well-known texts such as *My Secret Life*, published in around 1888 by the pseudonymous 'Walter'.[28] These essentially uncritical texts reveal to us a great deal about contemporary fears and attitudes to crime, but little about reality. A much more critical stance was developed through the scholarly apparatus of 'history from below', and particularly the Thompsonian conceptualisation of 'social crime', which helped historians to understand the way in which communities developed legitimising notions, a 'moral economy', to justify illegal activities in the face of social, economic and political marginalisation.[29] Probably the most impassioned of Thompson's disciples was Peter Linebaugh, who was always interested in applying Thompsonian models to eighteenth-century urban crime (rather than the rural and coastal illegalities which were the focus of much of this work).[30] Linebaugh, along with historians like David Philips and Jennifer Davies writing about the nineteenth century, did much to reveal the essential similarities between a dishonest 'criminal class' and the plebeian/working class.[31] Other studies, such as John Archer's work on poaching, have touched on the marginal relationship between criminal networks and economic activities. However, these accounts are not specifically interested in organised crime.[32] Clive Emsley writes: 'The notion of a criminal class was, indeed remains, a convenient one for insisting that most crime is committed on law-abiding citizens by an alien group. The more historians probe the notion, the more it is revealed to be spurious.'[33] Indeed, adventurous work by more culturally focused historians such as Randall McGowen have reinvestigated the notion, and argued that literary texts 'played a central role in helping Victorians to know their criminal class'.[34]

The spatial and territorial outlines of the underworld have been the concern of a number of historians of nineteenth- and early twentieth-century crime. This is perhaps not surprising given the redefinition of criminal areas during the nineteenth century, a process which, as we have seen, was aided and abetted by the formation of the Metropolitan Police, and further shaped by the vagaries of slum clearance and metropolitan improvement. The increasing preoccupation of the police with criminal area has frequently rested on understandings of metropolitan space.[35] However, criminality and gang activity has also been mapped in other urban spaces of the nineteenth and early twentieth centuries. For example David Jones discussed the 'China' district of Merthyr Tydfil in the nineteenth century, described by contemporaries as a criminal Alsatia.[36] A growing number of studies have investigated the 'turf wars' of Sheffield and Salford in the later nineteenth century and interwar Glasgow.[37] Andrew Davies's work, for example, focuses on the complex relationship between unemployment, gang formation and criminality in Glasgow during the 1930s, suggesting some of the problems of how we read and understand contemporary language and rhetoric. Thus what the police and contemporary press define as a criminal gang can clearly have a number of meanings and contexts.[38] The growing focus on urban, industrial spaces as 'underworld' sites is certainly a feature of later twentieth-century crime studies. Despite these forays into Britain's industrial conurbations, gravity time and again pulls the historian of the underworld back to London as the key site for criminal organisation, as we see in recent work on the metropolitan sex trade by Stefan Slater.[39] London's dominance again reminds us of the role of cultural production. In terms of literature, visual imagery, film and press media, the metropolis has a vividness and glamour with which few other cities can compete. Indeed, despite consistent representations of what might be called organised crime in London from at least the early modern period, the tendency of criminologists and sociologists has been to link the development of the underworld with the emergence of modernity.[40] Undoubtedly there are things that are 'new' in modern ideas about the underworld and organised crime (for example the impact of globalisation and the corresponding emergence of concepts like glocalisation and transnational organised crime).[41] But many inherent features and causal factors remain the same (for example the importance of kinship, territory, immigration and violence as a means of enforcement). This is particularly true of the criminal gang.

Whilst the gang has for a long time symbolised the human face of organised crime, there is a lack of consensus between modern gang scholars as to a clear definition of what a gang constitutes. Part of the problem is the hegemony of the youth and street gang in the literature. Thus from the late nineteenth century, the gang became most associated with the street activities of young men. Contemporaneously, academics were starting to examine the gang as a social phenomenon.[42] Perhaps most notable is the early criminological work of the Chicago School in the inter-war period of the twentieth century, particularly the research of Frederic Thrasher, who published *The Gang: A Study of 1313 Gangs in Chicago* in 1927.[43] Such youth street gangs can refer to a group defined in various ways: age, territorial alignments, ethnicity, violence and masculinity.[44] Indeed, some attempt at consensus has been worked out by gang researchers in the USA and Europe, who arrived at the following definition: 'A street gang is any durable, street-orientated youth group whose own identity includes involvement in illegal activity.'[45] This definition works very well for the historical research that has been undertaken into such street youth gangs. These are gangs that seem to have developed from the late nineteenth century in response to a certain set of economic and social conditions, and are perhaps described most eloquently by Geoffrey Pearson in his book, *Hooligan: A History of Respectable Fears* (1983).[46] A more detailed analysis of specific street-gangs can be found in Andrew Davies's research on later nineteenth-century Salford and interwar Glasgow.[47] The model is also recognisable in the postwar concern about gangs of Teddy Boys, who were frequently described as being involved in illegalities. The Teds were also strongly equated with the violent resolution of conflicts around territory and masculinity, as evidenced by the murder of John Beckley on Clapham Common in 1954.[48]

Whilst these historical street gangs may well have networked with older, more established criminals, the graduation of young men from street gangs to more sophisticated, organised criminal gangs is not at all clear-cut,[49] although in interwar Glasgow there is some evidence of progression, as Andrew Davies points out in his study of the Beehive Boys.[50] Philip Jenkins and Gary Potter have written about the 'golden age' of British gangsterdom in the postwar period.[51] Most notorious were the 1960s and early 1970s, when the family firm rose to prominence in the guise of east Londoners Reginald and Ronald Kray, and Charlie and Eddie Richardson south of the river. However, as Jenkins and Potter point out, the events of these years were far from novel. The 'family firm', for example, can be found in the interwar period, in the protection and gambling networks of the Sabini family, and in the activities of the vice networks of the Messina family in 1940s and 1950s Soho.

Organised crime itself is a heavily contested concept. Sociologists and criminologists started to debate the definition of organised crime in the 1960s. Much of this discussion took place in, and with reference to, the USA. Partly this was a response to the prevalence of fears about organised crime at that time, and particularly its conspiratorial nature and apparent links to American politics. Donald Cressey, author of the influential if contested work on the Mafia, *The Theft of the Nation*, became a key commentator.[52] One of the reasons why criminological attempts to define organised crime have been so contested is due to the problematic relationship between academics, practitioners and government. It is not easy to separate pure, academic explanations for organised crime from legal and political contexts. Moreover, as Alan Wright points out, these definitions are frequently resource-driven: 'It is clearly in the interests of legislators, policy makers and law enforcement agents to regard organised crime as a well-defined concept with identifiable structures. It is something about which they can make rational decisions.'[53] A recent, loose definition has come from the Serious and Organised Crime Agency (SOCA). This British body, established in 2006, described its remit as covering 'a very wide range of activity and individuals involved in a number of crime sectors'; however, the key targets are crimes relating to drug trafficking and immigration.[54] Why is this important to how we understand organised crime in the past? First, because historians have no theoretical model to explain criminal organisation, we need to draw from cognate disciplines to aid our explanations.[55] Secondly, now we are arguably in a state of late modernity, the 'modernity' of the nineteenth and twentieth centuries has become subject to historicisation. Thus the very process of contesting definitions has become part of the historical landscape. Understanding the extent to which definitions of organised crime are both contested and context-sensitive enables us to question the teleological view of organised crime. Certainly, modernity has provided society with structures, institutions and opportunities which may have increased the commission of crime. However, the organisation of crime is an historical constant. Thus in different times, in different ways, people have come together in alliances to commit events which are defined according to contemporary political and legal apparatus, as illegal.

4. Case Studies

a) The 'Making' of the Criminal Class

Several elements contributed to the making of the criminal class in nineteenth-century Britain. Social journalism and investigation arguably fused the literary genres that characterised the 1830s and 1840s, the Newgate novel and the Condition of England novel. Thus Dickens's and Gaskell's evocative portrayals of poverty and crime, both in London and in the growing industrial conurbations of the North, established a colourful and vital tradition of describing the poor, echoing elements of the rogue and picaresque literatures of an earlier period. Perhaps more original in the nineteenth century was the blending of these elements with social critique, laying the model for much of the quasi-literary commentary that was to appear over the subsequent decades. The sheer level of detail provided in the accounts taken by John Binny, published in Volume 4 of Mayhew in 1861, further strengthened the belief in crime as an organised activity, committed by a 'class' of criminals. The story of 'Dick', who described his life from his early 'career' as a pickpocket in the 1830s, would have been familiar to readers of Dickens's *Oliver Twist*.[56] The criminal class had historically been described as resourceful, flash, and prone to displaying their ill-gotten gain. For example, in the early nineteenth century contemporaries described the Swell-mob, gangs of young thieves and burglars who were frequently seen at the races spending money, escorting prostitutes and dressing 'swell'. As *Blackwood's Magazine* asked in 1841: 'Who would suppose, for example, that those young men at the corner, dressed in the height of the Cockney fashion, bedizened with mosaic jewellery, and puffing their cigars, are members of the swell mob – thieves, in short, and pickpockets?'[57]

The category of 'habitual criminal' was created with the passage of the 1869 Habitual Criminals Act and the 1871 Prevention of Crime Act, which gave the police extended supervisory powers over known offenders, and in consequence helped foster the notion of a criminal class.[58] Despite this, as Simon Stevenson has shown, the actual number of 'habituals' was very limited, and hardly representative of a class.[59] The idea of a skilled, professional and habitual criminal class came to dominate political and cultural, and to some extent practitioners', concepts of crime. Yet, the 'criminal class' was used to refer to a wide sector of the mainly urban poor. Gareth Stedman Jones and John Welshman have argued that this was a way of marginalising even further the 'residuum' or underclass.[60] The idea of the social residuum re-emerged with some force from the 1880s. A combination of factors explains its predominance from this period: new theories of degeneration, infrastructural problems with housing, unemployment and the resulting labour strikes such as the dock strike of 1889. However, more recently, historians have argued that there is rather more continuity with earlier ideas about the poor, which long predated the 'crisis' of the 1880s.[61]

During the early and later nineteenth century, the locale of this 'criminal class' would evolve. Dickens's Field Lane destroyed by the coming of the railway, and the slums around Seven Dials and Tothill Fields prison in Westminster had been removed.[62] Thus a mixture of slum clearance, transport infrastructure, public health legislation and philanthropic activity substantially altered the spatial map of crime in London. Acts such as the 1855 Metropolitan Local Management Act and the 1875 Artisans' and Labourers' Dwellings Improvement Act allowed local councils to do piecemeal slum clearance and rebuilding, which enabled them to focus very directly on areas with reputations for criminality. The latter legislation, also known as Cross's Act, sought out the 'rookeries' which had been identified by the social investigators of the previous decades. By the later nineteenth century, whilst criminal enclaves may have remained, there was generally a much greater segregation on lines driven by class and economic-basis.[63] As Richard Sennet commented, London was a collection of 'class homogenous, disconnected spaces'.[64] Thus the east side of London, both north and south of the river, now housed the working class and the new wave of immigrants which would appear from the later decades of the nineteenth century. As Gareth Stedman Jones pointed out, it was also from these areas that trade-union organisation and direct action would emerge. Thus 'Outcast London' would be set against the more affluent and prosperous West End. Whilst East and South London may well have been the habitus of working-class criminals, it was the commercial West End which, during the twentieth century, would increasingly be the site of organised criminal activity. Criminals were drawn to the clubs and businesses of this area as a commercial decision. However, there is no real evidence to suggest that these shifts, in both commercial and residential spheres, were particularly new.

b) Kinship, Territory and Violent Crime

Concern about violent street crime, 'turf' wars, and street-fighting gangs had periodically occurred throughout the later nineteenth century, particularly in London, Birmingham, Liverpool and Manchester. After the First World War concerns about such violence were fused with a growing awareness of organised protection rackets. During the interwar period, attention was particularly focused on the activities of the race gangs, or as they also became known, the razor-gangs. The Clerkenwell-based Sabini family (second-generation Irish-Italian brothers) were frequently implicated in the physical violence which was employed in order to gain control of lucrative pitches, but also to solve territorial clashes. Confrontations were widely reported in the press and the most celebrated of these was the 'Derby Day Battle' on 2 June 1921. A rival Birmingham gang had lain in wait for the Sabinis after the Epsom Derby, and hijacked and attacked a charabanc full of bookies from Leeds, having mistaken them for the Sabinis. A local police Sergeant named Dawson, fearing the men were Sinn Feiners, held the men at gunpoint. As the press reported, 'Pulling out his revolver, the sergeant said, "THE FIRST MAN WHO MOVES I WILL SHOOT".'[65] In many ways this event does much to help in our understanding of organised crime in this period. First, in terms of press involvement, the coverage of the racecourse gangs, and the Sabinis in particular, was extensive both in the local and national press. This was the first time that there had been such widespread press coverage of criminal gangs. Arguably there was a moral panic about violent crime at this time, although Clive Emsley believes this to have been overstated.[66] By the mid-1920s the racecourse conflicts seem to have metamorphosed into a much wider problem. Thus, in August 1925, after a series of incidents allegedly involving 'racing men', the *Daily Express* announced that the Home Secretary had declared war on the race gangs.[67] They also printed a list of 'gang outrages' which had apparently occurred in London and other parts of the country between March 1924 and August 1925.[68] The country, it seems, was gripped by rowdyism. Yet even at the time there was scepticism about the extent of the problem. As a response to the *Daily Express* reports, the Commissioner of Police held talks with the Secretary of State, as a result of which he initiated a full investigation into the 'alleged disturbances by race gangs' in London.[69] They found the version of events portrayed by the *Express* to be vastly overstated, with little evidence in many of the cases of any involvement of racing men.[70] Moreover, whilst the London gangs were perhaps the most visible, owing to the press coverage, similar conflicts could be found in other British cities during the 1920s and 1930s.

For example, the conflicts between the Park Brigade and Mooney Gang in Sheffield in many ways resonate with the events in London. Sam Garvin, the apparent head of the Park Brigade, according to J.P. Bean, 'frequented race-meetings' and 'occasionally stood as a bookmaker'.[71] The Sheffield gangs were 'stamped out' by Percy Sillitoe, the Chief Constable, who in the 1930s went on to offer 'a dramatic challenge to ruffianism in Glasgow'.[72] In Glasgow there was a strong press involvement in building up the drama of gang conflict. Andrew Davies's study draws from various feature articles from both local and national newspapers such as the *Sunday Mail*, *Sunday Dispatch* and *Evening Times*. As he points out, of the last of these mentioned, 'the *Evening Times* had itself carried hundreds of reports of the city's gang conflicts during the late 1920s and early 1930s, many of them highly sensationalised'.[73] One way of understanding the press preoccupation with gangsterdom from this period is to think about it in terms of contemporary cultural events. Thus the influence of American gangster culture can be sensed in the reporting of Sergeant Dawson's gunpoint arrest at Epsom. More generally, by the late 1920s and 1930s, before the censorship of the Hay's Code, gangster films were the dominant genre.[74] Films like *Little Caesar* (1930), *The Public Enemy* (1931) and *Scarface* (1932) were hugely influential in shaping ideas about organised crime both in the USA and Britain. Prior to this, 'true crime' was available in the form of pulp fiction which was available in Britain from the 1920s.[75]

c) Organised Vice

By the 1940s, metropolitan vice networks were dominated by the Maltese family, the Messinas.[76] The Messinas are important as they have been identified by scholars as being more closely associated with the American model of organised crime, and particularly with the emergence in Britain of 'syndicated' crime. Nevertheless, Philip Jenkins and Gary W. Potter have suggested that the Messinas 'were simply one manifestation of a long-standing urban phenomenon, a well-known system closely tied to networks of corruption and illicit finance'.[77] Much of the notoriety of the Messinas is due to their public exposure and 'exposé' by the crime reporter Duncan Webb. In 1950, *The People* published photographs of Messina girls, and the family were essentially accused of being white-slavers.[78] In his autobiography, *Crime is my Business,* published in 1953, Webb described his investigation into the Messina's 'empire'. Ordered by his editor to 'Smash this gang of ponces', Webb boasted: 'So I smashed it. And I drove the fragments whence they came; back to the brothels and gutters of the back streets of Europe.'[79]

Whilst the Messinas clearly played an important role in London's vice underworld, it is important to consider the relationship between their apparent notoriety and this 'exposé'. Thus contemporary accounts of the Messinas' activities have been questioned by scholars such as Edward Smithies.[80] The Messina exposé once again draws a triangular relationship between the press, the police and the villain, with Webb's suggestions of collusion between the Messinas and Scotland Yard.[81] In many ways the Messinas mark a new type of criminal organisation. Whilst territory was still important, the more prosaic world of racketeering, protection and gang violence with which the Sabinis were associated had been replaced by what was to become known as syndicated crime. Of course, the Messinas' notoriety also stemmed from their 'alien' origins. The five Messina brothers were the offspring of a Sicilian father and Maltese mother. Their father Giuseppe had apparently operated vice networks in Malta and Egypt.[82] The Messinas tapped into current fears about alienism and miscegenation which had already been raised by the concerns about foreign prostitutes in the interwar period.[83] Thus they were one of a number of family and community networks involved in illegal networks, whose characterisation in press and police commentary emphasised their 'foreignness'. Although, unlike the Sabinis or various Jewish and Irish criminals who were often second-generation Londoners, the Messinas' network had arrived fairly fully formed in the early 1930s.[84] The Messinas were finally 'broken' in Britain in the 1950s, although according to Jenkins and Potter they maintained their operations on the Continent, and kept interests in Soho at least until the 1970s.[85]

5. Conclusion

Most criminologists would agree that it was the latter part of the twentieth century in which organised crime made its most major transitions.[86]

Certainly the proliferation of capital from the late eighteenth century provided an earlier period of transition. The institutions and practices that arose out of urban, industrial, capital-based society in nineteenth-century Britain provided the conditions and opportunities for professional forms of crime to develop. Nevertheless, the meaning of organisation has to be considered. Thus organisation, in this case, suggests often loose networks drawn from communities, families or workplace relationships. For instance, the nexus of relationships that can be identified in the family firms of the interwar and postwar period of the twentieth century could be found in earlier generations. In the late twentieth century, on the other hand, striking changes converged which would help to shape a land of opportunity for the enterprising criminal. Drugs, finance, people trafficking and most latterly, the internet now dominate the international markets for organised crime.

According to Dick Hobbs, 'Professional crime has moved from an occupational foundation of neighbourhood-orientated extortion and individualistic craft-based larcenies towards an entrepreneurial trading culture driven by highly localised interpretations of global markets.'[87] Elsewhere, Hobbs has drawn on the concept of 'glocalisation' in order to illustrate the elements of the old-style 'underworld' that sit alongside the newer, global networks.[88] Hobbs stresses the relationship between the state, the local and the global. Moreover, he argues that the transition from the local nature of earlier forms of criminal organisation has to be understood against the contexts of deindustrialisation and the fragmentation of traditional working-class communities.[89] Short-term contracts and flexibility can be detected in the growing popularity of the long-firm fraud from the 1960s. This type of fraud involved obtaining goods on increasing credit until the company went into liquidation. The fraudulently obtained goods were then sold through the black economy. Such frauds had been running at least since the late nineteenth century.[90] However, they proliferated in the 1960s and were a particular specialism of the Richardsons and Kray brothers.[91] Along with other frauds, the long-firm fraud has gained a new lease of life with the emergence of the internet.[92] Similarly, short-term contracts characterise the major robberies and bullion raids which have occurred since the 1960s. The most notable of these was the theft of £26 million-worth of gold bullion from the Brinks-Mat warehouse at Heathrow airport in 1983. As Wright points out: 'This case is notable for the fact that it brought together a number of prominent criminals, who were free to operate without reference to a dominant criminal group or "crime family".'[93] The globalisation of the drugs market also illustrates how local networks have increasingly merged with global networks. For example, Curtis Warren initially began his 'criminal career' in street gangs in his native Liverpool. However, he developed an extensive network of global producers and traffickers in the 1990s. Warren was prepared to deal with a range of individuals and organisations, including corrupt officials and policemen.[94] This suggests that despite wide-ranging investigations into police corruption in the 1970s and 1980s, police involvement in organised crime operations continued to be a problem.

By the start of the twenty-first century, a new tide of regulation and professionalism was reflected in the creation of the Independent Police Complaints Commission in 2004. In many ways this new era of regulation marks the most recent transitions of organised crime. In previous eras the boundary between police and criminals was always fuzzy. Familiarity with local criminal networks and knowledge of 'faces' were seen as essential to good detection. For example, in his autobiography, published in 1960, the rather loquacious ex-Detective Chief Superintendent, Ted Greeno, active within CID and the Flying Squad in the 1920s, boasted: 'At no cost at all I got to know faces, until I have 10,000 or more "card-indexed" in this peculiar policeman's mind of mine.'[95] Whilst some elements of this 'traditional' localism remain, the paradigm of twenty-first-century organised crime is once again the ethnic crime group. Criminologists have, however, questioned the underlying assumption that organised crime is principally the responsibility of alien groups: 'To suggest that righteous citizens are being perverted, intimidated, and forced into vice by alien forces is far more palatable than suggesting that "native" demands for illicit drugs, sex and gambling invite the creation of organised crime groups.'[96] Finally, Gary W. Potter's perceptive remarks in many ways bring us full circle, at least for the last century or so: migration and immigration; the dissolving of old communities and establishment of new networks and new opportunities; the structures of information and media; the regulation and policing of vice, gambling, drugs, stolen goods and finance, have been the various strands which have colluded together to shape our perception and society's construction of the criminal 'underworld'.

Notes

1. A. Wright (2006) *Organised Crime* (Cullompton: Willan), 2–3.
2. *Fabian of the Yard* ran on BBC television from 1954 to 1956.
3. H.S. Becker (1963) *Outsiders: Studies in the Sociology of Deviance* (New York: The Free Press).
4. H. Shore (2007) '"Undiscovered Country": Towards a History of the Criminal Underworld', *Crimes and Misdemeanours*, 1, 1, 50–1.
5. G. Howson (1970) *Thief-taker General: The Rise and Fall of Jonathan Wild* (London: Hutchinson).
6. I.A. Bell (1991) *Literature and Crime in Augustan England* (London: Routledge) and S. Devereaux (2003) 'The Fall of the Sessions Paper: Criminal Trial and the Popular Press in Late Eighteenth-Century London', *Criminal Justice History*, 18, 57–88.

7. For example Edward Bulwer Lytton (1848) *Paul Clifford* (London: Routledge) and Harrison Ainsworth (1856) *Rookwood* (London: Routledge).

8. Henry Fielding (1755) *A Journey from this World to the Next and the Journey of a Voyage to Lisbon* (London: Harrison).

9. R. Paley. (1989) 'Thief-takers in London in the Age of the McDaniel Gang, c. 1745–1754', in D. Hay and F. Snyder (eds.), *Policing and Prosecution in Britain: 1750–1859* (Oxford: Clarendon Press).

10. J. Styles (1983) 'Sir John Fielding and the Problem of Criminal Investigation in Eighteenth Century England', *Transactions of the Royal Historical Society*, 5th Series, 33, 127–49.

11. TNA: TS 1/498/1–2, 'Memorial of Sir John Fielding for £400, the sum allowed for the expense of his "General Preventative Plan"'. However Fielding had been developing the plan at least since the 1750s; John Fielding (1755) *A Plan for Preventing Robberies within Twenty Miles of London, with an Account of the Rise and Establishment of the Real Thieftakers* (London: A. Miller).

12. C. Emsley (2005) *Crime and Society in England, 1750–1900* (3rd edn, Harlow: Longman), 229–30 and 238.

13. H. Shore (2003) 'Mean Streets: Criminality, Immorality and the Street in Early Nineteenth Century London', in T. Hitchcock and H. Shore (eds.), *The Streets of London: From the Great Fire to the Great Stink* (London: Rivers Oram), 151–64.

14. See L. Radzinowicz (1956) *A History of the English Criminal Law, Vol. 3 – The Reform of the Police* (London: Stevens & Son, 1956), 375–413.

15. For example see *SCPM*, 1816, 21, 48 and 147.

16. S. Petrow (1993) 'The Rise of the Detective in London, 1869–1914', *Criminal Justice History*, 14, 91–108.

17. On the spatial geography of the Victorian underworld see especially D. Green (1986) *People of the Rookery: A Pauper Community in Victorian London* (Kings College London: Department of Geography Occasional Papers, 26).

18. For further exploration of this idea see John Marriott's introduction to J. Marriott and M. Matsumura (eds.) (1999) *The Metropolitan Poor: Semi-Factual Accounts*, 1795–1910, Vol. 1 (London: Pickering & Chatto), xi–l.

19. D. Skelton and L. Brownlie (1992) *Frightener: The Glasgow Ice-cream Wars* (Edinburgh: Mainstream) and '"Ice-cream Wars" Verdicts Squashed as Justice System Faulted', *The Scotsman*, 18 March 2004.

20. P. Bean (2002) *Drugs and Crime* (Cullompton: Willan).

21. P. Reuter (1983) *Disorganised Crime: Illegal Markets and the Mafia – The Economics of the Visible Hand* (London: MIT Press).

22. For exceptions see A. Croll (2004) 'Who's Afraid of the Victorian Underworld?', *The Historian*, 84, 30–5 and Shore, '"Undiscovered Country"', 41–68.

23. J. Beattie (2001) *Policing and Punishment in London 1660–1750: Urban Crime and the Limits of Terror* (Oxford: Oxford University Press); Howson, *Thief-taker General*, passim and J.L. McMullan (1984) *The Canting Crew: London's Criminal Underworld*, 1550–1700 (New Brunswick, NJ: Rutgers University Press).

24. Paley, 'Thief-takers', passim.
25. J. Sharpe (2005) *Dick Turpin: The Myth of the English Highwayman* (London: Profile); R.B. Shoemaker (2006) 'The Street Robber and the Gentleman Highwayman: Changing Representations and Perceptions of Robbery in London, 1690–1800', *Cultural and Society History*, 3:4, 381–405 and G. Spraggs (2001) *Outlaws and Highwaymen: The Cult of the Robber in England from the Middle Ages to the Nineteenth Century* (London: Pimlico).
26. Sharpe, *Dick Turpin*, 9.
27. See for instance J.J. Tobias (1967) *Crime and Industrial Society* (London: Batsford); J.J. Tobias (1972) *Nineteenth Century Crime: Prevention and Punishment* (Newton Abbot: David & Charles); K. Chesney (1970) *The Victorian Underworld* (London: Maurice Temple Smith); D. Thomas (1998) *Victorian Underworld* (London: Murray); D. Thomas (2003) *An Underworld at War* (London: Murray) and D. Thomas (2005) *Villains Paradise: Britain's Underworld from the Spivs to the Krays* (London: Murray).
28. Thomas, *Victorian Underworld* and Anon. (1888) *My Secret Life* (Amsterdam: privately printed).
29. The most important exploration of the 'social crime' thesis can be found in D. Hay et al. (1975) *Albion's Fatal Tree: Crime and Society in Eighteenth Century England* (Penguin: Harmondsworth) and E.P. Thompson (1971) 'The Moral Economy of the English Crowd in the Eighteenth Century', *Past and Present*, 50, 76–136.
30. P. Linebaugh (1991) *The London Hanged: Crime and Civil Society in the Eighteenth Century* (London: Allen Lane).
31. J. Davis, 'Law Breaking and Law Enforcement: The Creation of a Criminal Class in Mid-Victorian London' (PhD thesis, Boston College, 1984) and D. Philips (1977) *Crime and Authority in Victorian England: The Black Country 1835–1860* (London: Croom Helm).
32. J.E. Archer (1999) 'Poaching Gangs and Violence: The Urban-Rural Divide in Nineteenth-Century Lancashire', *British Journal of Criminology*, 39:1, 25–38.
33. Emsley, *Crime and Society*, 178.
34. R. McGowen (1990) 'Getting to Know the Criminal Class in Nineteenth Century England', *Nineteenth Century Contexts*, 14, 33–54, at 35.
35. On metropolitan spatiality see S. Joyce (2003) *Capital Offenses: Geographies of Class and Crime in Victorian London* (Charlottesville: University of Virginia Press). See also Shore, 'Mean Streets', passim.
36. D.J.V. Jones and A. Bainbridge (1979) 'The Conquering of China: Crime in an Industrial Community, 1842–64', *Llafur: The Journal of the Society for the Study of Welsh Labour History* 2:4, 7–37.
37. For Sheffield see, J.P. Bean (1981) *The Sheffield Gang Wars* (Sheffield: D&D Publications). For Salford and Glasgow see A. Davies (1998) 'Youth Gangs, Masculinity and Violence in late Victorian Manchester and Salford', *Journal of Social History*, 32, 349–69 and A. Davies (1998) 'Street Gangs, Crime and Policing in Glasgow during the 1930s: The Case of the Beehive Boys', *Social History [London]*, 23, 251–67.
38. Davies, 'Street Gangs', 16–17. Glasgow has played a key role in the topography of 'hardness' that reoccurs in 'true crime' texts. For example, see

A. McArthur and H. Kingsley Long (1935) *No Mean City – A Story of the Glasgow Slums* (London: Longmans, Green & Co.) and J. Goodman and I. Will (1985) *Underworld* (London: Harrap), 64–83.

39. S. Slater (2007) 'Pimps, Police and Filles de Joie: Foreign Prostitution in Interwar London', *London Journal*, 32, 1, 53–74.

40. D. Hobbs (1994) 'Professional and Organised Crime in Britain', in M. Maguire, R. Morgan and R. Reiner (eds.), *The Oxford Handbook of Criminology* (Oxford: Oxford University Press), 441–68. For the medieval underworld see especially A. McCall (1979) *The Medieval Underworld* (London: Hamish Hamilton).

41. See P. Williams and E. Savona (eds.) (1996) *The United Nations and Transnational Organised Crime* (London: Frank Cass) and D. Hobbs (1998) 'Going down the Glocal: The Local Context of Organised Crime', *Howard Journal*, 37:4, 407–22.

42. H.D. Sheldon (1898) 'The Institutional Activities of American Children', *American Journal of Psychology*, 9:4, 425–48.

43. F. Thrasher (1927) *The Gang: A Study of 1313 Gangs in Chicago* (Chicago: University of Chicago Press).

44. A. Davies (2000) 'Youth Gangs, Gender and Violence, 1870–1900', in S. D'Cruz (ed.), *Everyday Violence in Britain, 1850–1950* (Harlow: Longman), 70–85.

45. See M.W. Klien (2005) 'The Value of Comparisons in Street Gang Research', *Journal of Contemporary Criminal Justice*, 21, 135–52, especially 136 discussing the work of the Eurogang researchers.

46. G. Pearson (1983) *Hooligan: A History of Respectable Fears* (London: Macmillan)

47. Davies, 'Youth Gangs', passim and Davies, 'Street Gangs', passim.

48. MEPO 2/9538: Murder of John Beckley by Michael John Davies at Clapham Common.

49. Wright, *Organised Crime*, 38–9.

50. Davies, 'Street Gangs', 259.

51. P. Jenkins and G.W. Potter (1988) 'Before the Krays: Organised Crime in London, 1920–1960', *Criminal Justice History*, 9, 209–30, especially 209.

52. D.R. Cressy (1969) *The Theft of the Nation: The Structure and Operations of Organized Crime in America* (New York: Harper & Row).

53. Wright, *Organised Crime*, 10.

54. See the website for the Serious and Organised Crime Agency: http://www. soca.gov.uk/index.html

55. For a recent discussion of such criminological theory and its application to history see Shore, '"Undiscovered Country"', passim.

56. John Binny, 'Narrative of a Pickpocket', in H. Mayhew (1864) *London Labour and the London Poor*, Vol. 4 (London: J. Bell & Sons), especially 324.

57. J. Murray (1841) 'The World of London', *Blackwood's Magazine*, August.

58. 32 & 33 Vict., c. 99; 34 & 35 Vict., c. 94.

59. S.J. Stevenson, 'The "Criminal Class" in the Mid-Victorian City: A Study of Policy conducted with Special Reference to the Provisions of 34 and 35 Vict., c. 112 (1871) in Birmingham and East London in the Early Years of Registration and Supervision' (DPhil thesis, University of Oxford, 1983).

60. G. Stedman Jones (1971) *Outcast London: A Study in the Relationship Between Classes in Victorian London* (Oxford: Clarendon Press) and J. Welshman (2006) *Underclass: A History of the Excluded, 1880–2000* (London: Hambledon Continuum).
61. Welshman, *Underclass*, 3–4.
62. See especially J.A. Yelling (1986) *Slums and Slum Clearance in Victorian London* (London: Allen & Unwin), 15.
63. J. White (1986) *The Worst Street in North London: Campbell Bunk, Islington, Between the Wars* (London: Routledge).
64. R. Sennet (1994) *Flesh and Stone* (London: W.W. Norton), 322.
65. *Surrey Advertiser and County Times*, 23 July 1921.
66. C. Emsley (2008) 'Violent Crime in England in 1919: Post-war Anxieties and Press Narratives', *Continuity and Change*, 23:1, 173–95.
67. *Daily Express*, 24 August 1925.
68. Ibid.
69. Minutes, HO 144/10430.
70. Ibid.
71. Bean, *Sheffield*, 41.
72. Sir Percy Sillitoe (1955) *Cloak Without Dagger* (2nd edn, London: Cassell), 152.
73. A. Davies (2007) 'The Scottish Chicago? From 'Hooligans' to 'Gangsters' in Inter-War Glasgow', *Cultural and Social History*, 4:4, 511–27, at 521.
74. J. Springhall (1998) *Youth, Popular Culture and Moral Panics: Penny Gaffs to Gangsta-Rap, 1830–1996* (Basingstoke: Macmillan), 101 and passim.
75. Davies, 'The Scottish Chicago?', passim.
76. E. Smithies (1982) *Crime in Wartime: A Social History of Crime in World War II* (London: Allen & Unwin), 140–7.
77. Jenkins and Potter, 'Before the Krays', 215.
78. *The People*, 3 September 1950.
79. D. Webb (1953) *Crime is my Business* (London: Frederick Muller), 111.
80. Smithies, *Crime in Wartime*, 140–1.
81. TNA: MEPO 3/3037, Activities of Thomas Duncan Webb, Press crime reporter (1946–56).
82. Jenkins and Potter, 'Before the Krays', 214.
83. Slater, 'Pimps', 56.
84. Jenkins and Potter, 'Before the Krays', 214. For police investigation into the Messina's see: TNA – various files in MEPO 2/9136, 10080, 9004, 9845, 8707, 8935, 9633; MEPO 3/2582; MEPO 26/85; CRIM 1/2152 – Defendant: MESSINA, Alfredo. Charge: Living on the earnings of prostitution and corruptly offering a bribe, 24 April 1951.
85. TNA – MEPO 2/9004, The Messina brothers: loss of British citizenship and deportations (1951–62). Jenkins and Potter, 'Before the Krays', 216–17.
86. Wright, *Organised Crime*, 174–82.
87. D. Hobbs (1995) *Bad Business: Professional Crime in Modern Britain* (Oxford: Oxford University Press), 115.
88. Hobbs, 'Going Down the Glocal', 407–22.
89. Ibid., 408.
90. E. Smithies (1984) *The Black Economy in England Since 1914* (Dublin: Gill & Macmillan), 51.

91. Wright, *Organised Crime*, 168–9.
92. 'Networking; Insight: Identity Fraud; Who's Being You?', *Accountancy Age*, 27 February 2003, 22.
93. Wright, *Organised Crime*, 176.
94. T. Barnes, R. Elias and P. Walsh (2001) *Cocky: The Rise and Fall of Curtis Warren, Britain's Biggest Drugs Baron* (Bury: Milo Books).
95. E. Greeno (1960) *War on the Underworld* (London: J. Long), 12.
96. G.W. Potter (1994) *Criminal Organisations: Vice, Racketeering, and Politics in an American City* (Prospect Heights, IL: Waveland Press), 10.

7 Fraud and White-collar Crime: 1850 to the Present

Sarah Wilson

1. Introduction

The contribution made by this chapter to the discussion of 'histories of crime' is an exploration of a number of dimensions of white-collar crime. The discussion will focus on exploring activity which in many respects does not appear to 'fit' with commonly held perceptions of criminal activity. Rather it is often presented as something which is somehow 'different from' other deviant behaviours, which are (much more readily) identified with criminality, and on occasions it is even suggested that it is seen as a 'special' type of deviance. Equally, these activities are perceived as causing considerable damage and being highly injurious across a range of societal interests. This is evident from the Attorney-General's announcement during 2007 that 'We are determined to tackle fraud – the "silent" crime that costs our economy and society so much: a minimum of £13.9 billion in 2005. If we can create a truly hostile environment for fraud in our society and economy, then we can reduce fraud.'[1]

As the above quotation suggests, much of this discussion of the significance of white-collar crime for exploring and understanding criminal histories will be pursued through types of white-collar crimes which can be classified as financial crimes, and often referred to as fraud. This will require some understanding of what might be meant by the term financial crime, and how and why many of these activities are commonly referred to as 'fraud', and of course of how they relate to the 'bigger picture' of white-collar crime – this allegedly 'special' type of deviance. Thus this chapter has two distinct, but closely related, purposes in respect of the remit to explore histories of crime. It wishes first to identify the significance of financial crimes for the discussion of white-collar crime, and thereafter it seeks to show how financial crimes can provide an illustration of 'issues' which arise in how criminal activities are perpetrated and also are perceived in society. In its illumination of a number of dimensions of white-collar crime histories, the chapter looks at the perpetration of financial crimes today and across a time frame of over 150 years. This is in order to point to the way in which current events can be seen as 'part of a broad cultural pattern with deep historic roots'.[2]

At the heart of bringing past and present together can be found distinctions which are commonly drawn between white-collar crime and 'ordinary', 'traditional' or 'common' crimes which subsist in society today. These can be found documented in academic commentary upon white-collar crime generally, in financial crime more specifically, and also in policy discourses oriented towards the 'problem' of financial crime. Both are central to this chapter and its examination of the historiography of white-collar crime, and also 'case studies' which are drawn from a number of points in time between 1850 and 2008. These case studies include notable banking frauds from the nineteenth century, as well as ones perpetrated by audacious individuals from the period, which are considered alongside the trial of the so-called 'Guinness Four' in 1990; the activities of Barings' 'rogue trader' Nick Leeson in 1995, and most recently the criminal trial of disgraced media tycoon Lord Conrad Black. It will become apparent that these case studies reveal much about the actual nature of financial crimes past and present, in terms of *what* they are and *how* they are perpetrated, and even *why* they are perpetrated, also pointing to the diversity of these activities. Furthermore, these illustrations can also cast light on how – if at all – the perpetration of these activities might have changed over the past 150 years.

It is also the case that examining these illustrations of high-profile financial crimes can even help to reveal some of the difficulties which the perpetration of these activities can present for actually aligning them with criminal activity at all. And whilst this latter consideration is largely beyond the scope of this chapter, these case studies can help to explain the very different views which subsist on whether these activities are considered 'real crime' which is perpetrated by 'real criminals'.

At one level, financial crimes are often perpetrated less openly than other types of criminal activity on account of their use of covert dishonesty or deceit, which also helps to make them less visible in official reports on crime (the so-called 'dark figure' of fraud[3]) and thus less easy to discover and expose to law enforcement than other types of crime. This can be seen in the allusion to the 'silent' victimisation of society in the opening quotation, and is also well documented in academic literature,[4] where it is also frequently claimed that the costs incurred by society resulting from fraud (as part of the sum of white-collar crimes) simply dwarf those arising from the 'street crimes' with which they are so often 'compared'.[5] However, research also actually points to the way in which notwithstanding this, financial crimes are often not seen as part of the '"real crime" problem' in societal consciousness, as illustrated in a famous study asserting that popular perceptions regard burglary as being far more serious than fraud.[6] This chapter tries to explain these mixed messages on the 'problem' of white-collar crime generally, and financial crime more specifically, and the implications of the subsistence of such a considerable spectrum of reactions and perceptions. It also looks at intellectual representations of financial crimes and also at ones oriented towards policy dating from the mid-nineteenth century to the present. This is to point to the presence of societal perceptions of a number of white-collar crimes which differ considerably from attitudes towards ordinary crimes, both in relation to the unlawful activities themselves, and also to those who perpetrate them. It will also point to the way in which much of the concern expressed across these discourses has become focused on the assertion made that white-collar crimes and their perpetrators are underrepresented in the workload of the criminal courts.[7]

Although suggestions that white-collar crime is often seen not really to 'fit' a number of attributes commonly associated with crime common in modern discourses, this chapter is focused on explaining how this can be seen as 'part of a pattern with deep historic roots'.[8] But it is also the case that the modern scholarship is actually deeply divided about whether white-collar crime is a 'special' type of deviance, or instead (whether as a matter of underlying quality and character) it is no different from any other type of crime, and that any assertion that it is different is socially constructed and even socially 'conditioned'.[9] It is also the case that while a number of scholars have questioned the harm caused to society by financial crimes, there is also much suggestion that these activities are capable of causing considerable damage across a range of societal interests, both economic *and* social in nature. In keeping with the histories of crime remit which is central to this collection of work, as the opening quotation suggests, in the UK there is currently very much prominence being given in policy discourses to the very real dangers presented by financial crime in the twenty-first century.

The very recent announcement that charges of fraud have been brought against two managers of the collapsed US investment bank Bear Stearns[10] suggests that financial crimes are likely, for the foreseeable future, to be closely associated with the onset of the 'credit crunch' currently gripping much of the world, and marked in the UK by the collapse of Northern Rock in September 2007. However, the 'problem' of financial crime has actually been a political priority 'of the highest' throughout these earliest years of the twenty-first century.[11] Most recently, the alleged fraud perpetrated by Société Générale trader Jérôme Kerviel forced further re-evaluation of the problem of financial crime. This is because of conflicting views found across academic scholarship and policy discourses simultaneously expressing doubt as to whether financial crime causes 'real harm', and also asserting it is a 'cancer' in society,[12] whose growth must be halted in the 'age of insecurity'.[13]

2. Chronology

The study of white-collar crime was pioneered by Edwin Sutherland, a sociologist who is most famous for his interest in the unlawful activities being committed by professional people operating within large and powerful businesses, which challenged deep-rooted conceptions of crime and criminality. In defining white-collar crime as that which is 'committed by a person of respectability and high social status in the course of his occupation'[14] Sutherland concluded that such behaviour suggested that criminology had to be more intricate than either traditional analyses of crime or those advocated by Marxism could account for. He was also deeply troubled by the way in which in the eyes of law enforcers, and beyond this across society, 'business men do not conform to the popular stereotype of "the criminal"'.[15] He proposed that it was for this reason that the workload of the criminal courts remained disproportionately dominated by 'traditional' or 'ordinary' crimes.[16] Sutherland believed that this reflected a bias in favour of those who did not 'conform to the popular stereotype of "the criminal"'.[17] In turn this called for all criminal activity to be brought under 'one unifying theory'[18] which would provide the first crucial steps for securing societal acceptance of white-collar crime *as* crime: in time this would allow the imbalances of law enforcement to be redressed, and would ensure 'all are equal in the eyes of the law'.[19] Furthermore Sutherland's work provides an important reference point for understanding the relationship between white-collar crime and the financial crimes of fraud around which this discussion is being cast. In the course of developing his own intellectual framework for analysing white-collar crime, Sutherland explained that activities falling under his definition of 'white-collar crime' could broadly be classified as one of two types of 'business crime'.

The first type concerned 'misrepresentation of asset values' and the second involved 'duplicity in the manipulation of power', and for Sutherland, the second represented crimes of corruption, and the first approximated with 'fraud or swindling'.[20] The academic scholarship which has grown up from its white-collar crime roots and become more specifically directed towards financial crimes shows very clearly that the terms 'financial crime' and 'fraud' are used synonymously and interchangeably. This does itself descend directly from Sutherland's description of fraud as a species of 'business crime' associated with 'asset values'. In English legal culture 'fraud' has long been recognised as 'a generic term for a type of offence, of which the ingredients are infinitely variable, but probably comprise the following: the dishonest non-violent obtaining of some economic advantage or causing some economic loss'.[21]

While it is the case that fraud can be found committed across the social and economic spectra of British society (with 'benefit' or 'social security' fraud found alongside a number of business frauds included under the rubric of 'common types of fraud'[22]), current policy discourses are most strongly focused upon those being committed 'in the commercial sphere'.[23] This is mirrored in the attention being paid to fraud by scholars, with both the academic literature and also policy discourses strongly aligning fraud with the much alluded to 'respectable offender'.[24] For scholars it is the 'respectable offender' who has traditionally best illustrated the discomfort white-collar crime is often believed to cause in societal consciousness, as captured in the assertion that '[t]he Jekyll-and-Hyde nature of crime committed by the respectable raises questions unlike those posed by other types of criminal behaviour'.[25] It is also the case that very recently scholars have started to take an interest in white-collar crimes of an 'everyday-life' nature,[26] and examine the significance and impact of fraud committed 'at the kitchen table, on the settee and from the home computer'[27] However, it is also noteworthy that this new focus on more everyday white-collar crimes – such as insurance fraud and obtaining credit using untrue information – has become fixed on persons labelled '*respectable opportunists*',[28] whose attributes are that they are 'members of the middle classes, and who would definitely reject the labels of "criminals" and "crime" for themselves and their actions'.[29]

While it is the case that not all frauds are 'business crimes', the dominance of crime committed in the 'commercial sphere' in discourses relating to responses to fraud can be seen in the huge concerns about the cost of fraud for the UK. For example a news release from the Attorney-General's office from 2007 was keen to publicise the government's determination to 'protect the public from crime and to keep the UK an honest, fair-dealing place to do business'.[30] For the current Attorney-General, Baroness Scotland, the prioritisation of measures to protect firms, taxpayers and the public 'from dishonest criminals' is 'good news for the financial sector and for the economy as a whole'.[31] Within this, reference to the business offender as a 'respectable offender' is implied in references made to the sophistication and intelligence behind many modern frauds, and the need for strategies to be put in place to 'thwart the inexhaustible ingenuity' of fraudsters.[32] This mirrors the long-established allusion in the scholarship to the way in which many key actors within legal processes (and society more broadly) 'admire and respect business men and cannot conceive of them as criminals', and this ensures that business people 'do not conform to the popular stereotype of "the criminal"'.[33]

Much of what has been said up to now has been written around the significance of financial crime in the twenty-first century, and by joining its readings of the modern literature alongside key works of historical enquiry. This chapter will now suggest that the 'fight against fraud'[34] actually began in Britain around 150 years ago and took shape in ways which are recognisable today during the years between 1850 and 1880. Although this is hardly a revelation, given that leading works on financial crime proffer that it is a 'mistake to view fraud as a new crime',[35] the case studies now drawn from past and present alike will be focused on some of the ways in which this observation is significant. By way of background, it has been suggested elsewhere[36] that the Victorian 'fight against fraud' was actually forged during crucial years between around 1850 and 1880, and that the impetus for this was generated very much by the railway boom and the aftermath of the collapse of the railway share market and the 1840s commercial crisis.

Contemporary accounts and works of historiography alike point to the way in which the climate of excitement created by railway speculation (which offered much higher returns than traditional securities, and especially government bonds) had exposed not simply a frenzy for investment, but also the 'inauguration, development and rapid progress of "high art" crime'[37] on account of the appearance of a number of attempts to exploit this appetite for investment. Within this there was a spectrum of dubious activities, accommodating at one extreme fraudulent bubble companies which were empty shells designed specifically and solely to dupe frenzied investors. However the spectrum also included greyer areas characterised by the desperate attempts of legitimate and *bona fide* railway schemes to attract investment in a highly competitive market, which meant that on occasion prospects were exaggerated even if they were not actually misrepresented. It would also transpire that even in *prima facie* legitimate (and accurately valued) schemes, shareholders' deposit monies were not always applied to business purposes, and were put to 'alternative use' by corporate officers. The collapse of the railway-share market reflected the way it became impossible for investors to make sound investment decisions. The very 'serious alarm for the future'[38] generated helped to perpetuate a sense that *business* activity was capable of amounting to *criminal* activity, and even that some business activities *should* amount to criminal conduct. Ultimately this would result in the appearance of the first criminal fraud trials in the early 1850s.[39]

3. Historiography

It is only comparatively recently that historians have started to appreciate the importance of white-collar crime and its perpetrators for enriching understanding of Britain's histories of crime and society alongside business, economy and finance. This commenced formally with the work of George Robb, but it was also part of a bigger movement towards illuminating the 'rise of respectable society'.[40] However it will become clear shortly that Robb followed a lead actually provided by Harold Perkin in the 1960s. Today, a small but learned cluster of writings on 'white-collar crime history'[41] has now emerged, and central to this was the appearance during the early 1990s of the strand of literature exploring the 'rise of respectable society', which would in many ways provide the initial intellectual space for forging historians' interest in white-collar crime. This was so notwithstanding that this literature characteristically presents a very positive, and indeed celebratory account of the achievements – social, economic *and political* – of the respectable, including the newly emergent middle classes, drawn largely from the increasingly numerous and increasingly powerful sector of manufacturers and industrialists.

This is because this literature base brought respectability and class sufficiently to the fore of historical enquiry to allow for a more comprehensive exploration of the respectable[42] and their professional activities[43] to be possible. This was the right point in time for Robb to suggest that it was during the nineteenth century, accompanying the arrival of 'big business', that white-collar crime made its appearance, articulating this towards exploring extensively the central role of fraudulent activities in the evolution of modern ideas on business regulation.[44] Perhaps the most important lead in this phase, ahead of Robb, was provided by Martin Wiener's assertion that a number of new types of crime which came to light during the nineteenth century implicated the respectable in ways which traditional crimes rarely had.[45] Wiener suggested that fraud was one of these 'new' crimes which exposed the 'criminal within respectability'.[46] Interestingly – given what is said elsewhere in this chapter about the nature of these activities – such conduct was described by one very prominent contemporary policy-maker as being 'divested of animosity on the part of the offender, of physical injury and physical alarm to the party defrauded'.[47] Wiener's intellectual lead provided the opportunity for the study of crime and society, law and policing to start to look at the respectable as *subjects of* the criminal law and its processes of enforcement. It also became possible for Britain's business and economic history to confront its points of connection with the emergence of *criminal* policy-making.

Taking the former first, the modern historiography of crime, society, law and policing has greatly enriched understanding of the revolutions in criminal policy which occurred during the early years of the nineteenth century, and during the early Victorian period. Numerous studies have helped to construct a picture of a society anxious to depart from its eighteenth-century regime of criminal enforcement and punishment. This had placed huge reliance upon a substantial (and ever-expanding) body of capital statutes and systems of secondary punishment embracing transportation and a range of 'physical' punishments, including principally whipping, branding and the pillory. But as the literature also makes plain, this was also a society which was very conscious of the high incidence of petty crime forever present in society. This was brought sharply into focus by the pressures and challenges arising from mass urbanisation, itself precipitated by the changing nature of the economy brought about by industrialisation. During the 1820s, this would lead to formal recognition of the essence of a 'joined-up' approach to crime, at the heart of which lay the need to increase the discovery and apprehension of criminals, and thereafter to ensure their punishment.

This would result in the revolution in policing, and the birth of the prison as an institution of punishment which occurred in earnest from the 1820s onwards, and these initiatives would themselves be supported by a new code of criminal laws. The new criminal law would bring *rationality* (in the form of clear requirements, most significantly that the commission of most unlawful acts must be accompanied by a guilty state of mind, or *mens rea*, for criminal culpability actually to arise). It also introduced parameters for courtroom consideration which would distinguish intention, voluntariness and rationality from 'personal circumstances' such as motivation and also *proportion* into the calculus of criminal liability. In presenting this narrative of the new 'economy of deterrence'[48] emerging during the early nineteenth century, historical discourses have traditionally focused on the respectable members of society as persons requiring the protection *of* the law *from* crime,[49] rather than being the subjects of criminal processes of enforcement. This does, of course, mirror the way in which societal consciousness of 'crime' and 'the criminal' became fixated upon the lower social orders during this time in Britain. This was so both *criminologically* (in the age of Beccaria and then Lombroso) and significantly also *politically*, as key figures such as Peel and later Chadwick sought to 'sell' the benefits of a society protected by efficient and proactive policing to a society which was actually very hostile to any possible infringements of liberties belonging to the 'free-born English man'.[50] Thus 'maintaining the illusion that socially dangerous and unacceptable activity was predominantly the province of the lower orders'[51] became a central tenet in securing these reforms.

A glance at the key literature demonstrates that the historiography of modern Britain's economic and financial development *has* long sought to chart the transformation of the British economy from its agrarian roots into the world's leading capitalist nation, brought about by its industrial revolution. This strand of literature has accordingly recognised distinct phases and patterns in economic stability, and provided extensive commentary on the need to regulate this new setting to ensure it could operate properly, and thereby encourage only those activities which were likely to reinforce wealth and prosperity, and not those which would undermine it. It is also the case that this literature base has a number of silences, including the ways in which understanding the nineteenth-century evolution of the free market and also the institutions and instruments of capitalism (including, respectively, the corporation and limited liability) both contributed to and were also challenged by the birth of modern white-collar crime as they emerged and secured domination as economic forces. This is so, notwithstanding that as early as the 1960s, Harold Perkin suggested that '[f]rom the "railway mania" of 1846–47 onwards the investing public was compulsorily educated in a whole new world and vocabulary of ingenious crime, which could only be perpetrated by business men and by large, prominent, wealthy or at least credit-worthy business men at that.'[52] Thereafter, it was not until 1992 that George Robb's pioneering work provided the first comprehensive study of the extensive perpetration of 'financial fraud' throughout the nineteenth century.[53]

Returning to the significance of the modern scholarship on white-collar crime, this literature base is dominated by explorations of crime which in many ways does not fit comfortably into established conceptions of crime and criminality. Much of this alludes to the oft-alleged 'special nature' of white-collar crime, which in simplest terms is acknowledgement of a perception that this activity is for some reason perceived as being somehow 'different' from many other manifestations of criminality. This discussion will point to the way in which assertions that white-collar crime is a 'special type' of deviance have become attached to the nature of the activities themselves, and also those who commonly perpetrate them. This can be seen within official discourses of law and policy-making and the administration of criminal justice, and wider public opinion alike. In turn this casts important light on the impact of financial crime in the UK today, and points to how and in what ways this might be similar to or different from concerns of past societies.

Notwithstanding the divisions within the literature, there appears to be, amongst scholars, a common understanding that issues which allude to the 'special nature' have been central in attempts to 'define the problem' of white-collar crime, and are at the heart of its discussion and debate across all discourses. Moreover, much of the white-collar crime literature aligns the *sociologically* crafted alleged 'special nature' in perceptions of financial crimes (and white-collar crime more broadly) closely to the *legal* language and rhetoric which has grown up around it. This can be seen embodied as the (popular) conception that financial crime is activity which is often claimed to be *mala prohibita*, as distinct from *mala in se*, with the former representing ('merely') technical violations of law, and the latter representing crimes in the true sense.[54] In more popular discourses such perceptions of a distinctiveness of white-collar crime translates into assertions that it is activity which is (or is at least regarded as being) 'less criminal'[55] than 'ordinary' crime, or even a manifestation of the operation of 'rich man's law'.[56] It is such considerations which scholars insist cut across the interests of academics, those concerned with policy formation, and 'lay' audiences alike, regardless of expressions of agreement.[57] In using both the modern literature and also the interest in white-collar crime now evident in historical enquiry, the chapter is able to introduce the experiences of the past into traditional understandings of white-collar crime as a '20th-Century Crisis',[58] with fraud itself described as the 'modern crime *par excellence*'.[59]

4. Case Studies

The 'fight against fraud' continues in earnest in the twenty-first century, and very recently it has been manifested in enactment of the Fraud Act 2006. This includes a new 'centrepiece' offence *of fraud* itself, addressing longstanding criticism that hitherto there has been 'no offence of fraud known to English Law – either common law or statutory'. Instead there was, in the words of former Solicitor-General Mike O'Brien, 'a wide and complex array of deception and theft offences ... and common law, [which] compiled somewhat haphazardly, have the task of encompassing the wide range of fraudulent conduct'.[60] The case studies which follow are very strongly tied into the way in which, prior to the Fraud Act 2006, fraud has been considered a generic term for activities which, while they might be ("infinitely") variable, do *characteristically* involve some deceit or *dishonesty*. This is perpetrated *non-violently* with a view to obtaining 'some economic advantage or causing some economic loss' – in other words, attaining some kind of *gain*. They also point to the centrality of the 'respectable offender' in the perpetration of financial crimes.

It is the case that both the variety, and also the unifying qualities of deceit and seeking some kind of economic gain identified by Kirk and Woodcock[61] can be seen in a number of high-profile 'frauds' from the late twentieth century and into the twenty-first. In chronological order, the trial of the so-called 'Guinness Four' regarded by many at the time as 'the trial of the [twentieth] century'[62] had arisen from an alleged share-trading fraud at the heart of a proposed takeover by Guinness of the Scottish drinks company Distillers. The allegations of misconduct centred on an alleged attempt to inflate the price of shares in Guinness which was crucial to raising the funds needed for the takeover. This had not been disclosed to shareholders by Chief Executive Ernest Saunders, who was tried, and it was also exposed that a total of millions were paid to co-defendants Parnes, Ronson and Lyons as 'fees' connected with securing and effecting the 'deal'. Like the Guinness saga, unlawful behaviour which was economically motivated and perpetrated using untruths was also at the heart of the collapse of Barings Bank in 1995, caused by the activities of 'rogue trader' Nick Leeson. In this case huge losses accrued from a number of unauthorised dealings which were concealed by Leeson using the now infamous '88888' account, and also by a number of falsifications and misrepresentations in accounting information which ultimately left a £827 million 'hole in the Barings balance sheet'.[63]

Moving into the twenty-first century, the affairs of media tycoon Conrad Black continue the narrative which associates fraud with seeking economic gain of some kind, and seeking to achieve this through use of some kind of deceit or dishonesty. Although a number of charges originally brought against Lord Black were discontinued and he was acquitted of others, he was actually convicted of fraud and obstructing justice. This occurred against a narrative backdrop of the extravagant lifestyle enjoyed by the tycoon, and allegations that this was achieved in part at the expense of his business empire, through a number of alleged 'unapproved' payments and bonuses, which he had paid to himself and to close associates over many years. However, at the time of the criminal trial, which eventually resulted from his 'alleged financial misconduct of diverting corporate funds to his personal use',[64] allusions to his high-profile (and even profligate) lifestyle were actually intimated by Lord Black himself, and closely tied into his concerns for his respectability and status. Indeed, Lord Black expressed concern that accusations (of misuse of corporate funds) against him would result in him being 'spurned by and shunned by persons who had personally accepted his hospitality in London, New York and Palm Beach'.[65]

Whether or not Lord Black's lifestyle was actually funded from the $47 million of company funds he was alleged to have applied to his personal use,[66] these allegations do provide a 'textbook' illustration of how financial crimes have become associated with non-violent and yet deceitful behaviour associated with economic gain. This is a pattern which can be seen throughout the case studies from the twentieth and twenty-first centuries illuminated above, and it can also be seen in the case studies which can be used as illustrations of the 'inauguration, development and rapid progress of "high art" crime' during the middle years of the nineteenth century,[67] notwithstanding that it remains much less well documented in the historiography. The term "high art" crime was coined by the *Times* financial journalist D.M. Evans, who also interestingly referred to the range of activities found beneath it as 'financial crimes' and even 'commercial crimes'.[68] According to Evans, this was a range which varied enormously both in the scale of activities which were possible, and also in terms of the persons who were responsible for their perpetration. This encompassed the 'gigantic forger or swindler' determined to outshine others; the 'reckless speculator' not content with working steadily for a distant reward and prepared to 'risk everything' in the hope of sudden gain; and even the 'apprentice boy' who takes to robbing the till at work for an evening's enjoyment.[69]

However, Evans also observed that these persons and their activities had a shared 'common passion' for quick gratification. Similarly, all these activities could be joined together through the way in which 'Without any great violence, all the incentives [to commit high art crime] may be brought under the one common rubric – the desire to make money easily and in a hurry.'[70] This does of course align Evans's work with observations on the perpetration of financial crimes in the twenty-first century, and aligns them with economic gain sought using some kind of deceit. It was suggested above that the first criminal trials to be associated with these activities were very concerned about where the boundaries for criminal liability in the context of business should be drawn. This can be seen in a number of case studies illustrating misconduct on the part of those who actually managed businesses, and also individual employees who were seeking to gain at the expense of a business. Illustrations of the first type – that concerning the criminal liability of those with managerial functions in business (often directors) – were actually very varied. These included fairly straightforward decisions concerning relatively well-settled legal positions on the misappropriation of property belonging to others (either the business itself, or its shareholders or customers), but also showed much more innovative considerations of criminal liability. The trial of London bankers Strahan, Bates and Paul in 1855[71] illustrates this with reference to the alleged misappropriation of money belonging to the customers of the defendants' private bank. Likewise the trials of the directors of the Royal British[72] and City of Glasgow[73] banks in 1858 and 1878–9, respectively, illustrate the way in which the boundaries of criminal liability were being actively pushed further. These latter cases both proposed and also established (evidenced by the conviction of those standing trial) that property did not have to be misappropriated to give rise to criminal liability. Moreover, actual attempts made to misrepresent the true state of a business (in terms of its asset values and liabilities) should be recognised as 'mainstream' criminal behaviour.[74]

For the purposes of this discussion it is interesting to note that the term 'fraud' was used to articulate alleged misconduct in business during the nineteenth century in all these earliest criminal proceedings. What is especially significant is the presence then of the associations which are made between fraud and the qualities which are believed to exemplify it today; that is, of course, some kind of deceit or dishonesty, and the pursuit of some form of economic gain. The nuances of activities which were 'non-violent' were present, but were altogether more subtle, and directed as references made to the way in which those standing accused of these activities were drawn from the cream of Victorian society. They were 'not prisoners such as are usually seen in that position, but gentlemen, hitherto standing high in the estimation of those who knew them'.[75] Although patterns of crime at the time indicated a surge in characteristically low-level crime, there was a clear element of violent crime within this calculus. This was certainly a more common manifestation of criminality than the activities of those whose position had brought not only the 'luxury which rank and wealth afford', but had ensured 'the unlimited confidence of those whose fortunes had been entrusted to their keeping'.[76]

What is perhaps most interesting about these early articulations of fraud is the way in which the association of fraud with securing an economic gain was very clearly found. It was present even in circumstances (such as these three banking scandals above) where the 'gain' being sought was apparently attributable to seeking to save a struggling business rather than self-advancement or greed. Nevertheless, use of the term 'fraud' reinforced that perpetrating such activities was capable of causing considerable harm, and was thus unacceptable, however apparently well motivated it might be. This was reinforced in legal jurisprudence of the time in the writings of Fitzjames Stephen, who suggested that there were two elements to a fraud. The first of which was 'deceit or an intention to deceive or in some cases mere secrecy', and the latter of which was, like today's discourses, articulated around the central quality of a gain which was intended or sought. However, significantly, Stephen articulated this around causing or even exposing another to loss, rather than emphasising especially seeking a gain for one's self. Accordingly, for Stephen the second element of a fraud was 'either actual injury or possible injury; an intent to expose some person either to actual injury or to a risk of possible injury by means of that deceit or secrecy'.[77]

There are of course a number of other notable Victorian fraud scandals, including several where, unlike the 'struggling business' cases, (economic) 'gains' *were* very strongly associated with greed and self-advancement. This can be seen in the fraud perpetrated by Walter Watts against the Globe Assurance Office with whom he held a position of employment, and for which he was tried and convicted in 1850, and also that committed in 1856 by W.J. Robson, who held a similar and fairly menial clerk's position in the Crystal Palace Company.[78] In both cases the frauds perpetrated were used to fund lifestyles which had many of the hallmarks of Conrad Black's in the twenty-first century, but by persons who lacked Lord Black's social and financial credentials. It was said of W.J. Robson that he was not a 'gentleman of simple tastes or habits'.[79] While a millionaire's lifestyle (without the millionaire's millions!) was not obviously present in Joseph Windle Cole's dockyard warrant frauds in 1854, it is clear that this behaviour was seen as crime for personal (economic) gain. This meant that the misconduct amounted to what scholars today call a 'crime of greed' rather than 'crime of need'.[80] Here there was very clear alignment of the term fraud with gain and even greed, and for the presiding judge this not only made Cole's conduct unacceptable, but because his activities lacked the extenuating influences of poverty, want, bad education and 'bad example', they were '[a]mongst the worst that can be brought under the notice of a court'.[81]

5. Conclusion

These illustrations of high-profile frauds from the nineteenth century[82] point to patterns in the perpetration of financial crime. There are a number of continuities in what amounts to fraud, in terms of what it is, and why it is perpetrated, and even in actual use of the term fraud in this context. These case studies also suggest the presence of patterns of continuity appearing to extend across a time frame of 150 years. At this point it must be wondered whether, if so much remains constant in the perpetration of financial crimes across this period of time which actually spans three centuries, whether anything has actually changed at all. It is now possible to suggest that there is something which can be added to the continuities seen in the perpetration of financial crimes across 150 years. This does very likely distinguish the 'problem' of financial crime in the twenty-first century, and suggests where realisation of this did in fact take shape in the closing years of the twentieth.

This twenty-first-century dimension of financial crime can be illustrated by the occurrence of the 'Soc Gen' fraud. This has not spawned the criminal charges against senior management which were expected in many quarters, especially given criticisms made about the lack of supervision of the activities of traders within Soc Gen's culture. However it remains to be seen whether some Soc Gen shareholders who did appear to know what was happening (and sought to sell their holdings accordingly) will face charges of insider dealing – namely, dealing in securities, in possession of information which is price-sensitive but not generally known to participants in financial markets. The 'rogue trader' himself, Jérôme Kerviel, has been charged, and the nature of these charges does cast light on the continuities with, and significantly the differences from, the past operating in the twenty-first century. Whilst it appears that Kerviel himself will not actually be charged with fraud,[83] he has been charged with abuse of confidence (a concept long associated with financial crime) and significantly, the illegal use of computers for his role in the scandal.

It is this reference to the role of computers in the Soc Gen fraud which provides an insight into the way in which the 'radical and multifarious advances in the use of modern technology'[84] have heightened, and possibly even fundamentally altered, the threat which is presented by financial crime in the twenty-first century. Certainly it is the case that current discourses on financial crime point to the way in which it is not only commercial dealings which have been revolutionised by technology, but also increasingly everyday life. Scholars are now accordingly pointing to the way in which financial crimes are becoming ever-more accessible across the social spectrum,[85] and this is likely to increase in an age which is increasingly one of universal computer ownership. However, it is also the case that sometime ahead of the technological revolution which was evident by the closing years of the twentieth century, scholars of white-collar crime had long feared that whilst these activities might be deeply entrenched in society (and as 'old as ancient Egypt' even), that it is actually technology which arms them with 'awesome powers' to cause considerable societal damage.[86] Indeed in relation to fraud itself, and as early as the 1980s, Levi suggested that technology not only makes new types of crime possible, but can actually make 'old kinds of crime more freely available'.[87] The possibilities provided for financial crime by technological advance increases vulnerability to financial crime, and it is for this reason perhaps that concern to 'create a truly hostile environment for fraud in our society and economy' is perhaps at its most visible and conscious ever in the UK.

In this respect, the Fraud Act 2006 currently has a very high profile, and is being presented as being able to 'get the law right'[88] and to protect the UK's economy and its wider societal interests against the 'silent predator'[89] of fraud. In this respect it is interesting to observe that the centrepiece fraud offence within the Act[90] is both a reflection of the observed qualities of fraud which might be regarded as 'timeless' (and which this chapter has shown to have subsisted throughout a time frame of 150 years), and also the significance of technology in the twenty-first century. The former are qualities of the non-violent use of deceit to secure a gain, and can be seen through the way in which the offence permits fraud to be committed through a variety of actual conduct.[91] However, it also requires the presence of both dishonesty and also an intention to secure a gain or cause (or expose) another to a loss for criminal liability to arise. The fraud offence has sought to accommodate the latter, arising from the way in which already considerable sophistication and rapid innovation in technology provides considerable assistance to fraudsters with already 'inexhaustible ingenuity'. This has 'targeted' underlying conduct (much of which attaches to the timelessness of fraud) rather than seeking to outlaw using specific ways and means to perpetrate financial crimes, where innovation is likely to be most prominent. It remains to be seen whether the new legal provisions will deliver what they are seeking to promise, but it is suggested that observing this should be of utmost importance not only to scholars of modern white-collar crime, but also to historians. This is because there is so much about the perpetration of financial crime today - both in terms of its essential characteristics and its underlying motivations, and even the threat it presents to a number of societal interests – which is demonstrably a broad cultural pattern with deep historic roots.

Notes

1. Baroness Scotland, Attorney-General 'Fighting Fraud Together', News Release, Attorney-General's Office (18 October 2007).
2. This is discussed in the main text shortly, and is referenced below in note 8.
3. M. Levi (1987) *Regulating Fraud: White Collar Crime and the Criminal Process* (London: Tavistock), 1.
4. For example, see A. Bequai (1978) *White Collar Crime: A 20th Century Crisis* (Massachusetts: Lexington Press), xvi.
5. D. Nelken (1994) 'White Collar Crime', in M. Maguire et al. (eds.), *The Oxford Handbook of Criminology* (Oxford: Oxford University Press), 355–92, at 368.
6. Levi, *Regulating Fraud*. This was Levi's assessment of the study of victims of crime by R. Sparkes et al. (1977) *Surveying Victims* (Chichester: Wiley).
7. E.H. Sutherland (1945) 'Is "White Collar Crime" Crime?', *American Sociological Review*, 10, 132–9.
8. S. Wheeler et al. (1982) 'Sentencing the White Collar Offender: Rhetoric and Reality', *American Sociological Review*, 47, 641–59, at 657–8.
9. See the reference which is made to the idea of a 'smokescreen' in Nelken, 'White Collar Crime', at 359.
10. See http://www.canada.com/calgaryherald/news/calgarybusiness/story.html?id=1614339f-7610-421a-91f3-39ec4057ad54
11. See Law Commission Consultation Paper (1999) *Legislating the Criminal Code: Fraud and Deception* (No. 155) (London: Stationery Office), 2.
12. B. Widlake (1995) *Serious Fraud Office* (London: Little, Brown), xii.
13. This is of course strongly associated with globalisation. See L. Elliott and D. Atkinson (1998) *The Age of Insecurity* (London: Verso).
14. E.H. Sutherland (1949) *White Collar Crime* (New York: Dryden), 9.
15. E.H. Sutherland (1945) 'Is "White Collar Crime" Crime?', 137.
16. Ibid., 137–9.
17. Ibid., 137.
18. Ibid., 132.
19. Ibid., 137.
20. E.H. Sutherland (1940) 'White Collar Criminality', *American Sociological Review*, 5, 1–12, at 3.
21. D. Kirk and A. Woodcock (1996) *Serious Fraud: Investigation and Trial* (London: Butterworth's), 1.
22. See Lord Roskill (1986) *Report of the Fraud Trials Committee* (London: HMSO), and more recently A. Doig (2006) *Fraud* (Cullompton: Willan).
23. Lord Irvine, quoted in the Law Commission's Consultation (1999) *Fraud and Deception*, 2.
24. M. Levi (2002) 'Suite Justice or Sweet Charity? Some Explorations of Shaming and Incapacitating Business Fraudsters', *Punishment and Society*, 4:2, 147–63, at 147.
25. Nelken, 'White Collar Crime', 355.
26. S. Karstedt and S. Farrall (forthcoming) 'The Moral Maze of the Middle Class: The Predatory Society and its Emerging Regulatory Order', in H.J. Albrecht,

T. Serassis and H. Kania (eds.), *Images of Crime II* (Freiburg/Br.: Max Planck Institute), 65–94.

27. Ibid., passim.
28. Ibid., passim.
29. Ibid., passim.
30. News Release from the Attorney General's Office, 'Fighting Fraud Together' (9 October 2007).
31. Ibid.
32. Law Commission (2002) *Report on Fraud*, No. 276 (Cm. 5560), para. 7.1.
33. Sutherland, 'Is "White Collar Crime" Crime?', 137.
34. Kirk and Woodcock, *Serious Fraud*, 4.
35. Levi, *Regulating Fraud*, 1.
36. See S. Wilson (2006) 'Law, Morality, and Regulation: Victorian Experiences of Financial Crime', *British Journal of Criminology*, 46, 1073–90.
37. D.M. Evans (1859) *Facts, Failures & Frauds: Revelations Financial, Mercantile, Criminal* (London: Groombridge), 1.
38. D.M. Evans (1848) *The Commercial Crisis 1847–1848* (London: Letts Son & Steer), 18.
39. See Wilson, 'Law, Morality, and Regulation', passim.
40. See F.M.L. Thompson (1988) *The Rise of Respectable Society: A Social History of Victorian Britain, 1830–1900* (London: Fontana).
41. See for example S. Wilson (2003) *Invisible Criminals? Legal, Social and Cultural Perspectives on Financial Crime in Britain 1800–1930* (PhD thesis, University of Wales).
42. Most famously in Michael Thompson's landmark work, referenced in note 40 above.
43. Including for example P. Corfield (1990) *Power and the Professions in Britain 1700–1850* (London: Routledge); G. Searle (1993) *Entrepreneurial Politics in Mid-Victorian Britain* (Oxford: Clarendon Press) and G. Searle (1998) *Morality and the Market in Victorian Britain* (Oxford: Clarendon Press).
44. G. Robb (1992) *White Collar Crime in Modern England: Financial Fraud and Business Morality, 1845–1929* (Cambridge: Cambridge University Press).
45. M. Wiener (1990) *Reconstructing the Criminal: Culture, Law, and Policy in England 1830–1914* (Cambridge: Cambridge University Press), 244.
46. Ibid.
47. This was of course Edwin Chadwick, in the *Report from the Royal Commission on the Constabulary Force*, PP 1839 XIX (169), 49.
48. See D. Eastwood (1993) *Governing Rural England: Tradition and Transformation in Local Government 1780–1840* (Oxford: Clarendon Press), 225–60.
49. D.J.V. Jones (1982) 'The New Police, Crime and People in England and Wales 1829–1888', *Transactions of the Royal Historical Society*, 33, 151–68, especially 157.
50. See S. Wilson and G. Wilson (2007) '"Getting Away With It" or "Punishment Enough"?: The Problem of "Respectable" Crime from 1830', in J. Moore et al. (eds.), *Corruption in Urban Politics and Society, Britain 1780–1950* (Aldershot: Ashgate), 65–89.

51. A. Norrie (1993) *Crime, Reason and History: A Critical Introduction to Criminal Law* (London: Weidenfeld & Nicholson), 85–6. This includes discussion of the characteristics of the new criminal law as indicated in the main text above.

52. H. Perkin (1969) *Origins of Modern British Society 1780–1880* (London: Routledge & Kegan Paul), 442.

53. See Robb, *White Collar Crime*, passim.

54. See Sutherland, 'Is "White Collar Crime" Crime?', at 139.

55. See Nelken, 'White Collar Crime', 365–7.

56. See Levi, *Regulating Fraud*, Preface, xxiv, xxvi.

57. Indeed (as documented in Law Commission Consultation Paper (1999) *Fraud and Deception*, 2), former Lord Chancellor Lord Irvine accepted that in respect of crime committed in the 'commercial sphere' the public has 'little confidence in the criminal justice process'.

58. Bequai, *White Collar Crime*, passim.

59. Levi, *Regulating Fraud*, 1.

60. *Hansard*'s Parliamentary Debates (12 June 2006), col. 534.

61. Kirk and Woodcock, *Serious Fraud*, 1.

62. See http://news.bbc.co.uk/1/hi/business/172316.stm

63. See http://www.riskglossary.com/articles/barings_debacle.htm

64. *Guardian* (28 February 2004).

65. *Guardian* (14 February 2004).

66. *Guardian* (19 November 2005).

67. Evans, *Facts, Failures & Frauds*, 1.

68. Ibid., 5.

69. Ibid., 1–2.

70. Ibid., 1.

71. The trial of Strahan, Bates and Paul in 1855 as transcribed in Evans, *Facts, Failures & Frauds*, 106–53.

72. The trial of the directors of the Royal British Bank, as transcribed in full in Evans, *Facts, Failures & Frauds*, 280–385.

73. The trial of the directors and manager of the City of Glasgow Bank at the High Court of Justiciary, Edinburgh, January 1879 (University of Glasgow Business Archive Centre, UGD Classification UGD/108 11).

74. This is considered further in Wilson, 'Law, Morality and Regulation', passim.

75. This was asserted during the trial of Strahan, Bates and Paul, as considered in Wilson and Wilson, '"Getting away with it"', passim.

76. Evans, *Facts, Failures & Frauds*, 117.

77. J.F. Stephen (1883) *A History of the English Criminal Law* (London: MacMillan), 2, 121–2.

78. The trial of W.J. Robson at the Central Criminal Court, London, 30 October 1856, as transcribed in Evans, *Facts, Failures & Frauds*, 417–31.

79. Ibid., 399.

80. Wheeler et al., 'Sentencing the White Collar Offender', 657.

81. The trial of Joseph Windle Cole at the Central Criminal Court, 26 October 1854, fully transcribed in Evans, *Facts, Failures & Frauds*, 197–225.

82. There is some discussion of how the infamous South Sea Bubble scandal from 1720 fits into this proposition in Wilson, 'Law, Morality and Regulation', passim.

83. As reported by Sky News (28 January 2008), Kerviel had apparently told police he had concealed his trades because he wanted to enhance his reputation as a trader, not out of any desire to hurt the bank. http://news.sky.com/skynews/article/0,,30000-1302639,00.html

84. Law Commission (1999) *Fraud and Deception*, 2.

85. For example the work of Karstedt and Farrall referenced in full in note 26 above.

86. See Bequai, *White Collar Crime*, Preface, iii.

87. Levi, *Regulating Fraud*, 3.

88. See reference made to this by former Solicitor-General Mike O'Brien in *Hansard* (12 June 2006), col. 535.

89. See Bequai, *White Collar Crime*, passim.

90. The fraud offence can be found located and also defined and illuminated within Sections 1–5 of the Fraud Act 2006.

91. According to Section 1, fraud can be committed by way of a false representation made; or a failure to disclose information while under a legal duty to do so; or through abuse of a position of trust.

8 Policing the Populace: The Road to Professionalisation

Chris A. Williams

1. Introduction

The law does not exist in a vacuum, but is imposed by a variety of agencies, the most important of which are the police. As the entry-point to the criminal justice system, police have immense influence on which crimes are prosecuted, and which behaviour repressed, thus in order to understand how the criminal justice system has evolved, we need to know how policing has changed. The most influential starting point in the definition of policing is that of Egon Bittner, who claimed that the most distinctive characteristic of the police is that they are 'a mechanism for the distribution of situationally justified force in society'.[1] The officially generated definition of the role tends to reduce the police function to two main elements – crime control and order maintenance: the oath taken by British constables since the late sixteenth century specifically refers to the enforcement of the law, and to the preservation of the peace. Policing necessarily involves the exercise of discretion, often in situations where (in contrast to other points in the prosecution process) there are no clear-cut legal guidelines on the correct action to take. Hence it is paradoxically true that one thing that defines policing is the deliberate *non-enforcement* of the law when to do so would threaten to compromise the authority of the officer(s) concerned. Thus, police institutions are very strongly influenced by their culture and traditions; one reason why the study of police history is essential, if we are to understand the present.

As well as their role in relation to the criminal justice system, it is important to remember the continuing role played by police forces in preserving the integrity and power of the state and its institutions to act. The first duty of any police force has been to protect 'the state, whose coercive arm they are'.[2]

2. Chronology

a) The 'Old' Police

Before about 1750, British police were paid and organised by local, not national, government. Every parish had its constable, a householder, picked every year to serve. He was usually selected by the vestry, the committee elected by all the parish's property-owners. If he refused to serve, or to find a substitute willing to take his place, he could be prosecuted and fined. He had a responsibility, through his powers of arrest and entry, to assist in the working of the criminal law, but his job also involved administrative tasks such as preparing the militia lists and moving unwelcome paupers through the parish. In theory he was an amateur – a free-born Englishman of the 'middling sort', carrying out a number of essential public duties. The constable mainly acted when called upon: he would follow up cases of theft, arrest suspects or receive them into custody, take them before the magistrates, and collect evidence for the prosecution, but it was up to the victim to ask him to do so, and to promise to reimburse his expenses.[3]

Often, the job of constable was taken year after year by the same man, who used the income from fees to supplement his trade at another occupation. In this way he would be in a position to gain experience and expertise as a constable over time. The rewards of thief-taking could be large: there were statutory rewards of up to £100 given out for the conviction of robbers in London.[4] So, if the same man volunteered as substitute every time, the post of constable could become full-time by default. These men were called 'acting constables' to distinguish them from the 'constable', which became an honorary post for a member of the middle classes. Often they were attended by assistant constables. Acting constables were men of some standing, who had to be literate and trustworthy. Their income put them in the class of respectable tradesmen.

The other element of the 'old' police was the night watches. These were financed by a tax on the wealthy inhabitants of a particular urban parish. Their job was to patrol the streets of their area, from a fixed box. They had powers of arrest, but these were limited to apprehending suspicious 'night walkers'. Many called the hour of the night to announce their arrival, although in some places they also sometimes walked their beats silently so as not to warn malefactors of their approach.[5] Before the arrival of gaslight in the early years of the nineteenth century, English towns generally had an informal curfew. If a watchman encountered anyone on the streets after dark, the onus was on the stranger to prove his business, or he would be searched as a matter of course for stolen property.

The eighteenth-century police were reasonably good at catching most criminals, and good at patrolling the streets at night, but they were less able to deal with public disorder, and very bad at imposing external moral codes (such as laws concerning drunkenness) on their communities. They could not be given orders at a national level, but, if the incentives were right, they could take part in nationally co-ordinated activity: for example, between 1798 and 1821 the Bank of England established a network of contacts around the country, who found 'energetic and clever' constables to fight the forgers of the paper currency. The result was hundreds of successful investigations.[6]

b) The Advent of the 'New' Police

The most famous major step in the construction of the 'new' police in England was the establishment of the Metropolitan Police. Sir Robert Peel had become Home Secretary in 1822 and, partly reacting to concerns over radical demonstrations, he argued for a new vigorous system of police – uniformed and supposedly both more efficient and more professional than their eighteenth-century counterparts. Although the validity of the statistics Peel used to 'prove' his case was probably minimal, in 1829 3,000 uniformed constables replaced the various local watch forces and took to their beats. However, throughout the 1830s, there was vociferous criticism of Peel's new force. Many commentators felt the uniforms of the new police betrayed their essentially 'military' and politically illegitimate character. Others griped at the cost of the new system, paid for by local government, which was more expensive than the old and often put fewer men on the streets.

It is worth bearing in mind that in some parts of London, the old watch forces were already uniformed, efficient, and closely supervised. The new kind of permanent police force was much harder to accomplish in the provinces, where regional authorities had a marked aversion to central government interference. Wrangling continued even as late as the 1850s, when there were a variety of different models in use as well as local authorities who had yet to set up any new provision at all. In 1857 the Police Act made police mandatory, but unlike the Met, who reported to the Home Secretary, provincial police reported to their local government authorities: Watch Committees of the corporations in the boroughs, and Police Committees of the bench of magistrates in the counties. Police reform was always linked to discussions and debates about the proper role of various branches of local government. For example, the creation of the Metropolitan Police was nodded through by radicals because at the time they were campaigning against the unelected parish vestries who controlled the old police.[7]

c) The Persistence of Detection

Unlike the new police, who were dedicated to the prevention of crime, old police constables were detectives in that they learned of crime after the fact, and helped to trace the perpetrator and collect and present evidence against them for a trial. Detection did not fit the rhetoric of the new police, but the need for it persisted. Since effective detection nearly always depends on cultivating links with informants who are themselves criminals, it has always created a potential for corruption and malpractice. This was particularly the case in the nineteenth century, when victims of crime and prosecution associations were offering substantial rewards for successful prosecution. In big cities like London, the milieu of a detective is often disturbingly similar to that of an habitual criminal.[8] Although police had operated in plain clothes before, the Metropolitan Police's Criminal Investigation Department (CID) was founded in 1842 (three years after the Bow Street and other police offices were closed). But it was plagued with the suspicion that its members were colluding with criminals, and in 1878, the Metropolitan CID was disbanded and re-formed when it was discovered that its upper ranks were actively engaging in frauds.

Despite these endemic problems, by the early twentieth century, the police detective was a celebrity, and his (often fictionalised) autobiography usually a bestseller. In the interwar period detectives were increasingly relying (or seeming to rely) on technology rather than 'information received' to catch criminals. In the 1930s the first government-funded forensic science laboratories were opened. Detectives were not the only source of police corruption. In the interwar period the uniformed police of Vine Street, whose West End beats presented them with many opportunities for taking protection money from prostitutes and drinking clubs, were purged three times, and a Vine Street sergeant, Goddard, was imprisoned for taking thousands of pounds' worth of bribes.[9] In the 1930s, newspaper editors had agreed with the Commissioner to suppress stories about police corruption: in 1969, faced with evidence of widespread misconduct in the Met CID, *The Times* publicised it. In the early 1970s the Met – from 1972 led for the first time by an outsider who had risen from the ranks, Robert Mark – struggled with limited success to punish corrupt detectives.[10]

Although new and old police had carried out political tasks for their master, until the end of the nineteenth century Britain was alone among European states in having no institution devoted to political policing.[11]

This changed after the Fenian (Irish Nationalist) attacks of the early 1880s, which led in 1883 to the Home Office creating the Special Branch within the Metropolitan Police: this was specifically tasked with maintaining surveillance on Irish nationalists and other individuals and groups who were suspected of political violence or the more broadly defined 'sedition'.[12] After this episode there was a surprising degree of continuity in police response to the terrorist threat from Irish republicans, calling for greater powers at periods of crisis, as much for symbolic reasons as for instrumental ones.[13] Detectives throughout this period had a vested interest in good clear-up rates.[14] They were always faced with the temptation to artificially massage these rates upwards. Thus the crime statistics which they generated were based on essentially fictitious levels of reported serious offences: one way that fear of crime was allayed was by suppressing its true extent.

d) Policing as a Career

The vast majority of men who tried their hands at being a new policeman failed to stick the job out for more than a year. It held out a prospect of secure employment and stable wages (a rarity for nineteenth-century workers).[15] But a policeman was on duty seven days a week, whatever the weather, under the close supervision of sergeants and inspectors. Discipline could be onerous, and there was no way to appeal against an oppressive superior. The work was tiring and monotonous, thus there was little wonder that many sought solace in alcohol, which was associated with many dismissals. Wages tended to be comparable to those of semi-skilled workers, but this was countered by the prohibition on policemen's wives working, lest they make contacts which could compromise their husbands. There was a usually a long wait before promotion to sergeant; although a highly literate minority who could work as clerks found promotion considerably easier and faster. Most forces offered pensions to men who had served more than 25 years, or been disabled by their service, but these were initially discretionary. Thus it is not surprising that after increases in wages, the first consistent (anonymous) political demand of police officers was that the pension be paid to all.[16] This agitation bore fruit with the 1890 Police Act, which made the pension mandatory.

During the First World War, inflation led to a calamitous fall in police wages, which increased membership of the clandestine police union, which had been formed with the co-operation of John Kempster, the editor of *Police Review*. On 31 August 1918 12,000 police officers went on strike over the non-recognition of the newly formed Police and Prison Officers Union, also demanding a £1 a week pay rise and a 12 per cent war bonus. They got the money and the Desborough Committee to look at the way that they were paid, but not the sought-for recognition. Desborough proposed nationally set pay, with a voice for men, but no recognition for the union. The union struck again in 1919 to get this craved recognition, but this strike was a failure. In the 1919 Police Act, police trade unions were prohibited and the Police Federation (barred from striking by its constitution) was set up to safeguard members' interests. The act simultaneously removed the police from the sphere of labour relations and dealt a blow to local control of the police when responsibility for pay and conditions was thus centralised.

e) Policing the Streets

From the very start, the new police were there primarily to protect property (notably at night) and to keep the streets clear. They were not especially good at policing private violence, or respectable crime. From their beginnings, one key innovative function of the new police was the attempt to impose order on unruly workers.[17] Their instructions to keep the streets clear and 'move on' groups of people led to many instances of friction with various sections of the public, especially young working-class men.[18] Of course policemen, usually patrolling alone and relying on a rattle or a whistle to summon help, often avoided conflict. Nevertheless, the constant pressure to 'move on', often accompanied by summary violence when the targets were juveniles, appear to have made an impact on the way that people behaved on the streets.

Perhaps the most startling statistic of the late nineteenth century is the vast reach of the police and the courts. It is likely that, at the very least, a third of working-class men in an industrial city like Sheffield had been arrested at least once.[19] The reach of the 'policeman-state' was further extended by legislation such as the 1880 Education Act, which made it a legal obligation to send children to school. The police were there to deal with those who refused to comply. Their particular attention was fastened on the very poorest and on the most mobile: the vagrants who were sometimes referred to as the 'residuum'. If anything, the problem of vagrancy loomed larger in the countryside than in the towns, and the threat of vagrants – who even if they were not criminal would need to be fed from the poor rates – was one of the factors that mobilised support for rural police reform in the 1830s.[20]

Often, policing was directed more against those seen as outsiders: this was often strangers to the area, but in many cases, particular police attention was fixed on ethnic minority groups: from the Irish in the nineteenth century to immigrants from the Commonwealth and Eastern Europe in the late twentieth. Close attention was rarely pleasant, and often led to friction between the police and some sections of these communities.[21] In the twentieth century this kind of policing was turned towards the middle classes in their cars. It was equally resented: the difference was that they had a means of articulating their dissatisfaction.[22]

f) Technology and Centralisation in the Twentieth Century

The police system of the nineteenth century changed little in the early years of the twentieth. It was still based almost entirely on foot patrol, delivered by a disciplined bureaucratically-controlled force. However, this came under strain from social and economic change. Dispersed settlement in suburbs, and the advent of widespread car-ownership, challenged a policing paradigm which had been designed for monitoring and controlling densely packed and largely static populations.[23] One way that they dealt with this was by turning to technological solutions: but this in turn created other problems.

Police were late to adopt telephones, but in the interwar period were quick to use radio; in the 1930s the modern scheme of control rooms responding to calls from the public directing officers in cars was introduced. [24] The widely copied 'Unit beat policing' system originated in Aberdeen in 1948, as a mixture of cars and foot patrols.[25] In the 1960s, the Lancashire force, faced with the problem of policing the new dispersed suburb of Kirkby, were among the first to move to a system where every police officer patrolled in a car.[26] For a time this was hailed as the way forward for policing, but soon it became apparent that these new systems had separated the police from the public, and meant that police officers rushing from problem to problem were more predisposed to aggression when they arrived.[27]

In a process that owed a lot to the fact that politically unreliable Labour members were becoming increasingly powerful on police authorities, the structures of police governance also changed. Before 1914, towns in England and Wales had almost complete autonomy over the way that they policed themselves, subject only to having a force that was large enough to qualify for a government grant. The police authority was the Watch Committee, a subcommittee of the town council, which had the power to hire, fire, discipline and direct its police force. The First World War had instigated a trend towards more involvement by central government in local policing. Issues such as the threat of espionage had redefined the police role as national rather than local, and the national government preferred to maintain a degree of control over them whilst evading ultimate responsibility for their actions. During the 1920s the Home Office also began to intervene in the appointment of chief constables. From 1936 they funded the training of a police 'officer class' for the first time at Hendon. The increasing provision of common police rules, conditions of service and services culminated in the 1964 Police Act, which in effect merged the city forces with their surrounding counties, and universalised the less democratic county police model.[28]

The counterpoint to this idea of technical progression was a worry that the police were now too remote from the public they were supposed to serve. This helped inspire the 1960 Royal Commission on Police, which was in the event characterised by reflexive moves by the government to back up the police rather than reform their practices.[29] By the 1980s, senior police officers had unprecedented independence from their authorities, and chief constables had in practice total independence from the Home Office.[30] Their organisation, the Association of Chief Police Officers (ACPO), tended to be the place where procedures and regulations common to all police forces were drawn up in concert with the Home Office. In this turbulent decade, police had to deal with industrial disputes and ethnic minority groups who were not prepared to endure inferior status. Some senior police officers brought to the fore in this period were known for their good sense. Others, such as Greater Manchester's James Anderton, were not.[31]

Then, the power of the chiefs was reined in. The main initiative came from the Home Office, who began to exert far greater detailed control over the 'independent' forces, via performance indicators, exhaustive audits and thematic inspections from a now far larger Inspectorate of Constabulary. During the 1990s, they began to stress the importance of 'community safety'. This was an implicit acceptance that police claims to a sole professional competence in fighting crime had not delivered. The 1998 Crime and Disorder Act mandated police forces to work in partnership with their local authorities. Despite this rolling back of police independence and claims to exclusive competence, a crucial development since the later 1980s has been the increased priority given to 'anti-terrorism' work. This has led to a massive expansion in the strength of Special Branch, and for the first time a permanent network of Special Branches in every police force in the country.[32]

3. Historiography

a) Whigs and Revisionists

The historiography of British policing falls into two chronological periods. The first, before the 1960s, was characterised largely by uncritical works of history, often written by insiders, which sought to celebrate the British tradition of policing, as much as to explain it. They took an uncritical attitude to the definition of crime, and repeated at face value the justifications advanced by police reformers. Exceptions to this trend were rare and uninfluential.[33] This tendency was exemplified by the work of Charles Reith, a journalist who in the 1930s began to write a series of books detailing the history of the British police, concentrating on the early days of the Metropolitan Police from its inception in 1829. The apotheosis of Reith's work was reached in 1943, with the publication of *British Police and the Democratic Ideal*.[34] This concluded that it was British policing, and only British policing, which stood between modern societies and dictatorship.

There were other motivations for writing this kind of history. One was the tradition of 'black-letter legal history', which is written from the starting point of the law itself, and seeks to explain how today's legal institutions and precedents developed. One exponent of this tradition was the pioneering criminologist Leon Radzinowicz, whose *History of the English Criminal Law* is also a history of police legislation.[35] While highly rigorous in its own terms, such history is by definition top-down, and often fails to take into account the wider social and political changes which have brought laws about.

The arrival of an alternative to this 'Whig' tradition of historiography preceded the emergence of a scholarly critique of it. In 1979; the article 'Ideology as History' by American sociologist Cyril Robinson pointed out that historians like Reith began with the premise that British police institutions were an example to the rest of the world, and proceeded to look for justification for this view.[36] The new attitude to police history pioneered by these revisionist historians of the 1970s was initially linked to interpretations that based themselves on a quasi-Marxist view of history, but the same spirit of critical attention was soon more often harnessed to a more empiricist view of the past. Particularly in the nineteenth century, policing was linked so closely to class conflict that nearly all historians stress the importance of class in the genesis and widespread adoption of police institutions.[37] The contrast between 'Whigs' and 'revisionists' is real, but in the 30 years since the revisionist interpretation arrived, hundreds of scholarly works on police history have been published, all rejecting 'Whiggism', and concentrating on a bewildering variety of aspects of police history. To a greater or lesser extent, most can be characterised through the way that they have addressed the two key issues of legitimacy and causation.

b) Legitimacy

The most influential critique of the 'Whig' view came from Robert Storch in the 1970s. He pointed out that opposition to the new police was not motivated purely by political spite, but often derived from deeper causes. In the early 1840s, notably in some Lancashire towns, there was sustained and organised opposition to the introduction of uniformed police, rooted in the working class.[38] This could be explained by the fact that, as well as being directed against ordinary criminals, new police were also 'domestic missionaries', tasked with instilling a tighter standard of behaviour in public which ultimately derived from middle-class values, and expressed itself in activities such as 'moving on' men who habitually congregated on streets and paths. In the 1840s a confident working-class movement had already developed a critique of legislation which criminalised workers' behaviour while ignoring the anti-social activities of the wealthy. This movement also saw in the new police a weapon fashioned to meet their challenge.

The new police were unpopular at their inception, but gradually received more acquiescence.[39] It is more difficult to decide whether acquiescence was the same as support, and if so, what was causing it. David Taylor's view is that 'The crucial distinction is between a dislike of (and even a violent response to) a specific police action and a general rejection of the legitimacy of the police *per se*.'[40] However, Williams has noted that in some cases, working-class reformers' opposition to the police was the other way round; the specific activity of the police and the new standard of order they represented were not opposed, rather the 'legitimacy of the police *per se*' was the target.[41] Legitimacy remains a slippery concept.

c) Causation

One crucial element of the 'Whig' interpretation was that the old police were so bad that the need for their reform was self-evident. Since the late 1970s, however, research on a number of periods and areas has shown that although some areas were badly policed at certain times, in the main the population of eighteenth-century Britain was perfectly happy with their police institutions. The old police were also capable of responding to perceived needs for reform.[42] Nevertheless, the old view of 1829 as the sole key moment in the history of British policing has meant that the nineteenth century has received far more attention than the twentieth until relatively recently.

The historiography of the introduction of the 'new police' into the UK has generally focused on three potential motivations for their introduction. The first is fear of serious crime, especially theft. This was the main reason that was advanced to justify the emergence of the new police at the time.[43] The second is the need to find politically acceptable ways of coping with large-scale potentially insurrectionary disorder. Much debate has concentrated on the 1839/1840 County Police Acts, and the extent that they were motivated by concern over crime or over Chartism. Brundage, Storch and Philips take the former view; Palmer the latter.[44] But those who stressed that the police were welcome, as well as those who pointed out how much they were opposed, looked to their new ability to act in groups to suppress and control hostile crowds.[45] The third motivation involves the use of the new police as 'domestic missionaries'. This has been best chronicled by Robert Storch in his influential article on the topic.[46] The new police spent a good deal of their time attempting to impose a new, middle-class standard of public behaviour on the working classes. They did this by moving on groups of men gathered outside pubs, and generally by suppressing popular customs.[47] In addition to this role it took some time before their exercise of wider powers of 'police' – which in the past meant the local government of space – was seen by historians as a crucial element of their role.[48]

One question still being debated by historians is the way that police expertise has diffused. The traditional view saw the fount of all innovation as the Metropolitan Police in 1829, but empirical research soon revealed a more complex picture.[49] In the nineteenth century, urban forces in particular developed their own ways of policing independently: in the twentieth they pioneered many technical innovations.[50] Policing was an international phenomenon. Stanley Palmer's pioneering work on the interplay between Britain and Ireland has shown how when Peel drew up the blueprint for London's Metropolitan Police in 1829, he was drawing heavily on his previous experience as Secretary for Ireland.[51] Several other attempts have been made by historians to link the genesis and development of British policing to the way that the Empire was policed.[52]

In the last decade, the idea that police must only be one monolithic state-controlled organisation with a monopoly of force has been challenged by a resurgence of various forms of private policing. In addition, attention is once more being paid to the victim, who in the mid-twentieth century had little or no formal involvement in the criminal justice system. While some historians have pointed out that many forms of private policing never went away, others have noted that in some respects the early twenty-first century is repeating some of the characteristics of the eighteenth century and earlier.[53]

4. Case Studies

The case studies listed below could be read as unfair to the police: they are largely about moments when policing was accused of being dysfunctional. Yet it is hard to avoid this kind of approach, for two reasons. The first is that the everyday application of policing by its nature tends not to be well documented, unless something goes wrong, thus resulting in the kind of inquiry that leaves good records. The second is that these revelations themselves are often highly influential in setting the agenda for changes in the practice of policing.

a) PC George Bakewell Arrests Some Chicken Thieves (1841)

In 1840 a failed businessman named George Bakewell joined the Birmingham police as a constable. He had already served as a parish constable, and acutely felt the low status, invidious and unrelenting supervision and lack of opportunity for advancement in the new police. The Birmingham force he was in was an especially militarised one, since it had been set up by the government largely to police the Chartists, whose National Convention was meeting in the city. Its Commissioner, Francis Burgess, was also keen to use the force to suppress crime, in an ultimately successful attempt to gain the support of the city's property-owning classes.[54]

On the morning of 15 February 1841, Bakewell made a successful arrest of the kind that Burgess approved of. The newspaper reported:

> George Bakewell ... stated that ... he was on duty in Edgbaston parish, when he saw two men advancing towards him. They were coming from towards Harborne, and each one carrying a bundle. Suspecting all was not right, he concealed himself in a plantation until they came up, when he suddenly sprang out and laid hold of Carr, whom he handcuffed and fastened to a gate, while he pinioned the other prisoner, who ran away and plunged into a pool, in which he nearly lost his life.[55]

In court, he presented himself as a passive patroller, whose innate suspicions were aroused, and who suddenly made an arrest. In his subsequent autobiography, his emphasis was different. He claimed to have been away from his beat during the arrest, and the passage is included as part of a condemnation of too-strict beat patterns.[56] Early in the morning he 'received information' that two men suspected of chicken-stealing had crossed into Warwickshire, and decided that 'as I imagined they would return between six and seven, the time when the duty was changed, I determined to watch in a plantation of firs'. After an hour's wait, he saw them, both carrying bundles, and stepped into the road 50 yards ahead of them. 'I immediately laid hold of one, and demanded of him to open his bundle, upon which a rather smart struggle took place, but I soon got possession of the bundle.' This time, the memoir tells a less abruptly violent tale than the court report, but it shows Bakewell as thief-taker rather than patroller: acting on information, hiding, and then springing out – not conforming to Peel's model of the new policeman as the passive preventer of crime.

This particular arrest gave him much kudos – one of the victims was a local magistrate, and after the case, the Chair of Worcestershire Quarter Sessions commended him, while Edgbaston Association for the Prosecution of Felons later voted him a reward.[57] These Associations were organisations of property-owners who clubbed together for mutual protection: in the era of the old police their common funds paid for prosecutions of anyone who stole from their members: later they provided rewards for new police who helped recover their stolen property.[58] They demonstrated the fact that for many middle-class Victorians, the protection of property was a key reason to support the new police.

This time, Bakewell had been fortunate in the operation of his discretion, departing from the script of the new police. But this was not always the case, and a few months later his career with the Birmingham police was (he claimed) ruined, when in a similar exercise of independent judgement, he arrested a respectable innkeeper on the mistaken word of a drunken farmer. He left the force – dismissed like so many of his contemporaries for drunkenness – in 1842. Like thousands of other men, for him policing was a stage they passed through.

b) Nott-Bower Suppresses the Liverpool Brothels (1890)

In 1890 the limits to local autonomy were tested when a pre-temperance group, the Vigilance Association, gained a majority on Liverpool City Council and hence its watch committee.[59] They ordered the city's chief constable, William Nott-Bower, to close down the city's brothels, which though technically illegal, had long been tolerated. This case demonstrates the extent to which Watch Committees could want to be 'domestic missionaries' imposing a new level of order, but it also demonstrates the limits to which policemen themselves shared this agenda. Nott-Bower was a trained police officer, originating from the upper classes (maternal grandfather a general, father a barrister), who obviously had a sense of his ability. He had received his initial training as a senior officer in the Royal Irish Constabulary before moving as a Chief Constable to England – first to Leeds at the age of 29, then Liverpool at 32. He had already been used as a consultant to a commission investigating the Dublin Metropolitan Police, and seen his recommendations adopted. Now eight years into his job at Liverpool, Nott-Bower protested that this closure of these establishments would merely spread the problem throughout the city and lead to more police work. His protest was important in that it prefigured a police claim to expertise that should (so he said) overrule the judgement of his police authority. As Brogden puts it:

> he utilised all the elements essential to the development of autonomy in the presentation of his case – legal discretion as a constable under traditional common law, professional expertise, experience as the practitioner and judicial knowledge of the nature of law. Early police managerialism was constituted by these elements.[60]

In the twentieth century, this view was to triumph: the landmark *Fisher* v. *Oldham* case concentrated on the first of these issues, when Judge McCardie made it clear that if the ordinary constable was responsible to the common law, then the chief constable also was responsible to nobody but the law. In 1890, though the position was clear, and the Liverpool Watch Committee overruled Nott-Bower, making it clear that they could give him detailed orders as to the policy of his force. This case was an important landmark in the debate (referred to above) about the organisational accountability of the police. Nott-Bower was eventually vindicated when the inhabitants of the areas into which the trade had moved put enough pressure on the watch committee that they tacitly reversed their zero-tolerance policy.[61]

c) Swamp '81 Precipitates the Brixton Riots (1981)

When substantial numbers of West Indian immigrants arrived in the UK after the Second World War, they tended to collect in areas which made them prey to discrimination and harassment. They rapidly realised that the Metropolitan Police was no help to them. Despite many attempts on the part of West Indian diplomats and community groups to raise the alarm, relations deteriorated, until by the 1970s, a young generation (which had seen their parents systematically discriminated against) came of age in an era of high unemployment, and a policing style which, while rarely racist in its intent, was felt as harassment.[62] Those black youths who turned to crime brought down an indiscriminate police response on the community as a whole, which further soured relations. In wider society, the threat of the 'mugger' was seen as a proxy for a whole host of social ills.[63] Criminologist Jock Young described the situation as 'military policing', characterised by

> policing without the consent of, and with the hostility, active or otherwise, of the community. The community do not support the police because they see them as a socially or politically oppressive force in no way fulfilling any protective functions ... the police force under such circumstances will not be in a position to receive the type of information from the community which would enable its activities to be characterised by the principle 'certainty of detection'. The crucial consequence of this situation is that an important part of police activity will come to constitute the random harassment of community at large irrespective of involvement in crime.[64]

It was in this kind of atmosphere that, faced with high figures for street robbery, the Met launched operation 'Swamp '81' in Brixton in April 1981.

A total of 112 officers stopped and searched youths (around half of whom were black) for evidence of wrongdoing. Many were charged under the 1824 Vagrancy Act with acting suspiciously: the infamous 'sus laws'. Of 943 stops, just one resulted in an arrest for robbery, and one for burglary.[65] This operation was the cue for three days of anti-police rioting in the area, which shocked many observers who had failed to realise the extent to which consensus between police and community had broken down.

Lord Scarman's subsequent inquiry concluded that although the riots were to be condemned, the police could make significant changes to the way that they went about their work. Notably, they sought to put into place permanent consultation schemes with representatives of local communities, and police training ought to be designed so that police officers were aware of the reactions of the communities that they were policing. Scarman did not, however, recommend that the police shift to the idea of 'community policing' which was being advocated at the time by some senior officers such as John Alderson, who called for 'the need for greater community cooperation between the police and other elements in society if the police were to halt the slide towards alienation from the public'.[66] Scarman's 1981 report problematised policing, and presented would-be reformers with a great number of standards against which to test it. It did not reduce the arguments about policing, which had been highly politicised since the 1970s, back to a series of technocratic discussions.

d) Macpherson's Inquiry into the Met (1998)

The murder of Stephen Lawrence in 1990 rapidly became a cause célébre. Lawrence was killed in an unprovoked racist attack in south-east London, but the failure of the police to catch his killers became a symbol of the Met's perceived unwillingness to support London's black population. In fact, the initial detection of the crime was not as badly botched as it sometimes seemed: the detectives' assumption that the killer(s) knew the victim would have been correct in the vast majority of murder cases: their problem was that they stuck for too long to their assumption that it was not a racist attack.[67] Like much scandal, it looked very different from the outside. In 1997, the incoming Labour government called a public inquiry into the case under the Judge Lord MacPherson.

The nadir of the Inquiry for the Metropolitan Police occurred when the author of the internal report into the investigation was called. DCS Roderick Barker, a former head of the Yard's elite Flying Squad, was unable to reconcile his positive report with the litany of failure that the inquiry had heard. During his cross-examination, it rapidly became clear that the internal report – an anodyne description of a routine investigation in which no mistakes had been made – bore no resemblance to the truth. Barker was a senior detective, a man whose job would have put him before judges in trials many times in the past: he had no excuses for his poor performance. MacPherson concluded of Barker: 'In our view, his value as a witness and his credibility in vital matters has already been much undermined for reasons which will be perfectly obvious for anyone here today. We feel we ought to indicate that this review is likely to be regarded by us as indefensible.'

Detective policing (Barker's speciality) is about presenting evidence that will stand up in court. For rational bureaucratic organisations to be governed, those in charge need to be sure that they are being told the truth by their underlings. The Metropolitan Police was under the control of the Home Office, which has always had an interest in making it more efficient, and a tendency to suspect that it could be more fit for its intended purpose. The multiple failures of internal administration discovered by MacPherson meant that the Met was forced to implement the majority of his recommendations. As well as more community consultation, this took the shape of family liaison teams, and the creation of a 'Racial and Violent Crimes Task Force'. The major departure, however, was the admission that policing could be institutionally racist. No longer were police defending their record on the basis of a series of discrete encounters: instead they had been forced to note the extent to which their institution as a whole impacts on society. Merely being accountable to the law was no longer enough.[68]

5. Conclusion

The history of the police institution has remained closely linked with the concrete experience within which British people have experienced the law. Moreover, the development of policing has reflected and amplified social changes: from the incorporation of the middle classes into the British political nation; through the development of secure working-class occupations; to the impact of the various massive changes of the twentieth century. Analogously, the historiography of policing has reflected changes in contemporary views of the role and legitimacy of the police.

As was stated at the outset of this chapter, policing culture is heavily influenced by the traditions and assumptions of the past. However, it is worth noting that some aspects of change have regularly been embraced, albeit sometimes slowly and sometimes in piecemeal fashion. This can most effectively be demonstrated by considering how, over the course of the historical period covered by this chapter, important elements within policing have changed. The motivations and professional orientation of policemen themselves have changed out of all recognition from its roots in the early nineteenth century. Similarly the experience of 'users of the police' – those who see them as a source of help and those who experience what it is to be 'policed' – has also altered dramatically. Nonetheless there are also enduring issues which appear with sustained regularity. Debates about the precise role of the police in both ideal and reality have been a constant theme since their inception, whilst issues of governance and account- ability (the latter currently dramatically in the ascendant) have similarly appeared with considerable regularity.

Notes

1. E. Bittner (1975) *The Functions of the Police in Modern Society: A Review of Background Factors, Current Practices, and Possible Role Models* (New York: Aronson), 39.
2. P.A.J. Waddington (1999) *Policing Citizens: Authority and Rights* (London: UCL Press), 64.
3. C. Emsley (1996) *The English Police: A Political and Social History* (Harlow, Essex: Longman), 8–23.
4. J.M. Beattie (2001) *Policing and Punishment in London: Urban Crime and the Limits of Terror, 1660–1750* (Oxford: Oxford University Press), 404.
5. P. Rawlings (2002) *Policing: A Short History* (Cullompton: Willan), 64–74.
6. R. McGowen (2005) 'The Bank of England and the Policing of Forgery, 1797–1821', *Past & Present*, 186, 81–116.
7. E. Reynolds (1998) *Before the Bobbies: The Night Watch and Police Reform in Metropolitan London, 1720–1830* (London: Macmillan), 5.
8. D. Hobbs (1988) *Doing the Business: Entrepreneurship, Detectives and the Working Class in the East End of London* (Oxford: Clarendon Press), 198.
9. Emsley, C. (2005) 'Sergeant Goddard: The Story of a Rotten Apple or a Diseased Orchard?', in A. Gilman Srebnick and R. Levy (eds.), *Crime and Culture: An Historical Perspective* (Aldershot: Ashgate), 85–104.
10. D. Ascoli (1979) *The Queen's Peace: The Origins and Development of the Metropolitan Police, 1829–1979* (London: Hamish Hamilton), 315–22.
11. H. Goddard (1956) *Memoirs of a Bow Street Runner* (London: Museum Press).
12. B. Porter (1991) *The Origins of the Vigilant State: The London Metropolitan Police Special Branch before the First World War* (Woodbridge: Boydell), 45–7.
13. M. Hassett (2007) '*British Government Responses to Terrorism, 1865–1975*' (PhD thesis, Open University).
14. B. Weinberger (1995) *The Best Police in the World: An Oral History of British Policing* (Aldershot: Scolar Press), 85.
15. C. Emsley (2000) 'The Policeman as Worker: A Comparative Survey c.1800–1940', *International Review of Social History*, 45, 89–110, especially 100.
16. C. Steedman (1984) *Policing the Victorian Community: The Formation of English Provincial Police Forces, 1856–80* (London: Routledge) 124–30.

17. R. Storch (1976) 'The Policeman as Domestic Missionary: Urban Discipline and Domestic Culture in Northern England, 1850–1880', *Journal of Social History*, 9:4, 489–501 and M. Neocleous (2000) *The Fabrication of Social Order: a Critical Theory of Police Power* (London: Pluto Press), 51–3.

18. M. Brogden (1991) *On the Mersey Beat: Policing Liverpool between the Wars* (Oxford: Oxford University Press), 98.

19. C.A. Williams (2000) 'Counting Crimes or Counting People: Some Implications of Mid-nineteenth Century British Police Returns', in *Crime, Histoire & Sociétés/Crime, History & Societies*, 4:2, 77–93.

20. D. Philips and R.D. Storch (1999) *Policing Provincial England, 1829–1856: The Politics of Reform* (London: Leicester University Press), 56–7.

21. R. Swift (1997) 'Heroes or Villains? The Irish, Crime and Disorder in Victorian England', *Albion*, 29, 399–421 and Emsley, *English Police*, 181.

22. C. Emsley (1993) '"Mother, What Did Policemen Do When There Weren't any Motors?" The Law, Police and the Regulation of Motor Traffic in England, 1900–1939', *Historical Journal*, 36, 357–82.

23. J.M. Klein (2007) 'Traffic, Telephones and Police Boxes: The Deterioration of Beat Policing in Birmingham, Liverpool and Manchester Between the World Wars', in G. Blaney (ed.), *Policing Interwar Europe: Continuity, Change and Crisis, 1918–40* (Basingstoke: Palgrave Macmillan), 216–36.

24. J. Bunker (1988) *From Rattle to Radio* (Studley: Brewin Books), 190–200.

25. Weinberger, *Best Police in the World*, 41–4.

26. E. St. Johnston (1978) *One Policeman's Story* (Chichester: Barry Rose), 169.

27. Weinberger, *Best Police in the World*, 73.

28. C.A. Williams (2007) 'Rotten Boroughs? How the Towns of England and Wales Lost their Police Forces in 1964', in J. Moore and J.B. Smith (eds.), *Urban Corruption* (Aldershot: Ashgate), 155–75, especially 159–63.

29. See for instance Williams, 'Rotten Boroughs?', passim and J. Hart (1963) 'Some Reflections on the Report of the Royal Commission on the Police', *Public Law*, 8, 283–304.

30. L. Lustgarten (1986) *The Governance of the Police* (London: Sweet & Maxwell), 125.

31. M. Prince (1988) *God's Cop: The Biography of James Anderton* (London: Frederick Muller).

32. Statewatch (2003) *Special Branch More than Doubles in Size* (Brussels: Statewatch).

33. For example J. Hart (1955) 'Reform of the Borough Police, 1835–1856', *English Historical Review*, 70, 411–27 and S. Pollard (1957) 'The Ethics of the Sheffield Outrages', *Transactions of the Hunter Archaeological Society*, 8, 118–39.

34. C. Reith (1943) *British Police and the Democratic Ideal* (London: Oxford University Press).

35. L. Radzinowicz (1948–86), *A History of English Criminal Law and its Administration from 1750* (4 vols, London: Stevens).

36. C.D. Robinson (1979) 'Ideology as History: A Look at the Way in Which Some English Police Historians Look at the Police', *Police Studies*, 2:2, 35–49.

37. D. Eastwood (1996) 'Communities, Protest and Police in Early Nineteenth-century Oxfordshire: The Enclosure of Otmoor Reconsidered', *Agricultural History Review*, 44:1, 35–46.

38. R.D. Storch (1975) 'The Plague of the Blue Locusts: Police Reform and Popular Resistance in Northern England, 1840–1857', *International Review of Social History*, 20, 61–89.

39. B. Weinberger (1981) 'The Police and the Public in Nineteenth-century Warwickshire', in V. Bailey (ed.), *Policing and Punishment in Nineteenth-century Britain* (London: Croom Helm), 67–93, especially 65.

40. D. Taylor (1997) *The New Police in Nineteenth Century England: Crime, Conflict and Control* (Manchester: Manchester University Press), 82.

41. C.A. Williams (2004) 'The Sheffield Democrats' Critique of Criminal Justice in the 1850s', in R. Colls and R. Rodger (eds.), *Cities of Ideas: Civil Society and Urban Governance in Britain 1800–2000* (Ashgate: Aldershot), 96–120.

42. See for instance R. Paley (1989) '"An Imperfect, Inadequate and Wretched System?" Policing London before Peel', *Criminal Justice History*, 10, 95–130; A.T. Harris (2004) *Policing the City: Crime and Legal Authority in London, 1780–1840* (Columbus: Ohio State University Press) and Reynolds, *Before the Bobbies*.

43. Emsley, *The English Police*, 25.

44. See A. Brundage (1986) 'Ministers, Magistrates and Reformers: The Genesis of the Rural Constabulary Act of 1839', *Parliamentary History: A Yearbook*, 5, 55–64; Storch and Philips, *Policing Provincial England* and S.H. Palmer (1988) *Police and Protest in England and Ireland 1780–1850* (Cambridge: Cambridge University Press).

45. For further discussion see D. Taylor (1998) *Crime, Policing and Punishment in England, 1750–1914* (Basingstoke: Macmillan), 75; Palmer, *Police and Protest*, 385 and A. Silver (1967) 'The Demand for Order in Civil Society: A Review of Some Themes in the History of Urban Crime, Police, and Riot', in D. Bordua (ed.), *The Police: Six Sociological Essays* (London: Wiley), 1–24, especially 10.

46. Storch, 'The Policeman as Domestic Missionary', 481–509.

47. V.A.C. Gatrell (1990) 'Crime, Authority and the Policeman-state', in F.M.L Thompson (ed.), *The Cambridge Social History of Britain 1750–1950, Vol. 3: Social Agencies and Institutions* (Cambridge: Cambridge University Press), 277.

48. See for instance M. Winstanley (1990) 'Preventive Policing in Oldham, c.1826–56', *Transactions of the Lancashire and Cheshire Antiquarian Society*, 96, 17–35 and D. Barrie (2008) *Police in the Age of Improvement* (Cullompton: Willan), 61–91.

49. T.A. Critchley (1967) *A History of Police in England and Wales: 900–1966* (London: Constable).

50. See R. Swift (1988) 'Urban Policing in Early Victorian England, 1835–86: A Reappraisal', *History*, 73, 211–37 and Klein, 'Traffic, Telephones and Police Boxes', 216–36.

51. Palmer, *Police and Protest*.

52. See M. Brogden (1987) 'The Emergence of the Police: The Colonial Dimension', *British Journal of Criminology*, 27:1, 4–14 and G. Sinclair and

C.A. Williams (2007) '"Home and Away": the Cross Fertilisation between "Colonial" and "British" Policing, 1921–1985', *Journal of Imperial and Commonwealth History*, 35:2, 221–38.

53. For further discussion see C.A. Williams (2008) 'Constables for Hire: The History of Private "Public" Policing in the UK', *Policing and Society*, 18:2, 190–205; L. Zedner (2006) 'Policing Before and After the Police: The Historical Antecedents of Contemporary Crime Control', *British Journal of Criminology*, 46, 78–96 and Rawlings, *Policing: A Short History*, 231–3.

54. M. Weaver (1994) 'The New Science of Policing: Crime and the Birmingham Police Force, 1839–1842', *Albion*, 26, 289–308, especially 308.

55. *Birmingham Journal*, February 20, 1841 ['Police Office'].

56. G. Bakewell (1842) *Observations on the Construction of the New Police Force, With a Variety of Useful Information* (London: Simpkin & Marshall), 14.

57. Bakewell, *New Police*, 43.

58. Philips, D. (1989) 'Good Men to Associate and Bad Men to Conspire: Associations for the Prosecution of Felons in England 1760–1860', in D. Hay and F. Snyder (eds.), *Policing and Prosecution in Britain 1750–1850* (Oxford: Clarendon Press), 113–70.

59. P. Waller (1981) *Democracy and Sectarianism: A Political and Social History of Liverpool 1868–1939*. (Liverpool: Liverpool University Press), 114–15.

60. M. Brogden (1982) *The Police: Autonomy and Consent* (London: Academic Press), 68–9.

61. J.W. Nott-Bower (1926) *Fifty-two Years a Policeman* (London: Edward Arnold), 141–6.

62. J. Whitfield (2004) *Unhappy Dialogue: The Metropolitan Police and Black Londoners in Post-war Britain* (Cullompton: Willan).

63. S. Hall et al. (1978) *Policing the Crisis: Mugging, the State, and Law and Order* (London: Macmillan).

64. J. Young and J. Lea (1984) *What is to be Done about Law and Order?* (London: Penguin), 172–3.

65. Cmnd 8427 (1981) *The Brixton Disorders, 10–12 April 1981: Report of an Inquiry by the Rt. Hon. The Lord Scarman, O.B.E.* (London: HMSO).

66. J. Alderson (1984) *Law and Disorder* (London: Hamish Hamilton), 139.

67. J. Foster (2008) '"It Might have been Incompetent, But it wasn't Racist": Murder Detectives' Perceptions of the Lawrence Inquiry and its Impact on Homicide Investigation in London', *Policing and Society*, 18:2, 89–112.

68. See *Sir William Macpherson's Inquiry into the Matters arising from the Death of Stephen Lawrence on 22nd April 1993 to Date, in order to Identify the Lessons Learned for the Investigation and Prosecution of Racially Motivated Crimes*. Report published February 1999.

9 Execution as Punishment in England: 1750–2000

Judith Rowbotham

I. Introduction

Capital punishment is the most extreme of the legislatively endorsed retributions dispensed by society to those convicted of offences deemed a serious threat to the community. This chapter examines execution in England in this socio-legal context, from the middle of the eighteenth century onwards.[1] It charts the radical shifts in attitudes towards this punishment strategy that mark this period; one which witnessed a clear reconsideration of the moral case for using the death penalty but also scrutinised the *manner* of executions. Today in the UK, parliament effectively accepts that execution is no longer morally justifiable in a 'civilised' state.[2]

Execution was an intrinsic element relating to the wider objectives of punishment, with debates stretching back to ancient Greece – debates that have been continually reinvigorated. These established that the offence needed practical as well as moral strategies in order to redress the balance and achieve justice. In that context, the very irreversibility of the death penalty established it as the ultimate sanction. Judeo-Christian thought added the exhortation in Genesis to justify the death penalty.[3]

Eighteenth-century Enlightenment thought reconsidered the purpose of punishment. This occurred amongst thinkers from Hegel to Nietzsche, and most notably in recent times in the ideas of Foucault. In his seminal work, *Discipline and Punish*, Foucault identified the shifting focus, from public to private and from the corporal aspects to the mental and moral aspects of punishment.[4]

The ethics of capital punishment provided a significant problem for eighteenth-century thinkers, at a time when society was reimagined in a more 'civilised' format. Utilitarians like Jeremy Bentham stressed a more compassionate, redemptive approach to wrongdoing.[5] However the death penalty's retributive quality made it problematic in a 'modern and civilised' age.[6] Then, as now, questions have remained about the appropriate context for this violent form of retribution.

2. Chronology

Hanging has a long pedigree in English memory as a form of execution for heinous criminal offences.[7] Literary depictions of executions indicate that hanging was relatively cheap and effective, and provided a good spectacle. These rituals were, with few exceptions, reserved for the most serious of offences such as treason. Beheading, burning and other elaborations, notably hanging, drawing and quartering, were generally reserved for high-profile or political figures.

The Treason Act 1351, its amendments and related legislation, such as the Sedition Act 1661, were rarely used after the end of the seventeenth century and after 1746, there were only four further executions for treason in that century.[8] During the nineteenth century, the trend moved strongly away from invoking the death penalty for treason. Fenian offenders, for instance, were charged either under the terms of the Treason Felony Act 1848 or (as in the case of the Clerkenwell Outrage of 1867) with murder.[9] While the sanction remained on the statute books until 1870, the Cato Street Conspirators in 1820 were the last in England to be so sentenced.[10]

The practice of hanging became the favoured method of execution for 'everyday' crimes, from murder to theft,[11] and is the focus of this chapter. Traditionally, crimes against the person most readily attracted a death sentence. Murder, rape, arson and robbery were tried as capital crimes in royal courts as the so-called 'Four Pleas of the Crown', but had latterly been joined by buggery and sodomy.[12] Property crime, however, dominated contemporary concerns during the eighteenth century, attracting a mandatory death sentence in the so-called 'Bloody Code'. There was a long tradition of high-profile capital property crime (such as the counterfeiting of coins), but the statute book was extended to include ever more minor property crimes.[13]

The eighteenth century confirmed the individual possession of property as a marker of social status and economic wealth. Thus contemporaries went to grotesque lengths to punish 'minor' crimes, from petty theft or insignificant damage to property. The process of expansion began with the notorious Waltham Black Act of 1723, which added 50 new property-related offences carrying a mandatory death penalty, with a further 60 being added during the reign of George III.[14]

The extraordinary rise in capital offences went alongside eighteenth-century society's perception of a rising crime wave.[15] The reality was (as today) the opposite of what contemporaries assumed. *Per capita* crime levels had been falling from the beginning of the eighteenth century, but rising population levels and urbanisation meant that numbers of crimes were going up in numerical, though not proportionate terms, and so, consequently, were actual prosecutions.[16] Also, thanks to the growing number of media outlets, criminality seemed both more visible yet anonymous, and more threatening.[17] The ultimate deterrent was sought because of the perceived incompetence of eighteenth-century policing methods. Thus by making the penalty disproportionate to the crime committed, such terror supposedly induced possible offenders to refrain from lawbreaking. As Block and Hostettler point out, the terms of the 1752 Act for the Better Prevention of Murder makes this particularly clear.[18] Commentators such as Henry Fielding justified this apparent individual injustice by emphasising the wider deterrent effect caused by the horrified reactions to such disproportionate punishment.[19]

By the early nineteenth century, over 230 crimes besides murder carried such a mandatory sentence.[20] This system (the 'Bloody Code') attracted fierce debate over its relevance as either deterrent or moral solution by the early nineteenth century. The arguments of figures like Montesquieu and Beccaria, who focused on its very irrationality and negative impact on a witnessing crowd, influenced figures like Jeremy Bentham and Samuel Romilly, key campaigners against the Bloody Code.[21] Hangings at Tyburn (today's Marble Arch) involved the procession by the condemned prisoners around three miles from London prisons, notably Newgate, adding to the spectacle.[22] Execution crowds were substantial in number, and often riotous and rude in behaviour, despite attracting men and women from all social levels – inviting much debate about human nature.[23] Edmund Burke insisted on the dramatic nature of the spectacle involved.[24] Samuel Johnson famously remarked in 1783 that 'Executions are intended to draw spectators, if they do not, they do not answer their purpose ... the public was gratified by a procession, the criminal supported by it.'[25]

However, by the middle of the eighteenth century, large numbers of sentences were commuted to transportation or pardons, making the Bloody Code seem ever more irrational and arbitrary.[26] It certainly made some unwilling to prosecute, as Gatrell points out.[27] However, as McLynn argues, a central justification of the Bloody Code was the supposed deterrence implicit in the horrible randomness of its operation.[28] Significantly, this created unwillingness amongst juries to convict, despite the evidence, because it became difficult to estimate the likelihood of a reprieve.[29] Few things emphasised this more than the continued use of the so-called 'neck verse', which conferred benefit of clergy, under a statute of 1350, on all who could recite from Psalm 51. Men like Blackstone saw it as providing an amelioration of the penal code, but Fitzjames Stephen later noted that it had 'reduced the administration of justice to a farce'.[30]

Yet the Code had its high-profile defenders into the nineteenth century. In 1817 for instance, the Lord Chancellor, Lord Ellenborough, stated that only 'terror alone could prevent the commission of that crime under consideration'.[31] But, when Tory Home Secretary in the 1820s, Sir Robert Peel, set about dismantling the English Bloody Code, his modernising policies echoed the *reforming* arguments of his political opponent, the Whig Attorney-General, Sir Samuel Romilly. Tellingly, Peel himself was not persuaded by arguments of the inhumanity of the punishment. Instead he concluded that the established strategy was failing in its intended purpose.[32]

a) 'Civilising the Process'

By the 1840s, the criminal code had been dramatically transformed in a remarkably short period of time. By the 1830s, offences carrying a mandatory death sentence had been reduced to 30; by the end of the 1840s the only offences warranting consideration of a death sentence were murder and crimes against the state, notably treason, arson in the royal dockyards or military stores and piracy on the high seas. Murder became established as the only crime where, in actual practice (except in time of war), conviction could result in execution.[33]

This indicates there was an active debate by the early nineteenth century about the usefulness of capital punishment. In punishing the relatively rare crime of murder, the debate focused on the appropriateness of hanging as a punishment, given its entirely retributive quality. In the post-1861 period, all death sentences saw subsequent petitions for clemency to the Home Secretary, usually including signatures from prosecution witnesses and jurymen. This suggests a gap between a general, morally driven popular support for the use of the death penalty and approval of the punishment in actual cases.[34]

The impact of executions on spectators constituted a debate where the official and populist advocates of public hanging were increasingly on the losing side from the 1840s onwards. [35] In his 1836 essay, 'Civilisation', J.S. Mill had argued that 'the spectacle, and even the very idea, of pain, is kept more and more out of sight of those ... who enjoy in their fullness the benefits of civilisation' because such spectacles hindered 'co-operation' within such communities.[36] Evangelical thought also opposed the public spectacle.[37] Overall, it was agreed that it was far more 'moral' for respectable society to witness the trial than the execution.[38]

Accepting this reality, the Capital Punishment (Amendment) Act 1868 maintained executions, but without public participation, though the presence of reporters as 'witnesses' for the public was permitted.[39] The last public hanging was that of the 'Clerkenwell Outrage' Fenian, Michael Barratt, in May 1868. In terms of the legislative context, efforts at reform concentrated upon the parameters of executions. Thus, while the last juvenile under 16 to be hanged was John Any Bird Bell, aged 14, in 1831,[40] public pressure saw an official restriction of capital sentences with the passage of the Children's Act 1908, which established the minimum age for execution as 16 (later raised to 18, with subsequent legislation in the Children and Young Person's Act 1933).

The scaffold's withdrawal behind the private walls of prisons also had more complex implications. One was provided by detailed reportage of capital trials. Importantly these were now better conducted than those discussed by Gatrell, leading to a substantial increase in the numbers of courtroom spectators, especially when it came to murder trials.[41] First defined in the modern sense in the Offences against the Person Act 1861, attempts to refine the common law of murder to permit a separation into categories of 'capital' killings and 'non-capital' killings failed. Nonetheless, only morally outrageous convicted murderers were executed in the last half of the century.[42] As Howard Taylor has pointed out, an average of 7 per cent of those convicted of murder actually went to the scaffold.[43]

Once hangings retreated from a direct public gaze, in the last decades of the nineteenth century experiments took place to refine the execution process to affirm its public acceptability in this new private guise. In 1885, for instance, the Home Office commissioned a standard gallows design, first used in 1890 at Kirkdale Prison (Liverpool), with an accurate and efficient execution drop. The use of this design spread throughout England and Wales and was later extended to the colonies.[44] By the start of 1890, the Home Office developed the formal training of hangmen, and in 1892 issued an official directive on the methods to be used.[45] Effectively, this modernised the process but ironically, as Gatrell suggests, took abolition off the political agenda for a substantial period.[46]

b) The Road to Abolition

As McGowen points out, both sides of the death penalty debate looked beyond the physical process to its capacity for psychological terror, thereby stressing the enduring importance of deterrence as a moral consideration. This emphasised the moral 'character of justice' and the visible exercise of the law's power.[47] Certainly printed matter dealing with the topic influenced the debate. Gatrell shows that execution ballads were an intrinsic part of the ritual for the masses in particular.[48] In addition, the nineteenth century (especially from the 1840s onwards) saw an increased discussion of these issues by 'respectable' society.[49]

From the early eighteenth century an organised opposition to capital punishment had sought to counter arguments for the extensive use of the death penalty. Cesare Beccaria had powerfully demonstrated that the deterrent effect of capital punishment did not work, thereby creating the modern case against the death penalty, with its emphasis on the need for appropriate punishment. For him, this also preserved what he saw as 'the social compact', binding together the rulers and the ruled, compelling the exercise of power to avoid excess.[50] In different ways, Beccaria's thesis was revisited by opponents of the death penalty up to the final debates in 1964.

Understanding the importance of the media's contribution to shaping abolition is essential, especially during the 1840s, 1850s and 1860s. There were many respectable members of society, like Charles Dickens, who did not oppose the death penalty but rather the current management of executions.[51] Particularly in the 1840s and 1850s, the press argued that the impressions acquired were negative in their individual and social impact.[52] Newspaper titles from the *Daily Telegraph*, with its predominantly working-class readership, to *The Times,* with its upper- and middle-class target audience, gave considerable, increasingly unwanted, detail about individual executions.[53] This was especially so when things went wrong, as they famously did in the execution of William Bousfield, who had so badly burned himself in an eve-of-execution suicide attempt that he could not stand unaided, and so was placed in a chair on the trapdoor of the scaffold. The hangman, William Calcraft, released the drop, and left the scaffold, as was his wont. Unfortunately, the method of hanging gave Bousfield a chance to try to save himself. According to *The Times* and the *Daily Telegraph*, the horrified crowd viewed him raising himself up no less than three times, until Calcraft and his assistants went below and held his legs until he expired.[54]

Just over a week later, the *Daily Telegraph* reported on a public lecture delivered by Reverend Dr Burns on the abolition of capital punishment. Burns effectively summed up the main issues in the Victorian debate:

> That capital punishment did not exert a virtuous influence on society was clear, from the fact that there is no scene more demoralising in its effect than that of seeing a fellow creature publicly strangled in the presence of some thousands of spectators, the majority of whom are persons of a vicious character; and it was also a notorious fact that criminals are even made and multiplied at the foot of the gallows.[55]

But he reinforced his arguments further by referring to the negative impact on the legal system and upon individuals implicated in the trial process:

> He adverted to the pernicious influence which the law exerted on jurymen, from the fact that a strong feeling existed in their minds

against bringing in a verdict of guilty when the severe sentence of death would be recorded, even in cases where the guilt of the criminal was clearly established; and when such is the case they must falsify the oath they take before taking their position as jurymen.[56]

The following year, though, another clergyman, Joseph Kingsmill, the Chaplain at Pentonville Prison, wrote to *The Times* to comment:

With regards to public executions, I do not hesitate to give my opinion that, even as they are at present managed in England, they are, upon the whole, salutary in their effects. You want to read a terrible lesson to those classes from which most danger is to be feared. The very scum of society become at once the audience, and a most attentive one.[57]

In the middle of the century opposition had included abolitionists, but also those opposed merely to the public spectacle.[58] The disappearance of the spectacle ensured that the abolitionist movement lost much of its impetus, once the immediate impression of suffering was no longer such a powerful factor operating on individual consciences.

Once unnecessary physical pain for the condemned had been prevented, individuals ignored the mental torture that the sentence undoubtedly inflicted. Possibly this indicates a continuity of the stern moral perspective expressed by the Revd Henry Cotton, prison chaplain at Newgate, who was gratified that Joseph Harwood, convicted of highway robbery in 1824, broke under the strain of awaiting either pardon or execution, indicating a suitable state of remorse.[59]

And yet, there was still a degree of physical horror associated with executions, if of a more voyeuristic nature.[60] After 1868, capital punishment's proponents argued for a silence over all but the barest details of executions (time, place, and by whom effected). Initially, however, a fair degree of detail was included in the coverage because of the use of lawyers as reporters, but this dwindled in the twentieth century.[61] As executions became less reported to a still interested public, the rumours about the reality of executions and occasional bungling grew to fill the space created by that interest.[62] Effectively, the visible reality was replaced by a gruesome imagined reality, which accorded with the moral terror deemed essential for the deterrent effect to work.[63] Certainly, once reporters disappeared from executions (after 1910), rumours about what had happened behind the closed doors of the prisons expanded significantly, especially in the interwar period.[64]

The British twentieth-century abolition campaign started with the Labour Party's abolitionist stance in its 1927 'Manifesto on Capital Punishment'. The events of 1930, however, reveal the purely theoretical nature of the Manifesto. Though a Royal Commission in that year recommended to the Labour government that an experimental five-year suspension of executions be implemented, its conclusions were ignored.

Even though the interwar years saw a real decline in crime and prosecutions, ironically the numbers of executions as a proportion of convictions had begun to rise after the 1920s.[65] This was encouraged by the diminishing public appetite for newspaper publicity and crime fiction. Such fiction hindered the use of petitions for mercy, as it (witness Dorothy L. Sayers's tale, *Strong Poison*, 1931) reinforced a new popular perception that once a sentence had been passed, without further evidence, the capital punishment process was unstoppable. It is during the twentieth century, when the state has such effective control over the information emanating from the scaffold, that Foucault's argument for use of the death penalty as a demonstration of state power has some validity for the UK.[66]

However, several postwar high-profile miscarriages of justice reinvigorated the abolition debate, leading to the long-delayed ending of the process.[67] In 1949 public concern over the conviction and execution of Timothy Evans, a man of low intelligence found guilty of the infamous Rillington Place murders, was compounded when it was established that the perpetrator had been another individual, John Christie.[68] This furore was followed by the controversial execution in July 1955 of Ruth Ellis, who proved to be the last woman hanged in Britain.[69] Soon after this, the death penalty was restricted further under the terms of the Homicide Act 1957 which achieved the distinction between capital and non-capital homicides which had eluded the Victorians. The only categories of murder eligible for the death penalty were: murder in the course or furtherance of theft; murder by shooting or causing an explosion; murder while resisting arrest or during an escape and finally murder of a police officer or prison officer. This tried to rationalise what had hitherto been identified as a moral choice for judges and Home Secretaries. This made capital punishment unpopular since it could no longer command public respect because it seemed as arbitrary as the Bloody Code.[70] Inevitably, then, the death penalty was suspended under the Murder (Abolition of Death Penalty) Act 1965.

In 1969, the Home Secretary proposed a removal of the five year limit on the death penalty's suspension, making it permanent, a motion carried by both Houses of Parliament. Thereafter it became traditional, until 1998, to hold a free vote on the restoration of the death penalty in every parliamentary session, which was always defeated.[71] Final removal of the option (except in times of war) appeared on the statute books in 1998. Under the terms of Protocol 13 of the European Convention (to which Britain signed up in 2003), the restoration of capital punishment under any circumstances is no longer available to British legislators. Even after 1965, the Privy Council carried the ultimate responsibility for hearing appeals and approving the capital sentence in former colonies. However, a continuing Labour Party campaign resulted in abolition in 2002 in the last British territory to retain it, though former colonies such as Jamaica severed links with the Privy Council in order to retain their power to execute people.[72] In addition, the fact that small numbers of Britons are regularly sentenced to death for crimes from murder to drug trafficking in non-Commonwealth countries ensures that the topic remains in the public domain.[73]

3. Historiography

The historiography of capital punishment and its abolition is not just a debate about punishment, but reflects the dominant agendas of historians seeking to investigate the moral status of societies. With some exceptions, such as Harry Potter's excellent survey of the religious dimension to capital punishment,[74] it is difficult not to see the twentieth-century historiography of this area of crime and punishment as being afflicted by what Peter Linebaugh termed a 'conceptual timidity'. This has resulted in a concentration by historians on narratives of the machinery of justice, while detailed discussion of the ethics of capital punishment have been largely left to legal scholars and criminologists.[75] A generation ago, the 'Bloody Code' was seen by Marxist historians, such as Linebaugh, as part of a system of tyranny practiced by the property-owning classes.[76] Douglas Hay's essay on 'Property, Authority and the Criminal Law' in *Albion's Fatal Tree* was the key text challenged by non-Marxist historians, most notably John Langbein. He noted that the statutes described were more obviously nervous reactions to individual encroachments rather then anything resembling a concerted policy.[77]

John Beattie has led a later more nuanced comprehension of law and the criminal justice system in the eighteenth century.[78] He, Langbein and others, like Peter King, have pointed out that the majority of the victims of crime were not the propertied elites suggested by Hay et al., but rather the 'small shopkeepers, artisans, lodging-house keepers, innkeepers and so forth'.[79] Beattie also suggested that searching for a property-led 'conspiracy' to implicate the poor had overlooked the importance of the jury and its famously recalcitrant nature.[80] As Langbein also points out, decisions reached by juries were in essence 'sentencing decisions', where the avoidance of a full guilty verdict was sufficient to avert execution.[81]

A major flaw in the analysis of many historians when dealing with punishment is the presumption that the passing of a sentence is the end of the criminal narrative. As long ago as 1948 as part of the abolitionist debate, Leon Radzinowicz first noted the discrepancy between conviction rates and actual executions. In the wake of *Albion's Fatal Tree*, research by Jim Sharpe and Peter King emphasised that the numbers of those hanged, rather than being reprieved, pardoned or transported, diminished during the period of the Bloody Code.[82] Gatrell argues convincingly that little changed after its repeal, since the process of avoiding actual execution of death sentences continued.[83] In the last half of the nineteenth century, the overwhelming majority of those convicted (by this time, only of murder) had their sentences reprieved to life imprisonment.[84] Some debate still continues, though, over the impact of executions on the crowd. Thomas Laqueur, back in 1989, argued that execution crowds were 'titillated' by the spectacle. Linebaugh still insists that the evidence he promoted in *Albion's Fatal Tree* indicates that crowds demonstrated their scorn at hangings alongside contempt for the legal process and established authority.[85]

Later historians have derived meaningful analysis from the issue of the punishment itself and its performativity. Foucault's concentration on capital punishment in *Discipline and Punish* related to the execution process as the ritual performance of state power.[86] However, in *The Hanging Tree*, V.A.C. Gatrell emphasised the role of the masses, as spectators of the execution spectacle, developing upon Laqueur's use of the word 'carnival'.[87] In England at least, the execution's witnesses were not the passive onlookers implied by Foucault's study.[88] Instead, they expressed their emotions and reactions to particular events and individuals on the scaffold.[89] The power of this was sometimes further emphasised by the behaviour of the prisoner, who was expected to be a didactic example to all.[90] What Gatrell's detailed study of execution crowds emphasises is that in the English execution process at least, the visible demonstration of state power was not a key feature of these events.[91]

For commentators like Samuel Johnson, and also Henry Fielding, who (unlike Johnson) desired a reform of the system, the point about the visibility of executions was that they demonstrated the justice system in action.[92] As Gatrell comments, while crowds frequently approved executions, when 'humbler people were hanged for humble crimes, they participated in an ongoing debate about the usefulness and purpose of the death penalty by acting like act like a Greek chorus, mocking justice's pretensions'.[93]

Some historians have probed the concrete experience of the death penalty and its use. Before the long drop, the horrific reality of executions for the victims, at least, has been passionately depicted, and in great detail, by Gatrell.[94] A number of important amplifying articles by scholars like Randall McGowen have also appeared in recent years.[95] The historiographical focus for the years after the removal of the Bloody Code and up to the ending of public executions does, to an extent, act as an afterword to the main debates discussed here. The way in which the body of those executed is depicted in the secondary literature provides a useful way for comprehending the shift in both the execution process and its historio-graphical depiction. Gatrell and McGowen, for instance, stress the grue-some and ghastly spectacle provided by the hanged body, and the extent to which a post-mortem dimension was added to those of murderers, through dissection.[96] However, the emphasis in the later period stressed that the 'professionally' executed body displayed minimal marks of violence.[97]

The apparent professionalisation of the execution process has been par-ticularly sustained by autobiographical texts.[98] The reportage from the prison scaffolds ensured that the professional 'secrets' of the new breed of executioner were widely known.

It is worth reflecting again on the extent to which historiographical developments are driven by present-minded concerns and that the gen-eral contexualising historiography of crime in the twentieth century is still sparse. Thus we still await work that may reveal the kinds of debates that have so invigorated and enlivened eighteenth-century historiography.[99] John Carter Wood's challenging work on violence, looking forward into the twentieth century, focused more on the social context of crime and criminals than on the punishment process *per se*.[100] Equally, Harry Potter and Hugh McLeod have focused on the Christian dimension to execution and the abolition process, but post-1918 realities are only one aspect of their texts.[101] Historical sociologist Christie Davies has also contributed to this aspect of the debate, with his argument that abolitionism in the 1960s was an element in modern permissiveness, but as Green and Whiting point out, it remains the 'the least discussed aspect of the [modern] state's involvement in civil society and personal life'.[102]

There are a number of detailed articles on aspects of the abolition-ist campaign, notably Victor Bailey's careful study of the attitude of the Labour Government 1945–51 which makes important, but still (in terms of thematic scope and chronology) limited contributions.[103] However, texts focusing on the capital punishment abolition and its politics in the twenti-eth century have not come from historians. Individual high-profile cases have attracted attention, but these are not linked to a historical discussion of the death penalty's socio-cultural impacts.[104] Works such as Block and Hostettler's *Hanging in the Balance* or Hood and Hoyle's *Death Penalty* are stimulating texts, but their legal or criminological perspective makes them narrative rather than analytical.[105] Thus, the historian interested in the social and economic dimensions of the twentieth-century abolition campaign awaits the equivalent of Gatrell or McLynn.

Amongst lawyers and criminologists, the debate continues (though mainly with a contemporary American focus) in terms which are familiar to the historian. Isaac Ehrlich, who argued in 1975 that executions pre-vented murders in the USA, continues to be cited while opposition, most recently from Paul Zimmerman, has voiced equally vehement denial of the concept.[106] These ideas must influence any future historical surveys of the history of abolition in Britain, since they help with an understanding of how the abolition debate, once the public spectacle issue was dealt with, became a matter mainly amongst professionals and politicians.

4. Case Studies

a) The Hanging

While the majority of hangings took place in London, provincial executions were also popular spectacles. The descriptions of the execution in August 1828, at Bury St Edmunds, of the man found guilty of the Red Barn or Polstead Murder, provides vivid insights into the realities of executions, and their popular presentation.

On the eve of his execution, William Corder, son of a yeoman farmer, confessed to shooting his pregnant mistress, Maria Marten, and to burying her body in the Red Barn in May 1827. It was a sensational case, not so much because of the fairly common and sordid facts, but because of the mechanism for the discovery of the murder. Maria's stepmother dreamed that her murdered body was buried in the nearby Red Barn, and persuaded her husband to search it.[107]

Once the body was found, the arrest and conviction of Corder was predictable, as was local and national interest. Elements of the case appealed to a wide audience, ensuring significant media attention: it featured a sensational murder and a criminal from a respectable background as popular titillations.[108]

According to such sources, Corder, as was expected of a 'good exit', repeated his confession on the scaffold and acknowledged the justice of his sentence. This ritual was important in assuring the direct and indirect witness to a 'just' execution.[109] Contemporary sources indicate that several thousand spectators arrived, representing a wide class and gender mix of society; emphasising the points made by Laqueur about the cross-class appeal of such events.[110] The crowd was apparently both noisy and cheerful, matching Gatrell's account of the complexity of crowd reactions at such events and the importance of the crowd's endorsement of the event.[111] Corder's progress to the scaffold was marked by due ritual (he shook hands with fellow felons, a process which deeply affected them), and equally appropriately, as a testament to justice, he needed physical support to meet his ghastly fate. Once hanging, his legs were hauled on by the hangman (Foxton) until he expired after several agonised minutes, when his body was cut down and delivered (still warm) to be anatomised.[112] What is striking in all this is the lack of squeamishness displayed by crowds and commentators. The rise of middle-class sensibility was by no means established even in 1828, despite the moves to dismantle the Bloody Code by that time. It did, however, manifest itself by the time of the second case study, focusing on hangman William Marwood in the 1870s.

b) The Hangman

Another way of illustrating issues such as the performativity within capital punishment is provided by an examination of the reportage of the performance of hangmen, their techniques of execution and the reaction to these, found in works like Howard Engel's *Lord High Executioner*, or Steven Fielding's *Executioner's Bible*.[113] Traditionally, hangmen had not been seen as savoury characters, with many, like the fabled Jack Ketch, being themselves criminals. Things had changed by the nineteenth century, however, with the arrival of public executioners of working-class respectability such as William Calcraft. Calcraft was the last of the 'traditional' hangmen: his successors were to claim the status of being professionals who had an expertise based upon training, practice or talent.[114]

William Marwood started his career as hangman in 1871, and quietly built a reputation as an efficient practitioner.[115] On becoming effectively the official 'national' hangman in 1874 when Calcraft retired, William Marwood made public statements, highlighting his claims to status. His self-description as 'Public Executioner', *never* as 'hangman' (a term he vehemently rejected), emphasised his 'professional' preparations for an execution, in contrast to Calcraft's technique (or lack of it).[116] Marwood is famously quoted as having insisted: 'He [Calcraft] hanged them – I executed them.'[117] He explained that by careful weighing and measuring of the condemned man or woman, the height of the drop could be calculated as to ensure almost instantaneous death through dislocation of the vertebrae.[118] In fact, the idea of using a longer drop to ensure a swifter death was already well known in England, but it was Marwood who popularised its use.[119]

From the start, the press coverage of Marwood's hangings emphasised his 'new' professional standards. In an early London hanging, inside the Surrey County Gaol in Horsemonger Lane, Southwark in October 1874, he despatched wife-murderer John Coppen. *Lloyds Weekly* reported to its working-class readership that Marwood's 'instruments' were 'very different' to those used by Calcraft: the rope was 'much larger and coarser and very much longer, so that the "drop" is nearly five feet when the scaffold falls'; while he also made use of an 'entirely new leather apparatus for confining the arms of the criminal', ensuring that there could be no attempt at resistance in what had become an orderly process.[120]

Marwood' had, according to *Reynolds News* (another title with a quintessentially working-class readership), a 'much more pleasing manner', dressing in what became identified as his 'uniform': superfine black cloth and with a 'massive' gold ring and chain.[121] In terms of performativity, Marwood's visibility compensated among the lower classes for the invisibility of the actual execution, as aptly summed up in the popular music hall couplet:

'If Pa killed Ma, who'd kill Pa?' – 'Marwood!'[122]

This explains why popular pressure for a removal of the death penalty made little headway in the decades following 1868. A very different context was required for the revival of the abolitionist campaign.

c) The Abolitionist

In British terms, the abolitionist campaign dates from the first efforts of John Howard (after whom the Howard League was named) in the late eighteenth century. Its continuation elsewhere ensures that the British experience forms part of the global movement today. The British context, of the 1960s, throws up a number of names including Sydney Silverman, Margaret Fry, Mrs Van der Elst and Roy and Theodora Calvert. Labour MP Silverman is usually, rightly, awarded the credit of persisting in bringing the issue before parliament from the 1930s on and realising the aspirations of the Labour Party's abolitionist tendency. However, the names of Mr and Mrs Calvert are much less familiar. They were, however, representative of a type of abolitionist that distinguished the campaign from the start. Both were convinced Christians, fuelling their passionate commitment to the abolitionist cause, a factor noted as important by Potter and McLeod. Nonetheless the Calverts did not rely solely upon that motivation for their arguments against the death penalty. Indeed, this would have been difficult, given the long-standing endorsement of capital punishment by leading Christians well into the twentieth century.[123]

Quaker Roy Calvert became convinced from an early age of the moral iniquity of the death penalty, using his position as a civil servant to accumulate material challenging its usefulness. In his Preface to his seminal text, *Capital Punishment in the Twentieth Century*, he went beyond sentiment and objected that the death penalty was 'both futile and immoral' on the basis of authoritative international statistical evidence.[124] So passionate was he about his cause that in 1922, aged 28, he abandoned the civil service to campaign full time for abolition, becoming a key figure in the National Campaign for the Abolition of Capital Punishment, founded in 1925. *Capital Punishment* had a profound effect, and can be credited with strongly influencing the course of the debate. Calvert died of septicaemia in 1933, aged only 33, but his wife Theodora continued the fight, ensuring that his work, especially *Capital Punishment*, was updated and reissued. Theodora (née Llewellyn Davies), the first woman barrister to be elected to the Inner Temple, continued as a campaigner for abolition, recruiting the support of other women in influential positions such as Maude Roydon, Lady Astor and Mrs Wintringham, JP.[125] The importance of the Calverts' contribution to abolition cannot be underestimated. When the Lords, in 1969, confirmed the permanency of the Murder (Abolition of Death Penalty) Act 1965, Lord Chorley paid tribute to 'the great work' done by Roy Calvert in his 'remarkable book', which – in his opinion – had subsequently done 'more than anything else' to 'build up informed opinion on this subject'.[126]

5. Conclusion

The drama of the scaffold has been a major element in this chapter, though a direct witnessing gaze on the execution process has long been a distant memory in Britain, but kept alive by media presentations of fact and fiction. At its strongest in the days of public hanging, the performativity of the scaffold ritual retained a fascination for the public, though that dimension has, sadly, been little explored for the last century. It was always an issue which had a strong class dimension, in that more men and women of the working class went to the scaffold than from any other class (unsurprising, given the standard expectation that social class determined responsibility for most crime). This made it far from surprising that in the twentieth century, the Labour Party has had the strongest association with that campaign amongst the political parties.

Christianity, or at least the attitudes of proclaimed Christian men and women, has always had a slightly more equivocal attitude, with both sides being prepared to emphasise biblical arguments. Today, there is little official or popular faith in the reformative potential of punishment, which seems to have been a key factor for most abolitionists up to the 1950s: but there is no longer any power to resort to the ultimate in retribution.[127] Where that leaves the Christian side in this debate remains unresolved.

Equally, the reasons for the final success of abolition are still a matter of debate. Whilst the position of the Anglican Church in the 1960s shifted to a pro-abolitionist stance, under the leadership of Archbishop Ramsey, it could not be claimed that abolition represented a triumph for the Christian perspective and its political influence. In explaining the 1965 decision, it is plain that a majority of politicians and lawyers became convinced that it was not a deterrent to crime by the 1960s. High-profile miscarriages of justice such as the cases of the Birmingham Six or the Guildford Four in the years since 1965 have damaged demands for a restoration of the death penalty.

Undoubtedly, as scholars from Gatrell to Hood and Hoyle have noted, the privatisation of the spectacle, alongside professionalisation of the actual process , was a crucial first stage in curbing the death penalty as the ultimate punishment strategy.[128] Today, when there are high-profile murders, as with the murder of Sarah Payne in 2000, there is a renewed public call for the restoration of hanging.[129] However, it is worth pointing out that even could this happen, it is likely that the late Victorian reality would reassert itself, with public indignation at a crime being always tempered, in practical reality, by an established public distaste for the actual execution. Petitions would return, and few, if any would actually be hanged at the end, thus making the restoration of the death penalty not only morally undesirable, but also practically useless as either deterrent or satisfactory social retribution.

Notes

1. Both Scotland and Ireland in had different jurisdictions. Thus if there were some commonalities between the methods of execution, and if in the later nineteenth and twentieth centuries, English hangmen served Scotland and Ireland also, the legal context within which this took place was significantly different. It can be pointed out that neither had a Bloody Code, however, and that proportionately as well as numerically, fewer people were hanged in either country. For further discussion see S.J. Connelly (1988) 'Albion's Fatal Twigs: Justice and Law in the Eighteenth Century', in R. Mitchison and P Roebuck (eds.), *Economy and Society in Scotland and Ireland, 1500–1939* (Edinburgh: John Donald), 117–25.
2. See for example the powerfully argued text, R. Hood and C. Hoyle (2008) *The Death Penalty: A Worldwide Perspective*, 3rd edn. (Oxford: Oxford University Press).
3. Genesis 9.6. Such sentiments were reinforced in several places in the Bible, as in Exodus 21.12; Deuteronomy 19.11–13.
4. M. Foucault (1977) *Discipline and Punish: The Birth of the Prison* (London: Allen Lane), especially 3–16.
5. See H.A. Bedau (1987) *Death is Different: Studies in the Morality, Law and Politics of Capital Punishment* (Boston: Northeastern University Press), Chapter 3, for a discussion of Bentham's perspective.
6. D. Garland (1991) 'Sociological Perspectives on Punishment', *Crime and Justice*, 14, 115–66, especially 116. See also B. Vaughan (2000) 'The Civilising Process and the Janus Face of Modern Punishment', *Theoretical Criminology*, 4:1, 71–89.
7. J.H. Baker (2002) *An Introduction to English Legal History*, (London: Butterworth), 501.
8. For a detailed narrative of such trials, see Francis Hargrave (1742) (ed.), *A Complete Collection of State-trials, and Proceedings for High-treason,*

Commencing with the Eleventh year of the Reign of King Richard II, and ending with the Sixteenth year of the Reign of King George III, 11 vols. (4th edn., Dublin).

9. See for instance P. Quinlivand and P. Rose (1982) *The Fenians in England* (London: John Calder).

10. The last similar event in Scotland also took place in 1820, after the '1820 Insurrection'. For a discussion of treason trials written by a lawyer, see A. Wharam (1996) *Treason: Famous English Treason Trials* (Stroud: Sutton).

11. See B. Bailey (1989) *Hangmen of England. A History of Execution from Jack Ketch to Albert Pierrepoint* (London: W.H. Allen), 3.

12. For a discussion of this see T.M. Cooley (ed.) (2003) *Blackstone's Commentaries on the Laws of England* (Boston: Lawbook Exchange), Book III, Chapter 4, 22–4.

13. See for instance J.M. Beattie (1992) 'London Crime and the Making of the "Bloody Code", 1689–1718', in L. Davison, T. Hitchcock, T. Keirn and R.B. Shoemaker (eds.), *Stilling the Grumbling Hive: The Response to Social and Economic Problems in England, 1689–1750* (New York: St. Martin's Press), 49–76.

14. For a full discussion of the Black Acts see E.P. Thompson (1977) *Whigs and Hunters: The Origin of the Black Act* (Harmondsworth: Penguin).

15. See for instance J.M. Beattie (1974) 'The Pattern of Crime in England 1660–1800', *Past and Present*, 62, 47–95, at 47.

16. Ibid., 47–95. See also J.A. Sharpe (1984) *Crime in Early Modern England 1550–1750* (London: Longman), passim.

17. See for instance C. Emsley (1983) *Policing and Its Context 1750–1870* (New York: Schocken Books) and J.M. Beattie (1986) *Crime and the Courts in England, 1660–1800* (Princeton: Princeton University Press).

18. See B. Block and J. Hostettler (1997) *Hanging in the Balance: A History of the Abolition of Capital Punishment in Britain* (London: Waterside Press), 30. Under the terms of that Act, execution was to follow immediately after conviction (within 48 hours, lessening the chance of a successful appeal) and the bodies of murderers were to be subjected automatically to post-mortem punishments such as a public dissection as a further gruesome part of the penalty for murder. Ibid., 30.

19. See F. McLynn (1989) *Crime and Punishment in Eighteenth-Century England* (London: Routledge), 249–51.

20. D. Phillips (1993) 'Crime, Law and Punishment in the Industrial Revolution', in P.K. O'Brien and R. Quinault (eds.), *The Industrial Revolution and British Society* (Cambridge: Cambridge University Press), 156.

21. See R. McGowen (1986) 'A Powerful Sympathy: Terror, the Prison, and Humanitarian Reform in Early Nineteenth-Century Britain', *Journal of British Studies*, 25:3, 312–34.

22. See A. Brooke and D. Brandon (2004) *Tyburn: London's Fatal Tree* (Stroud: Sutton Publishing), 11–13.

23. Gatrell, *Hanging Tree*, 56–8.

24. See E. Burke (1854) 'Essay on Sublime and Beautiful', *Works*, I, 81.

25. J. Boswell (1961) *The Life of Samuel Johnson, LLD* (Oxford: Oxford World's Classics), 1211.

26. Gatrell, *Hanging Tree*, 40–5.

27. Ibid., 19 and 406–8.
28. McLynn, *Crime and Punishment*, 254–60.
29. Ibid., 21.
30. J. Fitzjames Stephen (1883) *History of the Criminal Law* (London: Macmillan) I, 483.
31. Parliamentary Debates, 1810, 17, col. 197.
32. Randall McGowen (2000), 'Revisiting the Hanging Tree', *British Journal of Criminology*, 40:1, 1–13.
33. The Criminal Law Consolidation Act 1861 formally confirmed this 1840s reduction of offences, potentially attracting the death penalty.
34. This is based on the unpublished research of the author related to Home Office records.
35. See for instance McGowen, 'Powerful Sympathy', 314–15 and B. Faulk (1990) 'The Public Execution: Urban Rhetoric and Victorian Crowds', in W. Thesing (ed.), *Executions and the British Experience from the 17th to the 20th Century: A Collection of Essays* (Jefferson, NC: McFarland), 75–90.
36. See J.S. Mill (1836) 'Civilisation', in J.M. Robson (1977) (ed.), *Collected Works of John Stuart Mill* (London: Routledge & Kegan Paul). See also Gatrell, *Hanging Tree*, Chapter 15.
37. For further information see H. Potter (1993) *Hanging in Judgement: Religion and the Death Penalty in England* (London: SCM Press), passim.
38. For further discussion see D. Cooper (1974) *The Lesson of the Scaffold: The Public Execution Controversy in Victorian England* (Harmondsworth: Penguin) and R.D. Altick (1970) *Victorian Studies in Scarlet: Murders and Manners in the Age of Victoria* (London: Norton & Co.).
39. J. Tulloch (2006) 'The Privatising of Pain', *Journalism Studies*, 7:3, 437–51. See also Cooper, *The Lesson of the Scaffold*, for the history of the Royal Commission and the passage of the Act, 123–47 and especially 151. It is also worth noting that there was a very similar debate ongoing in the USA at the same time; see P.E. MacKey (1976) *Voices Against Death: American Opposition to Capital Punishment, 1787–1975* (New York: Burt Franklin).
40. J. Abbott (2005) 'The Press and the Public Visibility of Nineteenth Century Criminal Children', in J. Rowbotham and K. Stevenson (eds.), *Criminal Conversations: Victorian Crimes, Social Panic and Moral Outrage* (Columbus: Ohio State University Press), 23–39.
41. Gatrell, *Hanging Tree*, 531–3. See also D. Bentley (1998) *English Criminal Justice in the Nineteenth Century* (London: Hambledon Press).
42. L. Radzinowicz and R. Hood (1986) *A History of English Criminal Law*: V – *The Emergence of Penal Policy* (London: Stevens), 661–71.
43. H. Taylor (1998) 'Rationing Crime: The Political Economy of Criminal Statistics since the 1850s', *Economic History Review*, 51:3, 569–90.
44. See S.P. Evans (2004) *Executioner: The Chronicles of a Victorian Hangman* (Stroud: Sutton), 233–4.
45. Lord Callaghan, Foreword, in Block and Hostettler; *Hanging in the Balance*, 3 and Evans, *Executioner*, 368.
46. Gatrell, *Hanging Tree*, 610.
47. See McGowen, 'Powerful Sympathy', 315.
48. Gatrell, *Hanging Tree*, Part II.

49. For further discussion see J. Rowbotham and K. Stevenson (2005) 'Introduction', in Rowbotham and Stevenson (eds.), *Criminal Conversations*, xxi–xxxii.

50. C. Beccaria, *Of Crime and Punishment*: available at http://www.constitution.org/cb/crim_pun.htm

51. In 1846, Dickens famously wrote a series of letters on the topic: available at http://dickens.classicauthors.net/miscellaneous/miscellaneous4.html

52. *The Times*, 16 November 1849 (on the execution of the Mannings) and 1 April 1856 (on the execution of William Bousefield).

53. For further discussion see S. D'Cruze (2005) 'The Eloquent Corpse', and J. Rowbotham and K. Stevenson, 'Introduction', in Rowbotham and Stevenson (eds.), *Criminal Conversations*, 181–97, xxi–xxxii, as well as J. Rowbotham, K. Stevenson and S. Pegg (2003) 'Children of Misfortune: Parallels in the Cases of Child Murderers Thompson and Venables, Barratt and Bradley', *Howard Journal*, 42, 107–22.

54. *The Times*, 1 April 1856 and *Daily Telegraph*, 1 April 1856.

55. *Daily Telegraph*, 12 April 1856.

56. Ibid.

57. 'Capital Punishment and Public Executioners,' Letter, *The Times*, 7 January 1857.

58. See for example, Block and Hostettler, *Hanging in the Balance*, 60.

59. Gatrell, *Hanging Tree*, 43–4.

60. For further discussion see R. McGowen (2000) 'Revisiting the Hanging Tree', *British Journal of Criminology*, 40, 1–13.

61. J. Rowbotham and K. Stevenson (2003) 'Causing a Sensation: Media and Legal Representations of Bad Behaviour', in J. Rowbotham and K. Stevenson (eds.). *Behaving Badly: Social Panic and Moral Outrage. Victorian and Modern Parallels* (Aldershot: Ashgate), 31–46.

62. See for instance H. Engel (1998) *Lord High Executioner: An Unashamed Look at Hangmen, Headsmen and Their Kind* (London: Robson Books), 86 and Bailey, *Hangmen of England*, 30.

63. For further discussion see J. Carter Wood (2004) *Violence and Crime in Nineteenth-Century England: The Shadow of Our Refinement* (London: Routledge), passim, but especially 20–7.

64. Engel asserts there was 'hell to pay' if any details of executions emerged: I have found no substantial evidence of this, however, and suggest that the impression that executions were 'secret' was a useful fiction for the state. See Engel, *Lord High Executioner*, 86.

65. Taylor, 'Rationing Crime', 585.

66. L. Radzinowicz (1998) *Adventures in Criminology* (London: Routledge), especially Chapter 10, which provides a discussion of the issues discussed by the Royal Commission on Capital Punishment in 1949.

67. See for instance V. Bailey (2000) 'The Shadow of the Gallows: The Death Penalty and the British Labour Government, 1945–1951', *Law and History Review*, 18:2, 305–50.

68. See for instance B. Coffined (1987) *Miscarriages of Justice* (London: Hodder & Stoughton), Chapter 5.

69. See R. Hancock (1985) *Ruth Ellis: The Last Woman to be Hanged* (London: Robinson).

70. Lord Gardener confirmed that it had been the Homicide Act 1957 which had converted him to abolition. See *Hansard*, Lords Debates, 17 December 1969, 1110–11.

71. For further discussion see G. Dreary (1999) 'The Politics of Capital Punishment', in G. Dreary, G. Blake and C. Blake (eds.), *Law and the Spirit of Inquiry* (Geneva: Brill), 137–60 and Lord Windlesham (1996) *Responses to Crime* (Oxford: Oxford University Press), 3, 60–1.

72. *The Times*, 23 October 2002. After the shooting of a honeymoon couple in 2008, Antigua sought to reintroduce the death penalty, but this was blocked by the Privy Council. See *Daily Mail*, 10 March 2009.

73. 'This Futile Debate about Bringing Back Hanging', Leader, *Independent*, 22 August 2002. See also *The Times*, 23 October 2002. Many former colonies retain hanging, including India and Uganda, and at the time of going to press in August 2009 have made recent decisions, after public debate, to retain the sanction.

74. See Potter, *Hanging in Judgement*.

75. See P. Linebaugh (1991) *The London Hanged: Crime and Civil Society in the Eighteenth Century* (Cambridge: Cambridge University Press), xviii.

76. See D. Hay, P. Linebaugh, J. Rule and E.P. Thompson (1975) *Albion's Fatal Tree; Crime and Society in Eighteenth Century England* (London: Allen Lane).

77. See J. Langbein (1983) 'Albion's Fatal Flaws', *Past and Present*, 98, 96–120.

78. Beattie, *Crime and the Courts*.

79. Ibid., 101.

80. See for instance J.M. Beattie (1977) 'Crime and the Courts in Surrey, 1736–1753', in J.S. Cockburn (ed.), *Crime in England 1550–1800* (Princeton, NJ: Princeton University Press), especially 155, 163 and 176.

81. Langbein, 'Albion's Fatal Flaws', 107. It is interesting to note that his conclusion that eighteenth-century juries were harsh on those they perceived as 'professional' criminals was echoed in the nineteenth century. See also P.J. King (2000) *Crime, Justice and Discretion in England, 1740–1820* (Oxford: Oxford University Press), especially Chapter 7.

82. Radzinowicz, *History* of *English Criminal Law*, I, 15–16. See also J.A. Sharpe (1990) *Judicial Punishment in England* (London: Faber & Faber) and P.J. King (1984) 'Decision Makers and Decision Making in the English Criminal Law', *Historical Journal*, 27, 25–58.

83. V.A.C. Gatrell (1990) 'Crime, Authority and the Policeman State', in F.M.L. Thompson (ed.), *The Cambridge Social History of Britain 1750–1950* (Cambridge: Cambridge University Press), 243–310.

84. Meaning, in practice, a prison term of between 14 and 21 years.

85. For further discussion see T. Lacqueur (1989) 'Crowds, Carnival and the State in English Executions, 1604–1868', in A.L. Beier, D. Cannadine and J. Rosenheim (eds.), *The First Modern Society: Essays in English History in Honour of Lawrence Stone* (Cambridge: Cambridge University Press), 305–55 and Linebaugh, *London Hanged*, xx–xxi.

86. Foucault, *Discipline and Punish*, passim.

87. Gatrell, *Hanging Tree*, Part I.

88. Foucault, *Discipline and Punish*, 59.

89. Gatrell, *Hanging Tree*, especially 56–8.

90. See for instance J.A. Sharpe (1985) '"Last dying speeches": Religion, Ideology and Public Execution in Seventeenth Century England', *Past and Present*, 107, 144–67.

91. See for instance Gatrell, *Hanging Tree*, 62–3.

92. See for instance H. Fielding (1751) *An Enquiry into the Causes of the Late Increase in Robbers* (London).

93. Gatrell, *Hanging Tree*, 59.

94. Ibid., passim.

95. See for instance McGowen, 'A Powerful Sympathy', 312–34 and R. McGowen (1994) 'Civilizing Punishment: The End of the Public Execution in England,' *Journal of British Studies*, 33, 257–82.

96. See for instance Gatrell, *Hanging Tree*, 67–74; R. McGowen (1987) 'The Body and Punishment in Eighteenth-Century England', *Journal of Modern History*, 59, 651–79 and (2007) 'Cruel Inflictions and the Claims of Humanity in Early Nineteenth-Century England', in K. Watson (ed.), *Assaulting the Past: Violence and Civilization in Historical Context* (Newcastle-upon-Tyne: Cambridge Scholars), 38–57.

97. See McGowen, 'Civilising Punishment', passim and Bailey, *Hangmen of England*, 85–7.

98. See for example A. Pierrepoint (1974) *Executioner: Pierrepoint* (London: Harrap).

99. See S. D'Cruze, L. Jackson and J. Rowbotham (2005) 'Gender, Crime and Culture in the Twentieth Century: Conversations between Academics and Professionals', *History Workshop*, 60:1, 139–51 and S. D'Cruze and L.A. Jackson (2009) *Women, Crime and Justice in England since 1660* (Basingstoke: Palgrave Macmillan).

100. Carter Wood, *Violence and Crime*, passim.

101. H. Macleod (2004) 'God and the Gallows: Christianity and Capital Punishment in the Nineteenth and Twentieth Centuries', *Studies in Church History*, 40, 330–56 and Potter, *Hanging in Judgement*, passim.

102. S. Green and R.C. Whiting (2002) 'Introduction', in S. Green and R.C. Whiting (eds.), *The Boundaries of the State in Modern Britain* (Cambridge: Cambridge University Press), 341–74.

103. Bailey, 'Shadow of the Gallows'.

104. See for instance L. Bland (2008) 'The Trials and Tribulations of Edith Thompson: The Capital Crime of Sexual Incitement in 1920s England', *Journal of British Studies*, 47, 624–48. Criminologist Annette Ballinger discusses the experiences and executions of the 15 (out of 130 convicted) women hanged in the twentieth century. The text is valuable to historians, partly because it enables a link to the texts discussing the campaign for abolition produced by lawyers and other criminologists. See A. Ballinger (2000) *Dead Woman Walking: Executed Women in England and Wales 1900–1955* (Aldershot: Ashgate).

105. See Block and Hostettler, *Hanging in the Balance* and Hood and Hoyle, *The Death Penalty*.

106. For further discussion see I. Ehrlich (1975) 'The Deterrent Effect of Capital Punishment: A Question of Life and Death, *American Economic Review*, 65, 397–417; P. Zimmerman (2006) 'Estimates of the Deterrent Effect of

Alternative Execution Methods in the United States: 1978–2000', *American Journal of Economics and Sociology*, 65:4, 909–41 and H. Dezhbakhsh and J. M. Shepherd (2006) 'The Deterrent Effect of Capital Punishment: Evidence from a "Judicial Experiment"', *Economic Enquiry*, 44:3, 512–35. For critiques see J. Fagan (2006) 'Death and Deterrence Redux: Science, Law and Causal Reasoning on Capital Punishment', *Ohio State Journal of Criminal Law*, 4, 254–320 and R. Weisberg (2005) 'The Death Penalty Meets Social Science: Deterrence and Jury Behavior Under New Scrutiny', *Annual Review of Law and Social Science*, 1, 151–70.

107. See M. Gaskill (2003) *Crime and Mentalities in Early Modern England*, (Cambridge: Cambridge University Press), 219.

108. For further discussion see J. Curtis (1828) *The True and Faithful Account of the Mysterious Murder of Maria Marten* (London: Thomas Kelly) and C. Hindley (1878) *The Life and Times of James Catnach (Late of Seven Dials) Ballad Monger* (London: Paul & Co.), especially 186.

109. By no means all criminals made such a 'good' exit. See Gatrell, *Hanging Tree*, Part I. For the significance of confessions see also A. Mackenzie (2007) *Tyburn's Martyrs: Executions in England 1675–1775* (London: Hambledon) and J.A. Sharpe (2008) 'Review: Tyburn's Martyrs', *Reviews in History* available at http://www.history.ac.uk/reviews/paper/sharpe.html

110. *The Times*, 12 August 1828 and *Ipswich Journal*, 12 August 1828. See also Laqueur, 'Crowds, Carnival and the State', 305–56.

111. Gatrell, *Hanging Tree*, Chapter 2.

112. *The Times*, 12 August 1828 and see also Curtis, *Mysterious Murder of Maria Martin*, 290–300.

113. See Engel, *Lord High Executioner* and S. Fielding (2008) *The Executioner's Bible* (London: John Blake).

114. See H. Perkin (1989) *The Rise of Professional Society: England since 1880* (London: Routledge). Of course, such claims to professional status were not recognised by middle-class professionals. On the status of executioners see also G. Rubin (1964) 'The Executioner: His Place in English Society', *British Journal of Sociology*, 15:3, 234–53.

115. See Engel, *Lord High Executioner*, Chapter 4.

116. Major A. Griffiths (1904) *Fifty Years of Public Service* (London: Cassell), 340–3.

117. See *Oxford Dictionary of National Biography* available at http://www.oxforddnb.com/view/article/18244?_fromAuth=1.

118. See for instance 'A Personal Narrative by Marwood', *Hull Packet and East Riding*, 14 May 1880, where Marwood specifically laid claim to its invention and to his guarantee of swift death.

119. Gatrell, *Hanging Tree*, 51–4. For detailed descriptions of the development of a 'civilised' methodology of hanging, see Bailey, *Hangmen of England*, especially Chapters V, VI.

120. *Lloyds Weekly*, 18 October 1874; *Reynolds News*, 30 August 1874; *Liverpool Mercury* 1 September 1874; *Manchester Times*, 5 September 1874; *Lloyds Weekly*, 10 January 1875.

121. *Reynolds News*, 3 January 1875.

122. Evans, *Executioner*, 24.

123. From Archbishop Paley in the eighteenth century, to Archbishop Fisher in the 1950s, leading churchmen acted as vocal supporters of the death penalty in pulpits and in parliament. For the best discussion of this theme see Potter, *Hanging in Judgement*, passim.
124. R. Calvert (1928) *Capital Punishment in the Twentieth Century* (London: G.P. Putnam & Sons).
125. For further discussion see A. Logan (2008) *Feminism and Criminal Justice Reform: A Historical Perspective* (Basingstoke: Palgrave Macmillan), 32–3 and 83–5.
126. Lord Chorley, *Hansard*, Lords Debates, 17 December 1969, 1244.
127. For further discussion see J. Rowbotham (2009), 'Turning Away from Criminal Intent: Reflecting on Victorian and Edwardian Strategies for Promoting Desistance amongst Petty Offenders', *Theoretical Criminology*, 13:1, 105–28.
128. Gatrell, *Hanging Tree*, 530 and Hood and Hoyle, *The Death Penalty*, passim.
129. See for instance *Daily Telegraph*, 31 December 2001.

Further Reading

Introduction

Beattie, J.M. (1986) *Crime and the Courts in England 1660–1800* (Oxford: Clarendon Press).

Carter Wood, J. (2004) *Violence and Crime in Nineteenth Century England: The Shadow of our Refinement* (London: Routledge).

D'Cruze, S. et al. (2006) *Murder: Social and Historical Approaches to Understanding Murder and Murderers* (Cullompton: Willan).

Emsley, C. (2005) *Crime and Society in England 1750–1900* (2nd edn, Harlow: Longman).

Godfrey, B., Emsley, C. and Dunstall, G. (eds.) (2003) *Comparative Histories of Crime* (Cullompton: Willan).

Godfrey, B.S., Lawrence, P. and Williams, C.A. (2008) *History and Crime* (London: Sage).

McMahon, R. (ed.) (2008) *Crime, Law and Popular Culture in Europe, 1500–1900* (Cullompton: Willan).

Moran, L. and Skeggs, B. (2004) (eds.) *Sexuality and the Politics of Violence and Safety* (London: Routledge).

Rowbotham, J. and Stevenson, K. (eds.) *Criminal Conversations: Victorian Crimes, Social Panic, and Moral Outrage* (Columbus: Ohio State University Press).

Walkowitz, J.R. (1992) *City of Dreadful Delight: Narratives of Sexual Danger in late-Victorian London* (London: Virago).

Chapter 1   Moral Crimes and the Law in Britain since 1700

Bradlaugh-Bonner, H. (1923) *Penalties Upon Opinion* (London: Watts & Co.).

Cabantous, A. (2002) *Blasphemy: Impious Speech in the West*, trans. Eric Rauth (New York: Columbia University Press).

Cocks, H.G. (2003) *Nameless Offences: Homosexual Desire in the Nineteenth Century* (London: I.B. Tauris).

Goldsmith, N.M. (1998) *The Worst of Crimes: Homosexuality and the Law in Eighteenth Century London* (Ashgate: Aldershot).

Houlbrook, M. (2005) *Queer London: Perils and Pleasures in the Sexual Metropolis 1918–1957* (Chicago: University of Chicago Press).

Levy, L.W. (1993) *Blasphemy: Verbal Offense against the Sacred from Moses to Salman Rushdie* (New York: Knopf).

Nash, D.S. (1999) *Blasphemy in Britain: 1789–Present* (Aldershot: Ashgate).

Nash, D.S. (2007) *Blasphemy in the Christian World* (Oxford: Oxford University Press).

Nokes, G.D. (1928) *A History of the Crime of Blasphemy* (London: Sweet & Maxwell).

Weeks, J. (1989) *Sex, Politics and Society: The Regulation of Sexuality since 1800* (2nd edn, Harlow: Longman).

Chapter 2   Cruelty and Adultery: Offences against the Institution of Marriage

Amussen, S. (1994) '"Being Stirred to Much Unquietness": Violence and Domestic Violence in Early Modern England', *Journal of Women's History*, 6:2, 70–89.

Bailey, J. (2003) *Unquiet Lives: Marriage and Marriage Breakdown in England 1660–1800* (Cambridge: Cambridge University Press).

Bailey, J. (2006) '"I Dye [sic] by Inches": Locating Wife Beating in the Concept of a Privatisation of Marriage and Violence in Eighteenth-century England', *Social History*, 31:3, 273–94.

D'Cruze, S. (ed.) (2000) *Everyday Violence in Britain, 1850–1950: Gender and Class* (Harlow: Longman).

Doggett, M. (1992) *Marriage, Wife-beating and the Law in Victorian England* (London: Weidenfeld & Nicolson).

Foyster, E. (2005) *Marital Violence: An English Family History 1660–1857* (Cambridge: Cambridge University Press).

Hammerton, A.J. (1992) *Cruelty and Companionship: Conflict in Nineteenth-century Married Life* (London: Routledge).

Savage, G. (1998) 'Erotic Stories and Public Decency: Newspaper Reporting of Divorce Proceedings in England', *Historical Journal*, 41:2, 511–28.

Shanley, M.L. (1989) *Feminism, Marriage, and the Law in Victorian England* (London: I.B. Tauris).

Weeks, J. (1989) *Sex, Politics and Society: The Regulation of Sexuality since 1800* (2nd edn, London: Longman).

Chapter 3   Desperate Measures or Cruel Intentions? Infanticide in Britain since 1600

Arnot, M.L. (1994) 'Infant Death, Child Care and the State: The Baby-farming Scandal and the First Infant Life Protection Legislation of 1872', *Continuity and Change*, 9:2, 271–311.

Hoffer, P.C. and Hull, N.E.C. (1984) *Murdering Mothers: Infanticide in England and New England, 1558–1803* (New York and London: New York University Press).

Jackson, M. (1996) *New-born Child Murder: Women, Illegitimacy and the Courts in Eighteenth-century England* (Manchester: Manchester University Press).

Jackson, M. (ed.) (2002) *Infanticide: Historical Perspectives on Child Murder and Concealment, 1550–2000* (Aldershot: Ashgate).

Kilday, A.M. (2007) *Women and Violent Crime in Enlightenment Scotland* (Woodbridge: Royal Historical Society).

Kilday, A.M. (2008) '"Monsters of the Vilest Kind": Infanticidal Women and Attitudes Towards their Criminality in Eighteenth Century Scotland', *Family and Community History*, 11:2, 100–15.

Kilday, A.M. and Watson, K. (2008) 'Infanticide, Religion and Community in the British Isles, 1720–1920: Introduction', *Family and Community History*, 11:2, 84–99.

Marland, H. (2004) *Dangerous Motherhood: Insanity and Childbirth in Victorian Britain* (London: Palgrave Macmillan).

McDonagh, J. (2003) *Child Murder and British Culture 1720–1900* (Cambridge: Cambridge University Press).

Rose, L. (1986) *The Massacre of the Innocents: Infanticide in Britain 1800–1939* (London: Routledge & Kegan Paul).

Ward, T. (1999) 'The Sad Subject of Infanticide: Law, Medicine and Child Murder, 1860–1938', *Social and Legal Studies*, 8, 163–80.

Chapter 4   'Most Intimate Violations': Contextualising the Crime of Rape

Carrabine, E. et al. (2004) *Criminology: A Sociological Introduction* (London: Routledge).

Clark, A. (1987) *Women's Silence, Men's Violence: Sexual Assault in England 1770–1845* (London: Pandora Press).

Conley, C. (1991) *The Unwritten Law: Criminal Justice in Victorian Kent* (Oxford: Oxford University Press).

D'Cruze, S. (1998) *Crimes of Moral Outrage* (London: UCL Press).

Gatrell, V. et al. (1980) *Crime and the Law: The Social History of Crime in Western Europe since 1500* (London: Europa).

Home Office (2000) *Setting the Boundaries: Reforming the Law on Sexual Offences (London: Home Office Communications Directorate)*.

Kelly, L., Lovett J. and Regan, L. (2005) *A Gap or a Chasm: Attrition in Reported Rape Cases* (Home Office Research Study 293, Home Office Development and Statistics Directorate).

Rowbotham, J. and Stevenson, K. (eds.) *Behaving Badly: Social Panics and Moral Outrage – Victorian and Modern Parallels* (Aldershot: Ashgate).

Stevenson, K. (2004) 'Fulfilling Their Mission: The Intervention of Voluntary Societies in Cases of Sexual Assault in the Victorian Criminal Process,' *Crime, History & Societies*, 8:1, 93–110.

Wiener, M. (2004) *Men of Blood, Violence, Manliness and Criminal Justice in Victorian England* (Cambridge: Cambridge University Press).

Chapter 5   Murder and Fatality: The Changing Face of Homicide

Brookman, F. (2005) *Understanding Homicide* (London: Sage).

Cockburn, J.S. (1995) 'Patterns of Violence in English Society: Homicide in Kent 1560–1985', *Past and Present*, 130, 70–106.

Daly, M. and Wilson, M. (1988) *Homicide* (New York: Aldine de Gruyter).

D'Cruze, S. (1998) *Crimes of Outrage: Sex, Violence and Victorian Working Women* (London: UCL Press).

D'Cruze, S. (ed.) (2000) *Everyday Violence in Britain c1850–c. 1950: Gender and Class* (Harlow: Pearson).

D'Cruze, S. et al. (2006) *Murder: Social and Historical Approaches to Understanding Murder and Murderers* (Cullompton: Willan).

Eisner, M. (2001) 'Modernization, Self-control and Lethal Violence: The Long-term Dynamics of European Homicide Rates in Theoretical Perspective', *British Journal of Criminology*, 41, 618–38.

Emsley, C. (1996) *Crime and Society in England 1750–1900* (Harlow: Longman).

Polk, K. (1994) *When Men Kill: Scenarios of Masculine Violence*, (Cambridge: Cambridge University Press).

Wiener, M.J. (2004) *Men of Blood: Violence, Manliness and Criminal Justice in Victorian England* (Cambridge: Cambridge University Press).

Chapter 6   Criminality, Deviance and the Underworld since 1750

Chesney, K. (1970) *The Victorian Underworld* (London: Maurice Temple Smith).

Davies, A. (1998) 'Youth Gangs, Masculinity and Violence in late Victorian Manchester and Salford', *Journal of Social History*, 32, 349–69.

Emsley, C. (2005) *Crime and Society in England, 1750–1900* (3rd edn, Harlow: Longman)

McMullan, J.L. (1984) *The Canting Crew: London's Criminal Underworld, 1550–1700* (New Brunswick, NJ: Rutgers University Press).

Reuter, P. (1983) *Disorganised Crime: Illegal Markets and the Mafia – The Economics of the Visible Hand* (London: MIT Press).

Sharpe, J. (2005) *Dick Turpin: The Myth of the English Highwayman* (London: Profile).

Shore, H. (2007) '"Undiscovered Country": Towards a History of the Criminal Underworld', *Crimes and Misdemeanours*, 1:1, 41–68.

Springhall, J. (1998) *Youth, Popular Culture and Moral Panics: Penny Gaffs to Gangsta-Rap, 1830–1996* (Basingstoke: Macmillan).

Thomas, D. (2005) *Villains Paradise: Britain's Underworld from the Spivs to the Krays* (London: Murray).

Wright, A. (2006) *Organised Crime* (Cullompton: Willan).

Chapter 7   Fraud and White-collar Crime: 1850 to the Present

Bequai, A. (1978) *White Collar Crime: A 20th Century Crisis* (Lexington, MA: Lexington Press).
Doig, A. (2006) *Fraud* (Cullompton: Willan).
Evans, D.M. (1859) *Facts, Failures & Frauds: Revelations Financial, Mercantile, Criminal* (Groombridge: London).
Kirk, D. and Woodcock, A. (1996) *Serious Fraud: Investigation and Trial* (London: Butterworth).
Levi, M. (1987) *Regulating Fraud: White Collar Crime and the Criminal Process* (London: Tavistock).
Moore, J. et al. (eds.) *Corruption in Urban Politics and Society, Britain 1780–1950* (Aldershot: Ashgate).
Robb, G. (1992) *White Collar Crime in Modern England: Financial Fraud and Business Morality, 1845–1929* (Cambridge: Cambridge University Press).
Sutherland, E.H. (1949) *White Collar Crime* (New York: Dryden).
Wiener, M. (1990) *Reconstructing the Criminal: Culture, Law, and Policy in England 1830–1914* (Cambridge: Cambridge University Press).
Wilson, S. (2006) 'Law, Morality, and Regulation: Victorian Experiences of Financial Crime', *British Journal of Criminology*, 46, 1073–90.

Chapter 8   Policing the Populace: The Road to Professionalisation

Ascoli, D. (1979) *The Queen's Peace: The Origins and Development of the Metropolitan Police, 1829–1979* (London: Hamish Hamilton).
Beattie, J.M. (2001) *Policing and Punishment in London: Urban Crime and the Limits of Terror, 1660–1750* (Oxford: Oxford University Press).
Bittner, E. (1975) *The Functions of the Police in Modern Society: A Review of Background Factors, Current Practices, and Possible Role Models* (New York: Aronson).
Emsley, C. (1996) *The English Police: A Political and Social History* (Harlow: Longman).
Hobbs, D. (1988) *Doing the Business: Entrepreneurship, Detectives and the Working Class in the East End of London* (Oxford: Clarendon Press).
Philips, D. and Storch, R.D. (1999) *Policing Provincial England, 1829–1856: The Politics of Reform* (London: Leicester University Press).
Porter, B. (1991) *The Origins of the Vigilant State: The London Metropolitan Police Special Branch before the First World War* (Woodbridge: Boydell).
Rawlings, P. (2002) *Policing: A Short History* (Cullompton: Willan).
Reynolds, E. (1998) *Before the Bobbies: The Night Watch and Police Reform in Metropolitan London, 1720–1830* (London: Macmillan).
Taylor, D. (1997) *The New Police in Nineteenth Century England: Crime, Conflict and Control* (Manchester: Manchester University Press).

Chapter 9   Execution as Punishment in England: 1750–2000

Bailey, B. (1989) *Hangmen of England: A History of Execution from Jack Ketch to Albert Pierrepoint* (London: W.H. Allen).

Block, B. and Hostettler, J. (1997) *Hanging in the Balance: A History of the Abolition of Capital Punishment in Britain* (London: Waterside Press).

Cooper, D. (1974) *The Lesson of the Scaffold: The Public Execution Controversy in Victorian England* (Harmondsworth: Penguin).

Engel, H. (1998) *Lord High Executioner: An Unashamed Look at Hangmen, Headsmen and Their Kind* (London: Robson Books).

Evans, S.P. (2004) *Executioner: The Chronicles of a Victorian Hangman* (Stroud: Sutton).

Gatrell, V.A.C. (1994) *The Hanging Tree Execution and the English People 1770–1868* (London: Oxford University Press).

Hood, R. and Hoyle, C. (2008) *The Death Penalty: A Worldwide Perspective* (3rd edn, Oxford: Oxford University Press).

Linebaugh, P. (1991) *The London Hanged: Crime and Civil Society in the Eighteenth Century* (Cambridge: Cambridge University Press).

Potter, H. (1993) *Hanging in Judgement: Religion and the Death Penalty in England* (London: SCM Press).

Pratt, J. (2002) *Punishment and Civilization: Penal Tolerance and Intolerance in Modern Society* (London: Sage).

Index

Note: All texts cited in the index are primary sources and are listed in italics with the year of publication following. The abbreviations 'n.' and 'nn.' designate footnote numbers on the page cited.

of children 103, 108, 110
conviction patterns 106
defence of provocation 108, 110
definition of 106, 110, 184
and gender 107, 113–14
historiography of 104–11, 184
individual convicted of 101
insanity defence 108
and the media 108, 111, 113, 115
patterns of 101, 102–5, 106–7, 110
rates of 100–1
sentencing policy 107–9, 110
and servants 107
statistics for 100–1, 105–6, 110
and women 107, 108
Murder (Abolition of Death Penalty)
   Act (1965) 187, 194
My Secret Life (1888) 126

Nash, David 28
Nathan Committee (House of
   Lords) 110
National Campaign for the Abolition
   of Capital Punishment 193–4
National Secular Society (NSS) 23
National Society for the Prevention
   of Cruelty to Children
   (NSPCC) 85
National Vigilance Association 85
'neck verse' statute (1350) 182
Newgate Prison 182, 186
Nietzsche, Friedrich 180
Nilsen, Dennis 103
Nokes, G.D. 27
North, Judge Justice 31
Northern Rock Bank 143
Norton, Lord 84
Nott-Bower, William (Chief
   Constable) 172
Nott-Bowes, Sir John 26

O'Brien, Mike (Solicitor General) 150
Offences against the Person Act
   (1828) 42, 75 n.32, 84, 98 n.19;
   (1837) 108; (1861) 25, 75 n.32,
   84, 88, 108, 184
Old Bailey Sessions Papers 122
Operation Spanner 32

Ordinary of Newgate's Account 122
organised crime 11–12, 120–40
   definition of 121, 123, 124, 129
   and drugs 124, 129, 134
   historiography of 125
   and horse racing 124
   and nightclubs 124
   and people trafficking 129, 134

Paine, Thomas 19
   Age of Reason (1794, 1796, 1807),
      prosecution for publication
      of 20
Paley, Ruth 125
Pall Mall Gazette 84
Palmer, S.H. 169, 170
Park Brigade (gang) 132
Patel, Trupti 65
Payne, Sarah 195
Pearson, Geoffrey 128
Peel, Sir Robert 148
   and creation of Metropolitan Police
      force 162
   as legal moderniser 183
penal policy 3, 109
Pentonville prison 186
Perkin, Harold 147, 149
Pettiti, Judge 33
petty treason 107
Philips, David 126, 169
piracy 183
poaching 126
Police Act (1857) 162; (1919) 165;
   (1964) 166
police corruption 135, 163
Police Federation 165
policing 12–13, 113, 122–4, 127,
   148, 160–79
   arrest statistics 164
   careers in 164, 171–3
   County Police Acts (1839/40) 169
   and detection 163
   and 'domestic missionary
      work' 169
   of ethnic minorities 173–5
   historiography of 167–70
   impact of technology on 166–7
   and marital violence 43